Myanmar's Political Transition and Lost Opportunities

The **ISEAS – Yusof Ishak Institute** (formerly Institute of Southeast Asian Studies) is an autonomous organization established in 1968. It is a regional centre dedicated to the study of socio-political, security, and economic trends and developments in Southeast Asia and its wider geostrategic and economic environment. The Institute's research programmes are grouped under Regional Economic Studies (RES), Regional Strategic and Political Studies (RSPS), and Regional Social and Cultural Studies (RSCS). The Institute is also home to the ASEAN Studies Centre (ASC), the Temasek History Research Centre (THRC), and the Singapore APEC Study Centre.

ISEAS Publishing, an established academic press, has issued more than two thousand books and journals. It is the largest scholarly publisher of research about Southeast Asia from within the region. ISEAS Publishing works with many other academic and trade publishers and distributors to disseminate important research and analyses from and about Southeast Asia to the rest of the world.

Myanmar's Political Transition and Lost Opportunities
(2010–2016)

YE HTUT

YUSOF ISHAK INSTITUTE

First published in Singapore in 2019 by
ISEAS Publishing
30 Heng Mui Keng Terrace
Singapore 119614
E-mail: publish@iseas.edu.sg
Website: <http://bookshop.iseas.edu.sg>

All rights reserved. No part of this publication may be reproduced, stored in a retrieval system, or transmitted in any form or by any means, electronic, mechanical, photocopying, recording or otherwise, without the prior permission of the ISEAS – Yusof Ishak Institute.

© 2019 ISEAS – Yusof Ishak Institute, Singapore

The responsibility for facts and opinions in this publication rests exclusively with the authors and their interpretations do not necessarily reflect the views or the policy of the publisher or its supporters.

ISEAS Library Cataloguing-in-Publication Data

Names: Ye Htut, 1959–
Title: Myanmar's Democratic Transition and Lost Opportunities (2011–2016) / Ye Htut.
Description: Singapore : ISEAS – Yusof Ishak Institute, 2019. | Includes index.
Identifiers: ISBN 9789814843577 (paperback) | ISBN 9789814843584 (pdf) | ISBN 9789814843591 (epub)
Subjects: LCSH: Myanmar--Politics and government--1988-
Classification: LCC DS530.65 Y37

Typeset by Superskill Graphics Pte Ltd

Contents

Foreword by Robert H. Taylor — vii

Acknowledgements — xix

Introduction — 1

1. The National Convention — 5
2. The Constitution — 24
3. The Union Solidarity and Development Party — 33
4. Myanmar Spring and Aung San Suu Kyi — 46
5. The Union Government — 57
6. The Government and the Parliament — 101
7. Shwe Mann's Checkmates — 123
8. Turning Points — 154
9. Media Reform — 185

Epilogue — 216

Appendix A: President Thein Sein's Inaugural Address   227

Appendix B: President Thein Sein's First Address to the Cabinet   239

List of Interviewees   245

Index   247

About the Author   260

Foreword

U Ye Htut has written a book of a very rare kind. Few accounts of the inside working of a government are available so soon after it has left office. Even fewer, indeed almost none, are written about the working of the government of Myanmar by an author who could be considered an "outside insider". Ye Htut was not a key figure in the military government which preceded that of President Thein Sein in 2011. Having been an army officer on the cusp of becoming a colonel, he became a civil servant somewhat earlier in his career than many others would eventually become. Within the Thein Sein government he rose quickly, ultimately, in 2013, to the position of presidential spokesperson and then, the following year, minister for information. His talents and skills were clearly needed in Myanmar's transitional regime from military authoritarian to constitutional rule.

Moreover, Ye Htut's book is not merely his personal observations on the workings of the Thein Sein government from within. He has conducted extensive interviews with others more intimately involved in certain crucial decisions and events than himself, thus adding an additional dimension to his analysis. Many both inside and outside of Myanmar will be unaware of the crucial dynamics at work within the government for which he worked as a civil servant and ultimately as a minister. He was increasingly entrusted with greater responsibilities and increased inside knowledge because of not only his administrative competence but because of the high regard he was and is held as a result of his probity and open-mindedness.

Ye Htut's background is not unusual for someone of his age and position in Myanmar. Born in Yangon in 1959, his father, U Shwe Than, was a serving army officer and one of the earliest Myanmar graduates of the British Royal Military Academy Sandhurst. Shwe Than saw military service in various parts of Myanmar before being appointed first deputy head and then head of the police by General Ne Win in the 1970s. Subsequently, Ne Win moved Shwe Than to the headship of the country's national shipping company, then known as the Burma Five Star Line. Ye Htut, growing up in a military officer's home, could not be unaware of the intrigues that existed within the army and the army-dominated Burma Socialist Programme Party (BSPP) during his youth. Unusually, however, thanks no doubt to his father's great influence, he learned to read, write and speak English, a subject then not taught effectively as part of the national curriculum.

Accepted into the Defence Services Academy at Myamyo (now Pwin-Oo-Lwin) in 1977, after his second attempt, Ye Htut graduated in 1981 as a member of the 22nd intake. He initially served in the Kayin State and was heavily involved in major campaigns again the Kayin National Liberation Army (KNLA), the armed organization of the Kayin National Union (KNU). The KNLA/KNU were deeply involved in the smuggling trade that undermined the official but increasingly failing economy of socialist Burma. Fierce fighting in that area led to a significant flow of refugees into neighbouring Thailand in the mid-1980s.

Following the normal round of promotions and reassignments typical of an army career, Ye Htut served in other parts of Myanmar, including Tanintharyi Division, Kachin State, Mandalay Division and Shan State. He was chosen to be sent to Fort Bragg in the United States for further military training, but as a consequence of the reaction of the United States government to the anti-BSPP popular uprising and subsequent coup by the State Law and Order Restoration Council (SLORC) in 1988, that invitation was cancelled. As his military career reached its peak, he was appointed the chief instructor at the Military Advance Training School in the Southern Shan States in 2002. There he was able to pursue his interests in teaching as well as reading and writing. He occasionally contributed at that time to the army's *Military Science Journal*.

However, his military career was soon cut short as he was reassigned as a civil servant in the Ministry of Information. It was in his role as deputy director general in the Information and Public Relations Department of the Ministry that I first met Ye Htut. After the fall from power of General Khin Nyunt, the head of Military Intelligence, and the loss of his extensive personal network within the army and government in 2004, the information minister, General Kyaw Hsan, was apparently assigned the role of dealing with foreigners interested in Myanmar that members of Military Intelligence's former Office of Strategic Services (OSS) and selected ministers had undertaken after 1989. Prior to this, for a foreign scholar, contact with the government was extremely limited, if it occurred at all.

After a meeting with Kyaw Hsan, who was amazingly obliging, quickly gaining permission from various ministries for me and a Myanmar colleague to visit the Chin State, then a restricted area, the minister introduced me to Ye Htut. Ye Htut then took me off on his own and explained his role in the Myanmar Information Committee. Unlike my previous encounters with officials and ministers, who would be forthcoming only up to a point, for a subordinate official, Ye Htut was franker and more open than any met before. In contrast to other Myanmar government officials of his rank that I had encountered since 1989, Ye Htut was something new and perhaps a harbinger of changes yet to come. He even had an impish sense of humour and was also keen to inquire about how things were done elsewhere. Rarely had I met someone in Myanmar who, in dealing with a foreigner, was so confident of the latitude he had in providing information about the government and its plans. It was more like a meeting with my friends at Yangon University two decades before than an initial encounter in a ministry office.

During the next few years, I met with Ye Htut occasionally informally as well as formally with minister Kyaw Hsan. I often brought him English-language books from abroad to feed his incessant appetite for reading material. He in particular requested books on the political systems of Western states, particularly the United States. Amongst other books provided were William Riordan's 1905 classic *Plunkitt of Tammany Hall: A Series of Very Plain Talks on Very Practical Politics* and Robert Dahl's *How Democratic Is the American Constitution?* (2002). Years later, when the United States embassy began to cultivate relations with the Myanmar government, Ye Htut was asked by an American official what he had read about US democracy. He replied his knowledge was based in part on what I had provided. The embassy official promptly told him he had been reading the wrong books. I also supplied him with books on China, ASEAN and other current political and economic topics as well as contemporary fiction.

Ye Htut, as he mentions in this volume, was involved with Paul Pasch of the Friedrich Ebert Stiftung (FES), and former German diplomat P. Christian Hauswedell, in a series of track two diplomatic seminars and study trips organized by the Myanmar Institute for Strategic and International Studies (Myanmar-ISIS) in an attempt to get the member states of the European Union to understand Myanmar's planned political trajectory and related issues. If the Europeans could be persuaded to relax their economic sanctions, rather than just aping the United States, the possibility of a speedier transition would have been enhanced. I was included in these delegations of eight to ten Europeans and therefore travelled with Ye Htut and Myanmar-ISIS leaders up to the Myanmar border with China, the Shan, Kachin, and Kayin States and elsewhere meeting with ceasefire groups and visiting development projects as well as exchanging views in seminars with informed persons inside and outside the government. On our journeys and in our seminars, Ye Htut was a fount of useful information and, unlike some of his less forthcoming colleagues formerly in the Ministry of Foreign Affairs, was willing to share his views freely with the European delegates.

Separately I would occasionally visit Naypyitaw after the capital was moved there in 2005 to meet with Minister Kyaw Hsan and would then invariably meet Ye Htut. However, following the election of President Thein Sein's government, ministers and officials like Ye Htut became increasingly busy and opportunities to meet itinerant retired academics became fewer and briefer. Therefore the revelations in Ye Htut's book are as revealing to me as to other readers.

As the process of media reform developed, Ye Htut's central role grew until he seemed indispensable to the government. Having been promoted to director general of the Department of Information and Public Relations in 2009, he became deputy minister at the time that Kyaw Hsan was replaced as minister by U Aung Kyi in August 2012. Upon Aung Kyi's resignation, under conditions described in Ye Htut's text, he became minister of information on 1 August 2014, having been appointed presidential spokesperson in February 2013.

Whatever the degree to which readers of this volume followed the course of the politics of Myanmar since 1988, if not before, they will find aspects of events unknown to them up to now. Even seasoned observers will be unfamiliar with much Ye Htut tells us about the governments in which he served. The protracted process of shaping the eventual 2008

Constitution of the Republic of the Union of Myanmar is laid out in his first chapter, along with the unusual constraints placed on the president by three clauses of that constitution in chapter 2. Though attention is often drawn to the continuing role of the Myanmar army as set out in the constitution, less attention is given to the limitations on the president's authority vis-à-vis both the party structure and legislature (Hluttaw). As we shall see, these became as crucial to Myanmar's initial constitutional evolution as the remaining power of the army in and on the civilian government of Thein Sein.

Prior to this volume, little has been written on the army-created and backed political party, the Union Solidarity and Development Party (USDP), the successor to the Union Solidarity and Development Association (USDA). The victory of the USPD in the 2010 elections which created the legislature that made Thein Sein's government possible, owed far more to the decision of the major opposition party, the National League for Democracy (NLD), whose leader, Daw Aung San Suu Kyi, was barred from standing for election, than any action on the part of the USDP. The USDP was and apparently remains, as witnessed by the 2015 elections, highly dysfunctional. The product of military thinking and Myanmar's traditions of mixing business with politics, with no clear ideological perspective, created rivalries and schisms which could only be exacerbated by the ban on the nominal head of the party, President Thein Sein, from the typical majority party leadership role in republican constitutions, thus opening a door for others who felt his place should be theirs.

Enter the Machiavellian presence of Thura Shwe Mann, the third most powerful man in the ruling military council. He was widely expected to be chosen as the first president of the re-established constitutional order by the newly elected Pyidaungsu Hluttaw (Union assembly). When the then State Peace and Development Council (SPDC), the rebranded military junta that had ruled Myanmar since September 1988, dissolved itself, and the institutions of the 2008 constitution came into effect, most observers were highly sceptical that anything had really changed. Jaded from observing armies promulgating constitutions and returning former military leaders into elected politicians in other countries in Southeast Asia and beyond, both domestic and foreign analysts overwhelmingly discounted the significance of the inauguration of a new constitutional order under the leadership of the second tier of the old military order.

Events would prove them wrong on more than one account. Though many of the personnel in the new regime were former army officers, their new roles forced them to assume to the extent possible new modes of behaviour. Moreover, while formally the Pyidaungsu Hluttaw elected the president, in reality the choice it was given was predetermined by one of the last acts of the architecture of the new order, SPDC chairman Senior General Than Shwe. He surprised many, including the principals involved, in choosing not Shwe Mann as president but the number four officer in the old order, shy and retiring former prime minister Thein Sein. As Ye Htut details, in what is effectively a prologue to the ensuing drama, a scene was set for conflicts totally unexpected but with consequences still emerging.

Like all great dramas, while there were hints in the first act of what was to come, only a most acute inside observer could have known what they meant. All seemed to be set fair for the smooth functioning of the new order. The formal election of the president went to script and his inaugural address and first speech to his cabinet, while sounding fresh and novel, promising reform and perhaps even radical change, was dismissed by many as merely icing on an already old and stale cake. The shadow of the past hung heavily on the future. However, when President Thein Sein met with Aung San Suu Kyi five months after taking power and she eventually agreed to lead her party in joining in 2012 by-elections and entering the political process by being elected to the Pyithu Hluttaw (people's assembly), the realization became widespread that the Thein Sein administration was not just for show, but that the president meant what he had said about reform and change in his inaugural remarks. Ye Htut explains the inwardness of that process and its consequences in what he describes as Myanmar's Spring, in contrast to the so-called Arab Spring that was grabbing headlines at the same time. What he and no one else can explain except Aung San Suu Kyi herself is why she decided to lead her party into the political process under a constitution she had denounced as totally unacceptable just two years before.

Still, like a good dramatist, Ye Htut suspends the most gripping scenes to describe how, despite the legacy of its largely military inheritance, President Thein Sein and his ministers and other leading officials attempted to make the complicated institutions of Myanmar's new constitutional government work. These workings were made more complex as practices of the past proved more difficult to slough off

Foreword

than the many well intended and well remunerated foreigners who carried their bags of lessons learned elsewhere to Naypyitaw to lecture the executive on how to run an open, transparent, efficient, effective, gender regarding, and responsive administration. All easier said than done. What Ye Htut makes clear is that internal rivalries and conflicting interests within the Thein Sein administration posed problems that only the president could resolve. Thein Sein was not a dictator, but a listener and brooder, faced with many unenviable choices. Those with little or no experience of the complexities of governing a country as diverse and fractious as Myanmar often offered facile advice, which Thein Sein, with his decade of experience before assuming the presidency, knew better than most was largely irrelevant.

Having set the scene and introduced the principle characters and roles, the drama of Myanmar's transition from rule by the army under Senior General Than Shwe to the National League for Democracy under Daw Aung San Suu Kyi gets under way in earnest. However, neither of the key figures played a leading role, but their looming presence was always felt. The leaders of the action were President Thein Sein and Thura Shwe Mann in his role as the *primus inter pares*, initially in the Pyithu Hluttaw and then in the Pyidaungsu Hluttaw, as well as the nominally ruling party as acting chairman until his ouster in 2015. Shwe Mann's emerging alliance with, if not co-option of, Aung San Suu Kyi provides an unseen subtext of Ye Htut's detailed account of the increasing tension between the former number three and the former number four in the abandoned military order.

Given the central roles of President Thein Sein and Thura Shwe Mann in Ye Htut's account, it is important to note his relations with both men over the years. Ye Htut first met Shwe Mann in 1988 when he was a staff officer in the 44th Light Infantry Division and Shwe Mann was deputy commander of the No. 6 Light Infantry Regiment. They met again in 1992 in the Northern Command. Ye Htut admits Shwe Mann was something of a role model for him. As he notes in the text, it was Shwe Mann who nominated him to enter the Ministry of Information from the army. On the other hand, Ye Htut had never met Thein Sein until the new government was formed. After he became presidential spokesman in 2013, he travelled with the president on almost all of his foreign and domestic trips and sat in all important meetings with foreigners, ethnic armed group leaders, and others until the end of the presidency. Having observed at close hand the pressures on the president and the consequences of Shwe Mann's duplicity, he lost faith in his former military role model.

In what Ye Htut describes as "Shwe Mann's Checkmates", we see the attacking insurgent Hluttaw leader tie down the manoeuvrability of the president. The president, distracted from his reform plans by first sniping, and then artillery barrage, organized and led by Shwe Mann, becomes increasingly frustrated by the limitations on his authority and the conflicting advice offered by his cabinet and other advisers. In circumstances in which the past, both in terms of inherited traditions from the military experiences of most of the key actors, particularly hierarchical deference, made free and frank exchanges of views difficult when seen as between persons of unequal rank and stature, the robust arguments but common purpose which is normally expected within governments and ruling parties was difficult, if not impossible, to achieve.

Shwe Mann's lack of consistency in his views on the government's development priorities from his pre- to his post-military roles as revealed in the debates over the 2012–13 budget was just the beginning of the onslaught on the president. Others followed of which the issues of the appropriateness of a system of proportional representation to make Myanmar's electoral outcomes a better reflection of the majority views of the public, as opposed to results from the inherited first-past-the-post system, and the legal authority of the constitutionally mandated Constitutional Tribunal were perhaps the most crucial. The president's obvious worry about the implications of possible impeachment moves against him undermined his confidence in pushing his reforms.

The battle between Shwe Mann and Thein Sein was initially misunderstood by many observers, both Myanmar and foreigners, who, not studying the details, tended to see the initial conflict in either one of two ways. One, oft taken by those with a legalistic view of politics, was that the system of checks and balances that the previous government had heralded as a key feature of the new constitutional order was indeed working as intended. The other, more cynical, view was that the apparent conflicts between Shwe Mann and Thein Sein were merely for show. As two generals from the old order who had worked together for years in the SPDC government of the senior general could not really be at odds. They were play-acting in order to bamboozle the naïve into believing things had changed in Naypyitaw. The new order was merely mutton dressed as lamb. Even some former members of the army and civil servants far from the centres of conflict took this view. As Ye Htut documents, the conflicts were not only real but had consequences, largely negative, for Myanmar's political transition.

In addition to the president's stifled reform agenda and the instability created by the Shwe Mann orchestrated legislative attacks on the executive, events relating to pressing issues which invoked strong public opinion also drew the attention of the president and his far-from-united team. As a former British prime minister once allegedly remarked, what shaped what his government could do was "events, my dear boy, events". So President Thein Sein understood and, as Ye Htut explains, the issues of the Myitsone Dam conflict, the highly politicized drafting of the National Education Law, and the ethno-religious discord all posed challenges to the government. The outcome of decisions made by the government on these and other issues, as is often the case, had consequences unseen and unwanted at the time of action. Ye Htut takes his readers through these contortions also, drawing the drama away from just the battles in Naypyitaw to the wider context of Myanmar and continuing issues in its politics.

By way of a more personal reiteration, in his final substantive chapter Ye Htut's readers are told the story of his own part in one of the fundamental issues in Myanmar's transition. Stifling free debate and discussion in the media was one of the first consequences of the military coup of 1962, though the press in Myanmar after independence could also be said not to have been completely unfettered though relatively freer than what followed. The closing down of the independent media was one of the eventual causes of the collapse of the old order, for it had cut off the flow of ideas and criticism which is essential for any functioning state, economy or society to thrive and develop. Even Senior General Than Shwe understood this. As he explained in an unreported speech for newly inducted ambassadors in 2005, the necessity of a free press was obvious, but it had to be a press that would do more than just attack whoever was in power. As part of the transition following the adoption of the 2008 constitution, censorship would have to be terminated.

That, however, was easier said than done. Though the SLORC and the SPDC had allowed in various ways the emergence of private, non-government, media, this was kept under close supervision and control into the transition. The agency that imposed fetters on the private media was the Ministry of Information, having been assigned those duties after the fall of General Khin Nyunt and the transfer of censorship from the Home Ministry to the Information Ministry. That ministry, under the same minister who had been the media's bête noire, was now to become its liberator. Given the complete lack of trust that existed between the journalistic profession and the ministry, the deliberate and systematic liberation of the media was perhaps inevitably to have led to not merely doubts about but outright rejection of the ministry's plans.

The same distrust surrounded the Ministry of Information's intention to turn the state-owned newspapers and radio and television into public service media of the kind that existed in Western countries. Nothing like the BBC, Deutsche Welle or PBS had ever existed in Myanmar. The concept of public service broadcasting at arm's length from the government was totally foreign. Moreover, as too often forgotten in discussions about the private media, they must be run as businesses with the intention of making a profit for their owners. Public service broadcasters are seen as subsidized competitors for the private media's readers and advertisers, distorting the media market unfairly. Thus commercial interest, professional presumption and a severe lack of trust in the promises of the government meant that media reform would prove to be difficult.

Though Ye Htut does not raise his own role in the production of mass media during his years in government, his undoubted popularity with the public via his Facebook account perhaps raised the ire of journalists who were less well known and acclaimed. Known as the "Facebook minister", his public following reached a quarter of a million when he left office, having since then more than doubled to over half a million. His views, sometimes controversial, provoke the kind of public debate that a lively media should encourage, rather than pandering to received opinions and prejudices.

As Ye Htut explains, media reform was not only difficult but, in the end, incomplete. Before President Thein Sein stepped down from office, the possibility of fundamental reform to the media had become so politicized that it was not possible to continue to pursue. Opportunities were lost and chances to renew the drive for media reform by the successive government have been ignored. Now the old state media is extolled by the current minister for information, one of the vocal opponents of Kyaw Hsan's and his successors' gradual reform endeavours. Like so much else of the reform agenda of President Thein Sein, the past, in the form of vested interests, closed minds and the comfort of outmoded "standard operating procedures" hindered, and in crucial areas halted, the change that so many had hoped for in the preceding decades.

The failure of a thorough reform of the media is matched by the other failures of the Thein Sein administration to complete the president's reform agenda. In the epilogue, Ye Htut weighs up the major factors he sees as the cause of this. One is the legacy of the State Peace and Development Council government and its master for two decades, Senior General Than Shwe. Than Shwe had a vision of the kind of Myanmar he wanted to create, but not only did he not share this vision with others, the tools he used to craft his vision were those of the army, and were therefore incapable of building sustainable civilian institutions. The flawed 2008 constitution was just one of several inadequate tools he bequeathed his chosen successor, President Thein Sein.

As others besides Ye Htut have noted, Thein Sein was too nice to be president. He brought to the tasks he was assigned in the army and in government honesty and tenacity, but he did not possess within himself the ruthlessness and guile that most ambitious leaders wield in their climb to greater and greater power. Thein Sein, because of his competency, had power thrust upon him when he sought to avoid it. Noted as a good listener, he was also a deep, and doubtless lonely, thinker, displaying none of the garrulousness of many around him. Given a flawed and imperfect legacy from which to build, he tried his best. And, as Ye Htut notes in his concluding remarks, despite the lost opportunities of the Thein Sein presidency, there were great achievements. Thein Sein set a new standard for Myanmar's leaders.

Myanmar's Democratic Transition and Lost Opportunities (2011–2016) now joins the small corpus of important texts on Myanmar's modern political history. A few books by authors with unique access define their eras. *Guardian* Sein Win's *The Split Story: An Account of Recent Political Upheaval in Burma* (1959) does that for Myanmar's first effort to establish a civilian constitutional order. Ye Htut's does that for the second attempt. Whether there will have to be a third attempt remains in the balance. If there is, do not blame Thein Sein. The Thein Sein government attempted to establish a benchmark for open, listening and responsive government. Its achievements were not insignificant, and Thein Sein would probably be the first to say those achievements, as well as lost opportunities, were not the result of one person, though ultimately the president bears the greatest burden of office.

Dr Maung Maung, in the midst of his one-month presidency that led to the imposition of military government in 1988, reminded his listeners of Lord Acton's oft quoted aphorism "Power tends to corrupt, and absolute power corrupts absolutely. Great men are almost always bad men." Ye Htut has demonstrated that Acton's qualification on his words were well taken. Some great men are neither corrupt nor bad. They remain the exception to the rule, however.

Robert H. Taylor
11 January 2019

Acknowledgements

This book is based on my experiences during Myanmar's transition to democracy under President Thein Sein. I began as director general of the Information and Public Relations Department of the Ministry of Information under the president in 2011 and ended as minister for information and spokesperson for the president in 2016.

After I became presidential spokesperson in February 2013, I accompanied U Thein Sein on nearly all of the president's foreign and domestic trips, attending his meetings with foreign leaders, scholars, ambassadors, local people, leaders of ethnic armed organizations, and politicians, including Daw Aung San Suu Kyi. I observed how he tried to implement reforms and how much he suffered under the pressures created by his opponents over three years. I thank the president for selecting me to serve under him during a very critical time in Myanmar's political history.

My reflections in this book are not about the success of President Thein Sein's reform programme; it is about how and why the government lost opportunities to improve the governance of Myanmar through the reform process. I have tried to describe what went on behind the scenes of the Thein Sein government, and about the president, his policies, character, his rivals and the constraints with which he had to struggle.

Writing about your superior and your colleagues is not easy, since I have a personal attachment to many members of the cabinet, Hluttaw, Tatmadaw (Armed Forces) and USDP. Some of the individuals I discuss are my mentors, some are brother officers and some are classmates from the military academy. But thanks to Professor Taylor, who has always challenged my assumptions about Myanmar's politics, I have been able to reach reasoned conclusions supported by evidence.

I could not have written this book without the kind support from Director Choi Shing Kwok and Senior Advisor Tan Chin Tiong of the ISEAS – Yusof Ishak Institute. Being at ISEAS enabled me to reflect objectively on the events I describe, away from peer pressure. I also learnt from my colleagues at ISEAS who have vast experience in research by reading their papers and listening to their presentations. Thanks to ISEAS, I hope my book will contribute to a greater understanding of Myanmar's transition to democracy.

I wish to sincerely thank the individuals who allowed me to interview them and share their experiences and insights on many events and issues. I could not have written this book without the diligent efforts and research assistance of my former MOI colleagues Daw Moe Thuzar Soe and U Tin Maung Oo. I owe them a great debt of gratitude for a job well done. I also owe thanks to the dedicated group of journalists from *7Day* journal who provided me with news clips and who sometimes challenged my arguments about media reform in Myanmar.

Last but not least, my thanks go to my dad, mom and my family for their love, support and tolerance of my long absences from home.

Finally, all errors of fact, omission and interpretation are mine and I alone take all responsibility for that.

Ye Htut
30 January 2019
Singapore

Introduction:
Myanmar's Political Reforms

The "Myanmar Spring" or Myanmar's road to democracy commenced on 30 March 2011. That morning, newly elected President Thein Sein delivered his inaugural address to the Pyidaungsu Hluttaw (Union assembly). This was the first speech of the first competitively elected head of state by the parliament and, indirectly, the citizens of Myanmar since the 1962 military coup.

Although it was broadcast live, except for a few scholars and journalists, the majority of the people of Myanmar as well as the international community gave very little attention to the speech. As the ruling party, the Union Solidarity and Development Party (USDP), was backed by the military, and the elected president was a former general and the prime minister of the previous military government, they saw the new government as a quasi-military regime—the same old wine in a new bottle.

Myanmar had held a general election on 7 November 2010 under a new constitution. The constitution had been formally adopted following a referendum in 2008. The previous military government stated that this election was the starting point for a democratization process,[1] but given the contentious nature of the election process, the international community rejected the election result. For example, the International Crisis Group took the following view of the elections and the subsequent government under President Thein Sein:

> [the] Union Solidarity and Development Party (USDP) won a landslide victory leaving the military elite still in control. Together with the quarter of legislative seats reserved for soldiers, this means there will be little

political space for opposition members in parliament. The new government that has been formed, and which will assume power in the coming weeks, also reflects the continued dominance of the old order with the president and one of the two vice presidents drawn from its ranks and a number of cabinet ministers recycled.[2]

The United States government, the leading power critical of the military government, stated that the elections "were neither free nor fair and failed to meet any internationally accepted standards" and that "Myanmar missed an opportunity to begin genuine transition toward democratic governance and national reconciliation."[3]

President Thein Sein was aware of this mistrust and was eager to send a strong positive message to both the public and the international community. In this regard, the salient points of his speech included the following:

1. Moreover, it is still necessary to show our genuine goodwill towards those who have not accepted the constitution because of being sceptical about the seven-step road map in order that they can discard their suspicions and play a part in the nation-building tasks. Likewise, we need to convince some nations with negative attitude towards our democratization process that Myanmar has been committed to implement a democratic system correctly and effectively.
2. In transition to democracy, it is obligatory to promote democratic practices not only among the Hluttaw representatives but also among the people. To do so, I promise that our government will cooperate with the political parties in the Hluttaws, good-hearted political forces outside the Hluttaws and all social organizations.
3. Democracy will develop only hand in hand with good governance. This is why our government responsible for Myanmar's transition to democracy will try hard to shape good administrative machinery.
4. To safeguard the fundamental rights of citizens in line with the provisions of the constitution in the new democratic nation is high on our government's list of priorities. We guarantee that all citizens will enjoy equal rights in terms of law, and we will reinforce the judicial pillar. We will fight corruption in cooperation with the people as it harms the image of not only the offenders but also the nation and the people.

5. So, we will amend and revoke the existing laws and adopt new laws as necessary to implement the provisions on fundamental rights of citizens or human rights.
6. Particularly, I would like to exhort all to work together in the national interests, ignoring any negative attitude such as from the government and the opposition, which was conventional in Myanmar politics.[4]

The president's future reform agenda, including reconciliation with opposition groups, especially with Daw Aung San Suu Kyi, rapprochement with the West, good governance, promotion of human rights and the abolition of repressive laws, was based on this speech. However, at that time Thein Sein could not openly say these things. He had to pass his message indirectly to the citizens of Myanmar and the international community.

These were strong and sincere words, words that before 2011 no high official would have dared to speak. The president's words were completely different from the utterances of the previous military government. Even though critics of the government said that these were all just sweet words and that the president would not implement them, for the people of Myanmar such words would have been unthinkable only a few months earlier, and many came to sense that a wind of change was blowing.

President Thein Sein's reforms were very different from "Colour Revolutions" or the so-called Arab Spring. This was not a popular uprising causing the fall of a repressive government. These reforms were implemented by the military that had seized power in 1988. Senior General Than Shwe, who led the country from 1992 until President Thein Sein assumed office, established the political mechanism that enabled the bloodless reform, and General Thein Sein, another military leader, launched the reform process based on this mechanism. It was a unique transition to democracy that led to the peaceful transfer of power to Aung San Suu Kyi as leader of the National League for Democracy (NLD) government in 2016.

In retrospect, President Thein Sein's five-year term of reform was a struggle to implement a new political landscape in Myanmar after twenty years of military government and isolation from the Western international community. However, though there have been many achievements, there remain many challenges. Also, there were many lost opportunities and setbacks, which future governments might learn to avoid. This is the story that I wish to tell.

Notes

1. Information Minister Kyaw Hsan relayed this message to the UN special representative to Myanmar, Ibrahim Gambari, many times, but Gambari thought this was just the junta's propaganda.
2. International Crisis Group, "Myanmar's Post-Election Landscape", 7 March 2011, p. 1.
3. The White House Office of the Press Secretary, "President Obama on Burma's November 7 Elections", press statement and Secretary of State Hillary Clinton's statement on 7 November 2010.
4. The entire speech is printed as Appendix A along with President Thein Sein's remarks to the cabinet and other officials as Appendix B.

1

The National Convention

Senior General Than Shwe and other military leaders established a new political system under the 2008 constitution. The National Convention played an essential role in the drafting process. Although the military State Law and Order Restoration Council (SLORC) organized the National Convention, in 1989, prior to national elections the following year, the Tatmadaw (armed forces) had no intention of drawing up a new constitution.

After the military took power in 1988, SLORC chairman Senior General Saw Maung explained that the army government would not write a new constitution, and that it was the responsibility of the political parties that won the forthcoming national elections to do so. "The coming Pyithu Hluttaw will write and adopt a new constitution. After its adoption, power will be transferred to the constitutionally formed government", he explained.[1]

This position was clearly stated at the SLORC's 43rd press conference on 9 June 1989. The SLORC spokesperson said:

> It has been said that power will be transferred to the government that will come into being in accordance with the law after the elections are held.

Power could not be handed over immediately after the elections are held as government will have to be formed on the basis of a constitution. If power will be transferred hastily [without a proper procedure], it would lead to a shaky and weak government; any rational person can understand it. Only if the power is transferred to a government formed systematically on a basis of a constitution, will the government to be constituted be stable. We have two constitutions at present, namely the 1947 constitution and the 1974 constitution. If the Hluttaw members unanimously selected one of the two constitutions and formed a government then, power would be transferred to them. We are ready to transfer power to the government formed in accordance with the constitution. If both the constitutions are not acceptable, a new one should be written. The Tatmadaw will not draw up a new constitution. The SLORC will not do it either. The representatives elected are to draw it.[2]

Although the SLORC promised to hold an election, it never explained that this election would be held under the previous, 1974 constitution. The 1947 constitution was abolished following the 1962 military coup and eventually replaced by the 1974 constitution. The election held in 1990 was for a single-house parliament as under the 1974 constitution. However, the 1974 constitution established a one-party political system and not a multiparty democratic system, which was the ostensible objective of the 1990 election. Surprisingly, the NLD and other contesting political parties never questioned the SLORC's plan for the transfer of power. Also, the SLORC never defined the coming parliament as either a constitutional assembly or a legislative assembly that would form the government and take power.[3]

On 12 April 1990, six weeks before the election, SLORC secretary 1, Major General Khin Nyunt, said:

> The party that wins in the 27 May elections will have to form a government. Only if a firm constitution can be drawn up and a government formed in accordance with it will the government be a strong one. So we will continue to carry out the responsibilities even after the elections. We will continue to do so till a strong government has been formed.[4]

In this ambiguous situation, the 1990 election was held, and ninety-three parties contested. Aung San Suu Kyi's NLD won 392 out of 447 seats. After the election, the NLD prepared for a transfer of power. The party sent a letter to the SLORC on 21 June requesting to discuss future political programmes based on the national interest. No response was received from the SLORC.

The NLD Central Executive Committee met on 28 and 29 June and adopted three objectives as urgent political tasks: (1) the release of Aung San Suu Kyi and former general Tin Oo from house arrest; (2) the transfer of power from the SLORC; and (3) the re-opening of all universities.[5] To implement these tasks, the NLD drafted an interim constitution and planned to hold a plenary meeting of all the elected parliament members from the NLD on 28 and 29 July. It was to be held at Gandhi Hall, Yangon, and would later be referred to as the Gandhi Hall meeting.

While the NLD was planning for the plenary meeting, the SLORC chairman, Senior General Saw Maung, and secretary 1, Major General Khin Nyunt, said that the recently elected parliament should draft a new constitution and that the SLORC would hand over power when a new constitution was adopted by a referendum and new elections held under that constitution.[6]

NLD members and the public debated whether the proposed Gandhi Hall meeting was for the preparation of a new constitution or to form a new government under the NLD that would then take power.[7] The SLORC was concerned that the NLD would declare an interim government during that meeting and start another crisis like that of 1988 when unrest led to a declaration of martial law. One day before the start of the Gandhi Hall meeting, 27 July, the SLORC released Declaration No. 1/90, stating that power could not be transferred simply by convening the Pyithu Hluttaw (lower house or people's assembly) and that the elected representatives had a duty to first draft a constitution. The SLORC warned that they would not accept the NLD plan to form the government by the adoption of an interim constitution, and that such efforts would be dealt with by strong legal action.[8]

In 1991, Saw Maung and Khin Nyunt proposed the holding of a National Convention by elected members of parliament and ethnic representatives. Khin Nyunt pledged to assist the convening of the National Convention with political party leaders, elected members, ethnic representatives and other politicians.[9] This idea reflected the attitude of the military leaders that they should avoid the drafting of the constitution. But this attitude changed shortly after, following the retirement of Saw Maung from the SLORC chairmanship for reasons of a nervous breakdown. General Than Shwe, the vice chairman of the SLORC and Tatmadaw commander in chief, succeeded him. For General Than Shwe, the uncompromising nature of the NLD led to a deadlock in Myanmar's political transition and he apparently believed he had to find a way to move forward. He sought to establish a political structure that could create a civilian government in line with the Tatmadaw's idea of nation building, and consequently decided the SLORC must lead the constitution drafting process and manage the political transition.

The Military and the Constitution

Prior to 1988 there were two periods in which the army was directly involved in the country's government. The first was the assumption of power as a caretaker government in 1958 following the negotiations between Prime Minister Nu and commander in chief General Ne Win; the second was the seizure of power in 1962 during a national debate on demands from ethnic leaders for an amendment of the 1947 constitution, which the military believed would contribute to the disintegration of the Union.

The 1958 caretaker government transferred power to the party that won the elections in 1960. Within the short span of its rule, the caretaker government was able to bring much needed stability and economic development and won the support not only of the public but also of the international community. The military leaders hoped that the politicians who had been their comrades in the independence struggle would maintain the situation as restored by the caretaker government. However, Nu's ruling Union Party suffered an intra-party crisis between two factions and faced demands from ethnic groups to amend the constitution. Ethnic leaders wanted a new federal constitution; the Tatmadaw saw this as a threat to the Union.

This situation led to the military coup of 1962. Prior to the coup, General Ne Win and his colleagues had concluded that the Westminster system of parliamentary democracy was not working to realize the socialist goals aspired to by General Aung San. As a first step, they set up the Burma Socialist Programme Party (BSPP) as a political wing of the military, and General Ne Win served as its chairman. The BSPP then drafted a single-party constitution, designated their party as the leading party, and implemented their variety of socialism. General Ne Win become president after the introduction of the 1974 constitution. Nearly all of the top positions in the government were filled by retired military officers. The BSPP's socialist policies eventually led to the bankruptcy of the economy, and, following widespread public protests in 1988, the SLORC came to power.

In 1992, Senior General Than Shwe selected a different approach to that of his predecessor, Ne Win. He did not seek to transfer power to the NLD, as Ne Win did to the Anti-Fascist People's Freedom League (Clean) in 1960; nor did he want to take command as Ne Win did in 1962. His plan was to create a political system that would result in a peaceful transition to multiparty democracy. In this the military should not have a leading role, but should rather be an important partner as in a coalition government. The military would control certain important ministries, and its support would be needed in order to pass important decisions such as constitutional amendments. This is the reason Than Shwe changed Saw Maung's policy and decided to convene a National Convention to draft a new state constitution.

Preparation for the National Convention

On 24 April 1992, the SLORC issued Notification No. 11/92 stating that it would meet with elected representatives from political parties and elected independent representatives within two months, and that it would call a National Convention within six months to draft the basic principles for a new state constitution.[10] Under Order No. 13/92 issued on 28 May 1992, the SLORC formed a fifteen-member National Convention Convening Committee (NCCC), with Yangon Command commander Major General Myo Nyunt as chair. On the same day, the SLORC announced that a coordinating meeting for the National Convention would be held at 9 a.m. on 23 June 1992. According to the announcement, the SLORC invited the following numbers of representatives from political parties:

(a)	National League for Democracy	15
(b)	Shan National League for Democracy	6
(c)	National Unity Party	3
(d)	Union Pa-O League	1
(e)	Mro (a) Khami National Solidarity Party	1
(f)	Shan State Kokang Democratic Party	1
(g)	Lahu National Development Party	1

At the same time, the SLORC informed the NLD that if they wanted to attend the National Convention, the party would have to abolish their Pyithu Hluttaw Representatives Group that had been set up on 9 October 1990. The demand put the NLD leaders of the time in a very difficult position. As NLD chairman Tin Oo and general secretary Aung San Suu Kyi had been detained in July 1989 and acting chairman Kyi Maung in September 1990, former brigadier general Aung Shwe became the acting chairman of the NLD Central Executive Committee (CEC). The SLORC demanded that the NLD accept their Declaration No. 1/90 and expel Aung San Suu Kyi from the NLD. The SLORC threatened to dissolve the party if it failed to do so. Aung Shwe and the remaining CEC members believed that maintaining the NLD as a political party during Aung San Suu Kyi's house arrest was strategically more important than resisting the SLORC's demands. After much consideration they agreed to all of the SLORC's demands and issued Declaration No. 5/90, which accepted the drafting of a new constitution and expelled Aung San Suu Kyi from the NLD on 11 December 1991. These decisions faced strong protests from NLD members. Aung Shwe and the NLD CEC then faced the difficult decision of whether or not to attend the National Convention, a situation they discussed in meetings on 2 and 4 June. They decided to attend the National Convention and agreed to abolish the Hluttaw committee.[11] Like previous decisions, the decision to attend the National Convention was denounced by hard-line NLD supporters. However, because of this decision, many detained NLD elected Hluttaw members were released and the NLD was able to hold a series of meeting under the pretext of preparations for the convention.[12]

The National Convention Convening Committee met on three days, 23 and 30 June and 10 July. The discussions were concerned mainly with how to select representatives for the convention. The committee eventually agreed to hold a national convention composed of the following eight categories of delegate groups:[13]

1. political parties
2. representatives-elect
3. national races
4. peasants
5. workers
6. intellectuals and intelligentsia

7. state service personnel
8. other invited guests

The SLORC insisted on the following principles in the drafting of the new constitution:

1. non-disintegration of the Union;
2. non-disintegration of national solidarity;
3. consolidation and perpetuation of sovereignty;
4. emergence of a genuine multiparty democratic system;
5. development of eternal principles of justice, liberty and equality in the state;
6. participation of the Tatmadaw in a leading role in national politics.

Disagreements with the NLD

Disagreements between the SLORC and the NLD began during the coordination meeting for the National Convention. First, they differed on the selection of delegates to the National Convention. The NLD wanted all the elected representatives from the 1990 election to attend the convention, but the SLORC wanted to use a proportional system based on seats won by each party. That meant that the NLD, which won 392 seats, would only have 88 representatives. Another dispute concerned the selection of the other groups: ethnic minorities, peasants, workers, civil servants, intellectuals and intelligentsia, and other invited guests. According to the NCCC plan, government officials were responsible for the selection process for these groups. The NLD wanted a more transparent and inclusive process in the selection of delegates, especially for representatives of peasants, workers, and intellectuals and intelligentsia. The NLD also wanted to add youth and women as delegate categories.[14]

The SLORC refused to accept these suggestions and announced that 702 delegates from the eight delegate groups would be invited to attend the National Convention (see Table 1.1). The NLD sent 49 delegates in the "political parties" group and 107 delegates in the "representatives-elect" group. Among those invited, the NLD representatives and those of the ethnic armed groups were the only independent delegates, as all the others were handpicked by the government. Elected delegates represented just 15.24 per cent of the total membership, accounting for 107 out of the total 702. With this ratio the SLORC effectively marginalized the NLD.[15]

TABLE 1.1
National Convention Participants (1993)

Group	Total
Political parties	49
Elected representatives (1990 election)	12[a]
National races	215
Peasants	93
Workers	48
Intellectuals and intelligentsia	41
Civil servants	109
Other invited delegates[b]	57[b]

Notes: (a) The NLD and the SNLD boycotted the National Convention; (b) 42 of the "Other invited delegates" were from ethnic armed groups that had ceasefire agreements with the government.
Source: National Convention Convening Commission, *Amyotha Nyilarkan Thamine* [History of the National Convention], 2008.

The NLD criticized the leading role of the SLORC in organizing the National Convention. They argued that it was contrary to Declaration No. 1/90, which stated that the drafting of the new constitution was the responsibility of the elected representatives. They also criticized the last in the list of fundamental principles for the National Convention, that the constitution must allow for "participation of the Tatmadaw (military) in the leading role of future national politics". They saw this as opposed to the principles of democracy.[16]

Another dispute was over the convention procedures. According to National Convention Convening Committee procedures, the NCC Working Committee first explained the adoptable basic principles for each chapter during a plenary session. The eight delegate groups were then to hold separate sessions and prepare their respective responses to these basic principles. But the NLD saw these processes as complicated and tightly controlled, and as not allowing a full and free discussion of the issues involved. According to the NLD, the instructions of the NCCC were as follows. As a first step, delegates who wanted to participate in group discussions would have to prepare position papers, which would be submitted to the chairman of the group's panel. The third step would allow the panel chairman to suggest modifications to the paper. In the fourth step, the panel would present its papers to the Working Committee, which could send them back with suggestions for change.[17] The papers were to be amended in accord with these suggestions in the fifth step. In the sixth step, papers were to be read in respective group discussions. The panel chairman would then send all papers to the Working Committee again as a seventh step. Sometimes the Working Committee would edit a previously approved paper. The eighth step was the submission of the papers at a plenary session, and the papers would finally be sent to the Working Committee with comments from the chairman of the plenary session. Afterwards, the Working Committee, with the approval of the NCCC, announced the adoption of the principles at the next plenary session.

NLD representatives objected to this process and accused the National Convention of becoming a tightly controlled seminar lacking serious and open discussion. They also opposed the practice of dividing papers into "majority opinion" and "minority opinion" because elected representatives were always in a minority in the convention. They complained that the idea of scrutinizing the papers by a panel had not been mentioned in National Convention procedures.

The NLD submitted their complaints to the Working Committee on 9 September 1993. The Working Committee replied that SLORC Order No. 13/92 on the National Convention stated: "The Commission shall make arrangements to enable the representatives attending the National Convention to submit systematically their wishes, suggestions and proposals at the National Convention", and that their process was in accord with this order. They also pointed out that NLD representatives should also be panel members and participate in this process.[18] The objections of the NLD were to no avail.

Departure of the NLD from the Convention

While the National Convention was in session, the SLORC sent an overture to Aung San Suu Kyi by allowing her husband and two sons to visit in August 1993. They also allowed some foreigners to meet with her, including US congressman Bill Richardson.

On the evening news of 20 September 1994, the people of Myanmar were surprised to see SLORC chairman Senior General Than Shwe and secretary 1 Major General Khin Nyunt holding talks with Aung San Suu Kyi. On 28 October 1994, secretary 1 Major General Khin Nyunt, judge advocate general Brigadier General Than Oo, and Defence Services inspector general Brigadier General Tin Aye met with her. According to the state-run dailies, the meeting discussed the prevailing national political and economic situation, the political and economic reforms of the SLORC, and measures for long-term national interest in a cordial and frank atmosphere. But according to Khin Nyunt, Than Shwe never discussed politics during his meeting with Aung San Suu Kyi. Rather, he discussed other issues such as regional development. Whenever Aung San Suu Kyi raised political issues, he cleverly changed the topic. He only met with her to reduce international pressure and never intended to enter serious political dialogue.[19]

The relationship between the SLORC and NLD showed improvement on 15 March 1995 when the NLD chairman, former general Tin Oo, and CEC member Kyi Maung were released from prison. Not long after, on 10 July 1995, Aung San Suu Kyi was released from house arrest. From that day, however, instead of moving towards reconciliation between the two sides, relations deteriorated, primarily because of NLD opposition to the National Convention.

The day after she was freed from house arrest, Aung San Suu Kyi held a press conference at which she stated that some procedures of the National Convention should be changed. At another press conference, held at NLD headquarters on 22 November, she criticized the National Convention for ignoring the parties that won the 1990 elections. She claimed that the processing of the papers by panels and the lack of open debate was contrary to SLORC Declaration No. 1/90. She also urged that the National Convention should have a timetable, and she requested a dialogue with the SLORC in regard to the National Convention.[20]

When reporters asked about boycotting the National Convention, Aung San Suu Kyi replied that although the NLD was still undecided, all options would be considered, and she added that the NLD was not rejecting the National Convention but was merely opposed to the manner it was being conducted.[21] On 27 November the NLD sent a letter to the Working Committee that called for a dialogue with the government and asked the committee to reply by the next day. Instead of directly replying to the NLD, Lieutenant General Myo Nyunt, as chairman of the NCCC, addressed the plenary session on 28 November. He defended the convention procedures and accused certain elements of trying to sabotage the constitution drafting process. He made no mention of a dialogue with the NLD.

After that plenary session the NLD again sent a letter to the Working Committee stating that since there had been no response to their requests they would not attend the convention but would wait for the government's decision on holding a dialogue. Then, on the evening of 28 November, the eighty-six NLD delegates to the National Convention, led by Aung Shwe, walked out of the convention. The NLD explained that the walkout was not an act of boycott but merely a pause while awaiting a dialogue with the government.[22] The government, however, did not accept that position. On 30 November the Working Committee announced the expulsion of the eighty-six delegates from the NLD based on their alleged violation of the convention's rules and regulations by being absent without leave for two days.[23] The NCCC also issued a press statement accusing the NLD of attempting to abolish all agreed basic principles for the constitution and replace the convention with one of their own. The statement said that the NLD was only interested in partisan politics and thus neglected the national interest. The commission reaffirmed that in order to fulfil the national interest the convention would proceed without the NLD.[24]

The National Convention continued until it was finally adjourned on 31 March 1996. Between 1993 and 1996 the National Convention met in six sessions and agreed on 104 basic principles formulated as the basic principles for eight chapters of the constitution (see Table 1.2).[25] Although the National Convention was adjourned in 1996, the commission and Working Committee continued their work. They studied other national constitutions, drafted principles for the remaining chapters, held discussions with relevant government departments, and briefed Senior General Than Shwe and other top leaders.[26]

TABLE 1.2
National Convention Sessions (1993–96)

Session	from	to
First	9 Jan 1993	11 Jan 1993
Second	1 Feb 1993	7 Apr 1993
Third	7 Jun 1993	16 Sep 1993
Fourth	18 Jan 1994	9 Apr 1994
Fifth	2 Sep 1994	7 Apr 1995
Sixth*	28 Nov 1995	31 Mar 1996

Note: *The NLD delegation walked out on 28 November 1995.

Confrontation

After the NLD walked out from the National Convention, relations between the SLORC and the NLD deteriorated further. On several occasions between 1996 and 2001, government security forces prevented Aung San Suu Kyi from leaving Yangon. Whenever she attempted to travel to another state or region, her convoy was stopped outside Yangon and sent back. Sometimes she was also stopped from travelling to NLD township offices in Yangon Division. The NLD responded by holding weekend meetings in front of Aung San Suu Kyi's house, where she and other leaders, in responding to questions from an audience of supporters, would attack SLORC policies. Aung San Suu Kyi also asked the international community to pressure the SLORC by supporting sanctions on Myanmar and opposing the country's application for membership of the Association of Southeast Asian Nations (ASEAN). On 23 June 1998, the NLD sent a letter to Senior General Than Shwe demanding he call a session of the Pyithu Hluttaw before 21 August. The SLORC viewed this as an ultimatum and responded by temporarily detaining all NLD elected representatives at army guest houses in order to prevent the NLD from convening the Hluttaw themselves.

While all its elected representatives were detained, the NLD and its allies formed the Committee Representing the People's Parliament, or CRPP, on 16 September 1998.[27] This committee was headed by Aung Shwe, as chairman of the NLD, and had nine members, including Aung San Suu Kyi. The committee appointed Rakhine NLD elected representative Saw Mara Aung as Hluttaw Speaker, formed ten Hluttaw committees, and added another nine members, mostly from ethnically designated parties.[28] The CRPP announced that they would try to convene the Hluttaw and that they would act as the Hluttaw until that time.[29] This led to increasing tension with the SLORC.

The confrontation reached its highest point on the evening of 21 September 2000, when Aung San Suu Kyi arrived at Yangon Central railway station for a proposed trip to Mandalay, Myanmar's second-largest city. When her supporters arrived they were barred by security forces from entering the station. And when Aung San Suu Kyi arrived, station staff informed her that all tickets had already been sold. She decided to stay at the station and catch another train the next morning, but the station staff asked her to leave. When she refused, security forces

The National Convention

arrested her, vice chairman Tin Oo and other NLD members. The next day, the government announced that Aung San Suu Kyi and Tin Oo were under house arrest.

Unlike during previous house arrests, the SLORC allowed Razali Ismail, the United Nations Secretary-General's Special Envoy to Myanmar, to visit her and attempt to negotiate between Aung San Suu Kyi and the SLORC. He travelled to Myanmar nine times between 5 November 2001 and the end of 2002. Very little was revealed of these negotiations, but General Than Shwe invited Aung San Suu Kyi for lunch on 29 January 2001. Also present at this lunch were General Maung Aye, Lieutenant General Khin Nyunt, Lieutenant General Thura Shwe Mann and Lieutenant General Thein Sein from the SLORC, and Aung Shwe, Tin Oo and Lwin from the NLD. Talk during the lunch was mainly on personal matters—political issues were not discussed. General Than Shwe said the meeting was about getting to know each other better, and that in future he intended to invite their spouses. He also spoke about his recent trip to China.[30]

Aung San Suu Kyi was released from house arrest on 6 May 2002. Aung Shwe and Tin Oo had been released on 15 February 2002. The government now allowed Aung San Suu Kyi to travel freely around the country. She travelled to many states and regions and visited some government development projects, such as for bridges and dams. Government officials briefed her about these projects. On 17 August 2002 she said that she saw positive developments in the current situation. On a trip to Rakhine State in December 2002, however, she faced difficulties when the local authorities prevented NLD supporters from greeting her. She strongly denounced the authorities, and the government accused her of returning to a policy of confrontation.

Two weeks before this, on the anniversary of her release from house arrest, she held a press conference at which she said now was not the time for building trust but was rather a time for meaningful dialogue, and she questioned the government's sincerity about national reconciliation. In May she visited Mandalay and Sagaing Divisions and Kachin State. There she accused the local authorities of harassing NLD supporters during her visits—the government accused her supporters of disturbing public order and blocking traffic. The government allowed members of the government-sponsored Union Solidarity and Development Association (USDA) to stage counter protests against the NLD. Tensions between NLD supporters and those who protested against them were high, and small clashes between the two occurred. This ended on 30 May 2003 with the tragic Depayin incident, when Aung San Suu Kyi's convoy was attacked by a mob. According to official reports, four died and fifty were wounded, but this claim has been contested by the NLD and by human rights groups. Aung San Suu Kyi and members of her entourage were evacuated by security forces, and according to state media they were put under protective custody.

With international pressure mounting, Senior General Than Shwe introduced new initiatives for political reform. General Khin Nyunt, military chief and secretary 1 of the SLORC, was appointed as prime minister, the post held by Than Shwe since 1992. On 30 August 2003, Khin Nyunt addressed government and army officials and announced a seven-step road map to disciplined democracy. His statement had three parts. The first was concerned with economic and infrastructural development undertakings by the Tatmadaw government since 1988, while the second dealt with political developments since 1988. The third part laid down a political road map for establishing democracy in Myanmar. The seven-step road map was as follows:

1. Reconvening of the National Convention that had been adjourned since 1996;
2. After the successful holding of the National Convention, step-by-step implementation of the process necessary for the emergence of a genuine and disciplined democratic system;
3. Drafting of a new constitution in accordance with basic principles and detailed basic principles laid down by the National Convention;
4. Adoption of the constitution through national referendum;
5. Holding of free and fair elections for Pyithu Hluttaws (legislative bodies) according to the new constitution;
6. Convening of Hluttaws attended by Hluttaw members in accordance with the new constitution;
7. Building a modern, developed and democratic nation by the state leaders elected by the Hluttaw and the government and other central organs formed by the Hluttaw.[31]

The idea of the road map for democratization had begun to be formed following three meetings General Khin Nyunt had in the 1990s with Prime Minister Lee Kwan Yew of Singapore. Premier Lee gave three suggestions to Khin Nyunt: (1) deal tactfully with the opposition, avoiding harsh measures; (2) change the image of the government from a military one to a quasi-civilian one; and (3) re-engage with the international community. Khin Nyunt understood that Lee had indirectly encouraged him to find a way to work with Aung San Suu Kyi. Another ASEAN leader to encourage him to find a means to work with the opposition was President Suharto of Indonesia. Khin Nyunt began to think about how to bring the NLD into the process, but he did not dare mention this openly to the senior general at the time.[32]

In 2001, while Razali Ismail was negotiating between the military leaders and Aung San Suu Kyi, Khin Nyunt thought it was an appropriate time to propose the road map idea to Than Shwe. Than Shwe accepted the idea but decided it was too early to announce it because he had many things to do to prepare for a transition to democracy. But Khin Nyunt, after consulting with the chief justice and attorney general, laid out a seven-step road map and kept it to himself. After the Depayin incident, Than Shwe ordered Khin Nyunt to draft the seven-step road map and to announce it. Than Shwe's decision to appoint Khin Nyunt as prime minister and for him to announce the road map was because he did not want to attend the international meetings to attempt to reduce international pressure.[33] The NCCC was hence reorganized with SLORC secretary 1 Lieutenant General Thein Sein, General Khin Nyunt's successor, as chair, chief justice Aung Toe and minister Lieutenant General Tin Htut as vice chairs, minister Brigadier General Kyaw Hsan as secretary, and Major General Khin Aung Myint as joint secretary. Twelve other members were also appointed.[34]

Reconvening the Convention

When the SLORC declared the reconvening of the National Convention, suspended since 1996, the question as to whether the NLD would rejoin it became an important issue. Since their demands in 1996 had never been met, the SLORC had to find a new means to bring the NLD into the convention in order to enhance its creditability.

First, Major General Kyaw Win, deputy chief of military intelligence, and others were sent to explain the desire of the State Peace and Development Council (SPDC) for NLD participation in the convention. When Aung San Suu Kyi requested to meet with other NLD CEC members, the government arranged a meeting at her house. After the CEC meeting, Aung San Suu Kyi replied to the government with the following conditions for the NLD's participation in the forthcoming convention:

1. Unconditional release of all political prisoners, including Aung San Suu Kyi and Tin Oo;
2. Recognition of the 1990 election results;
3. Permission to reopen all NLD offices; and
4. Selection of NLD delegates to be done solely by the NLD.

When Aung San Suu Kyi met with CEC members for a second time, she informed them that Kyaw Win had told her that SLORC leaders might be willing to agree to her demands. The CEC then started preparations to attend the convention. Subsequently, however, Major General Kyaw Win visited again and informed them that his boss (*Lugyi*) would not concede to the NLD's demands. According to the NLD, the party then decided not to attend the convention.[35]

According to Khin Nyunt,[36] the idea of sending minister for home affairs Colonel Tin Hlaing, deputy military intelligence chief Major General Kyaw Win, and head of the Political Department of Military Intelligence Brigadier General Than Htun to Aung San Suu Kyi was his own. He believed that without the NLD the National Convention would not be considered legitimate by the people or the international community. However, he knew that if he presented the proposal for the meeting with her to Senior General Than Shwe and Vice Senior General Maung Aye, they would reject it. He therefore secretly started to have discussions with Aung San Suu Kyi through his team and promised them he would try his best to ensure the release of Tin Oo and Aung San Suu Kyi from house arrest, but they should not be members of the NLD delegation to the convention. When Aung San Suu Kyi agreed, he proposed to Than Shwe that the government should release them from house arrest but not allow them to attend the convention. Than Shwe rejected this and the deal collapsed. Khin Nyunt suspected that Kyaw Win, who was close to Than Shwe, informed the senior general about the secret deal with the NLD, and this is one of the reasons Than Shwe decided to remove him.[37]

In the government's official version, the SLORC said that although the NLD delegation had been expelled from the convention in 1996, for the sake of national reconciliation an invitation letter had been sent to them. The NLD issued a statement on 14 May that they refused to attend. They gave various reasons for this decision, including the refusal to release Tin Oo and Aung San Suu Kyi. The SLORC responded that neither of these two were members of the NLD delegation in 1996, and their release should not be linked with participation in the convention. The government asked Aung San Suu Kyi and Tin Oo to remain at their homes in order to maintain stability during the convention.[38]

The National Convention that had been adjourned for nearly seven years was reconvened on 17 May 2004 under the terms of the road map. It was attended by 1,086 representatives from the eight categories of delegate groups. Sixty per cent, or 633 delegates, were from the delegate groups of national races. Working Committee chair Aung Toe told diplomats that they included one national race representative from every township.[39] There were accusations that those national race representatives were USDA members controlled by the government (see Table 1.3).[40] Although the NLD refused to rejoin the convention, seven elected representatives from the NLD decided to attend in their personal capacities, and they were expelled from the party. From the political parties, the Shan National League for Democracy (SNLD) and the Arakan National League for Democracy (ANLD) were also absent from the convention.

There were also accusations about the lack of a timetable for the National Convention, and a claim the government was using delaying tactics. Former information minister Kyaw Hsan refuted these allegations and stated that the government indeed had a timeframe for the convention but was unable to make it public so as to avoid any disturbances created by the opposition on the basis of the timetable.[41]

The National Convention thus reconvened without the NLD. Five sessions were held before it concluded on 3 September 2007. From 1993 to 2007 it held eleven sessions, and the basic principles and detailed

TABLE 1.3
National Convention Participants (2004)

Group	Total
Political parties	29
Elected representatives (1990 Election)	15
National races	633
Peasants	93
Workers	48
Intellectuals and intelligentsia	56
Civil servants	109
Other invited delegates*	105

Note: *90 of the "Other invited delegates" were from ethnic armed groups that had ceasefire agreements with the government.
Source: National Convention Convening Commission, *Amyotha Nyilarkan Thamine* [History of the National Convention], 2008.

principles for the future constitution were adopted. After the National Convention was concluded, the SPDC formed the State Constitution Drafting Commission under Notification No. 2/2007 of 18 October. The commission was chaired by Chief Justice Aung Toe. Eight months later, a new constitution was adopted by a referendum.

It can be said that the military leaders were able to achieve their strategic political objective of setting up the political system that could implement a peaceful transition to democracy. However, the NLD's refusal to rejoin the National Convention made the new constitution and government appear less creditable in the eyes of many of the people of Myanmar and the international community. The NLD made its stance abundantly clear through its Shwegondine Declaration of 29 April 2009.

Because of the Tatmadaw's failure to persuade the NLD to participate in the National Convention, internal and external support for the road map was weak. The impact of that weakness was visible during the early period of Thein Sein's government, and the first priority of the president was therefore to bring the NLD into the political process.

Notes

1. Senior General Saw Maung's concluding speech at the General Staff College, 11 November 1989.
2. *Loktharpyithu Naezin* [Working People], 10 June 1989.
3. For a fuller discussion of this issue, see Derek Tonkin, "The 1990 Election in Myanmar: Broken Promises or a Failure of Communication", *Contemporary Southeast Asia* 29, no. 1 (April 2007): 33–54.
4. *Loktharpyithu Naezin*, 13 April 1990.
5. Aung Shin (Monywa), *Amyotha Democracy Apwegyoke Mattan 1988–2010* [Chronicle of National League for Democracy (1988–2010)] (Yangon: Pyinsagan Literature House, 2016), p. 45.
6. Remark by Senior General Saw Maung on 3 July 1990 and Khin Nyunt's press conference on 13 July 1990.
7. Aung Shin, *Amyotha Democracy Apwegyoke Mattan*, p. 46.
8. SLORC Declaration No. 1/90, 27 July 1990.
9. SLORC Press Conference, 14 May 1991.
10. National Convention Convening Commission, *Amyotha Nyilarkan Thamine* [History of National Convention] (Yangon, 2008), p. 11.
11. Aung Shin, *Amyotha Democracy Apwegyoke Mattan*, p. 80.
12. Ibid., p. 85.

13. National Convention Working Committee Chairman, Chief Justice Aung Toe's clarification to diplomats and the press on 21 March 2006.
14. *Loketha Pyuithu Nazin*, 11 July 1992.
15. Aung Shin, *Amyotha Democracy Apwegyoke Mattan*, p. 87.
16. Ibid., p. 85.
17. Ibid., p. 95.
18. Interview 001.
19. Interview with Khin Nyunt, 11 July 2016.
20. Aung Shin, *Amyotha Democracy Apwegyoke Mattan*, pp. 131, 152.
21. Ibid., p. 155.
22. Ibid., p. 154.
23. Paragraphs 5(b), (d) and (e) of the National Convention regulations.
24. Press release of NCCC, 29 November 1995.
25. National Convention Working Committee chairman Chief Justice Aung Toe's clarification to diplomats and the press on 21 March 2006.
26. Interview 001. When the NCCC briefed Senior General Than Shwe, other top leaders General Maung Aye, Khin Nyunt and Tin Oo were also present. After 2004, General Maung Aye, Soe Win, Shwe Mann, Thein Sein and Tin Aung Myint Oo were present.
27. Aung Shin, *Amyotha Democracy Apwegyoke Mattan*, p. 263.
28. Ibid., p. 265.
29. Aung San Suu Kyi's letter to the public on 19 September 1998.
30. Aung Shin, *Amyotha Democracy Apwegyoke Mattan*, p. 314.
31. General Khin Nyunt's speech at a press conference, 30 August 2003.
32. Interview with Khin Nyunt, 11 November 2016.
33. Ibid.
34. SLORC Declarations Nos. 10/2003 (6 September 2003) and 11/2003 (23 September 2003).
35. Aung Shin, *Amyotha Democracy Apwegyoke Mattan*, p. 428.
36. Interview with Khin Nyunt, 11 November 2016.
37. Ibid.
38. *Myanma Alinn*, 15 May 2004.
39. National Convention Working Committee chairman Chief Justice Aung Toe's clarification to diplomats and the press on 21 March 2006.
40. "Money for National Convention Delegates Families", *Democratic Voice of Burma*, 17 June 2004.
41. Minister for information Brigadier-General Kyaw Hsan's lecture at Myanmar and International Studies Course 12 of the USDA, 14 May 2007.

2

The Constitution

President Thein Sein began his reform agenda under the 2008 constitution. There were two aspects of the 2008 constitution that affected his reform agenda. The first were perceptions of its legitimacy, and the second were articles of the constitution that restrained the president's ability to implement his reform agenda.

Legitimacy

Although the military leaders intended to use the 2008 constitution as the main platform for their democratization process, their means of drafting the constitution was questionable. Senior General Than Shwe saw the constitution as a transitional one that could be amended in the future to achieve fully fledged democracy in Myanmar. State Peace and Development Council (SPDC) leaders said that the constitution and coming election were not the end of the democratization process but were just the beginning, and that the constitution would be amended based on the maturity of all stakeholders.[1] Even though most of the stakeholders, including the National League for Democracy (NLD), could accept the 2008 constitution as transitional, there were strong objections to the drafting process. At the

National Convention, the decision of the State Law and Order Restoration Council (SLORC) to form eight delegate groups to represent political parties, ethnic minorities and various sectors of Myanmar society was a correct approach for the participatory process. But the government's selection process created opposition, not only from the NLD but also from ethnic parties. Also, the lack of open debate at the convention contributed to the peoples' mistrust of the constitution. People saw the entire process as highly undemocratic and as manipulated by the Tatmadaw (armed forces) in order to continue military dominance in politics.

When the National Convention concluded in September 2007, the ruling SPDC formed a Drafting Committee headed by Chief Justice Aung Toe.[2] The committee drafted the constitution based on the basic principles and detailed principles adopted by the National Convention. They began the drafting process on 3 December and finalized a draft on 19 February 2008. Ten days earlier, on 9 February, the SPDC announced that a referendum on the new constitution would be held in May 2008 and that general elections for Union, state and regional *hluttaw* (legislatures) would be held in 2010.

On 26 February 2008 the SPDC announced the formation of a forty-five-member referendum commission.[3] This commission set the date of the referendum as 10 May 2008.[4] Although the draft constitution had been completed, the government did very little to create public awareness of its contents. The government printing house produced only a few thousand copies of books on the constitution and published only a few articles about it in the government newspapers. There was no opportunity for open debate, since SLORC law no. 5/96 provided for a prison sentence of up to twenty years for anyone undertaking activities to disturb the National Convention process or expressing criticism of its principles. When the referendum commission refused to accept international observers, the government lost its last opportunity to win the trust of the public. Although the SLORC had its reasons to avoid any disturbance by opposition groups, these extreme measures did not advance nation building or national unity and failed to satisfy those concerned with the constitution drafting process. The military mindset of using coercion instead of persuasion or negotiation prevented national consensus on the future constitution.

On 2 May 2008, Myanmar was hit by cyclone Nargis. It was the deadliest cyclone in Myanmar's history. Thousands of people were killed or went missing and millions were made homeless, with the Ayeyawady delta region being particularly affected. With the referendum scheduled for 10 May, many thought it would be postponed because of the national disaster. But on 6 May the commission declared the referendum would still be held on the 10th, with the exception of forty-seven townships that had been particularly badly hit by Nargis, where the referendum would be postponed to the 24th, just two weeks after Nargis. The decision was widely criticized, but the government responded that Nargis had hit only small parts of the country and that the referendum should not be postponed. Very few people accepted this explanation, however, and many accused the government of manipulating the voting process and coercing the people in order to achieve a *yes* vote. People later named the new constitution the Nargis Constitution. Thein Sein who became president under that constitution had to work hard to overturn this image.

Restraints

Under the new constitution, Myanmar would have an Executive Presidency[5] and practise separation of powers. Section 11(a) stated that "The three branches of sovereign power namely, legislative power, executive power and judicial power, are separated, to the extent possible, and exert reciprocal control, check and balance among themselves." But three sections restrict the executive power of the president—namely, sections 64, 105 and 228(a).

Section 64

Section 64 states that "If the President or the Vice-Presidents are members of a political party, they shall not take part in their party activities during their term of office from the day of their election." Such provisions can be found in the constitutions of some countries following the Westminster system of government, where the president or head of state has few executive powers. However, it is hard to find this kind of provision in executive presidential systems. The inclusion of this section in the constitution of Myanmar, which practices an "Executive Presidency", is therefore peculiar. The 1947 constitution, which was based on the Westminster system, did not have such a provision, although the president was just a ceremonial head of state.

When asked about this restriction, National Convention Working Committee vice chair Attorney-General Aye Maung explained that Senior

General Than Shwe's idea was that the president should be free from partisanship and represent the entire nation and people, and should avoid representing a particular party. For example, he said, "When the President visits to the regions, he should meet with all people, not just his party supporters, and the people should see that he represents all the people regardless of politics or religion or ethnicity."[6]

Another senior member of the USDP had an alternative explanation, that Senior General Than Shwe took stock of lessons from the 1958 political crisis when the leadership dispute in the ruling party spilled out into parliament and ended in a military caretaker government. He wanted to separate the executive not only from the legislature but also from the president's own party.[7]

There is also another theory regarding section 64. That Senior General Than Shwe intentionally designed the political structure to balance power between the government, parliament and the military.[8] However, a former Amyotha Hluttaw (upper house or house of nationalities) Speaker and joint secretary of the National Convention Convening Committee, Khin Aung Myint, has rejected this view. He is of the opinion that the senior general's idea was based on his experience during the parliamentary democracy period (1948–62), with no thought about the effect of this clause for the future. According to Khin Aung Myint, everyone thought the future president would be Senior General Than Shwe, and they therefore paid little attention to issues of presidential power or the subtleties of checks and balances.[9]

Section 64 is a noble concept but is impractical in reality. As this section barred President Thein Sein from involvement in USDP activities, he had to temporarily appoint the Speaker of the Pyithu Hluttaw (lower house or people's assembly), Thura Shwe Mann, as acting party chairman. This would not have been a problem had relations between President Thein Sein and Speaker Shwe Mann remained cordial. But when a rivalry between the two developed, the president found himself in a position where he was unable to influence the party's policies and legislative agenda.

There are similar clauses in sections 232(k) and 233(f) that prohibit Union ministers and deputy ministers from being involved in party activities. When the USDP formed the new government on 30 March 2011, it automatically split into two factions—the one with the president and his cabinet members and the other with Thura Shwe Mann and members of parliament. On 2 July 2012, at a meeting between the government and

USDP Hluttaw leaders, Thein Sein proposed to amend sections 64 and 232(k), but Shwe Mann and his powerful ally former minister Aung Thaung objected to this proposal.[10] There were different opinions on the definition of the words "party activities". From the viewpoint of Shwe Mann and his supporters, the holding of the party chairmanship meant getting involved in party activities. They therefore interpreted the president's act of holding the post as a violation of the constitution. But the president's supporters responded that the restriction was only on involvement in the party's daily activities and not about holding the position of chairman.

When the USDP's first party congress[11] was convened on 14 October 2012, there was speculation that Shwe Mann would formally replace President Thein Sein as party chairman, but after many behind-the-scenes meetings among the top leaders, the president remained as chairman; however, most of the Central Committee members were members of parliament selected by Shwe Mann. Elections for Central Committee members were not conducted by secret ballot, and many of those elected were former government officials who joined the party just before the general election. Grass-roots members who worked for the party while it was a non-political association, the Union Solidarity and Development Association (USDA), complained about the process, but Shwe Mann rejected their pleas. During his speech on the third day of the congress, Thura Shwe Mann said he was responsible for the party's reorganization and he made his decisions based on the party's interests. After the congress, the president and some senior ministers remained as Central Executive Committee (CEC) members, but the Central Committee was packed with Shwe Mann's allies. According to one USDP CEC member, Thein Sein made a mistake at the congress by allowing Shwe Mann to stay as acting chairman as well as vice chairman of the USDP. He should have made Shwe Mann patron and kept him only as Speaker of the Pyithu Hluttaw. If Thein Sein had done that, he could have controlled the party and the Hluttaw.[12]

Shwe Mann was thus able to control both the party and the parliament. In his concluding speech, he said, "After the party congress the cooperation between USDP controlled parliament and the government will be improved",[13] but this never happened. After the congress, Shwe Mann never again consulted informally with the president on policy matters or legislative measures. In 2013 he and another CEC member, Aung Thaung, the former minister for industry under the military government, met with

President Thein Sein and asked him to resign from the chairmanship and to serve as patron of the party. President Thein Sein replied that he would resign but could not accept the post of patron. He indicated he would serve only as an ordinary member.[14] Shwe Mann then withdrew the proposal because if the president had resigned the chairmanship and served as an ordinary member it would have created a backlash against Shwe Mann from the party rank and file. Nonetheless, he began to undercut the president's power from within.

Subsequently, USDP MPs began openly criticizing government policy. Shwe Mann, as Speaker of the Pyithu Hluttaw and the Pyidaungsu Hluttaw (Union assembly), took no action to control their activities, and sometimes even encouraged them.[15] As the rivalry between Thein Sein and Shwe Mann increased, USDP members in both houses—rather than NLD members—turned into the main opposition force to the government. As a consequence, President Thein Sein's legislative agenda in both houses faced an even harder time than that of Democrat President Obama with the Republican-controlled Congress in the United States. After 2013, the impact of that situation caused much delay and many complications for the reform process.

Section 105

Unlike with other executive presidencies, the 2008 constitution did not give the president veto power over legislation. Even a failure to sign enacted bills does not stop them from acquiring legal effect. According to section 105, the president shall sign bills approved or bills deemed to have been approved by the Pyidaungsu Hluttaw within fourteen days of receipt, and shall promulgate them as law. If the president does not send the bill back to the Pyidaungsu Hluttaw together with his signature and comments within the prescribed period, or if the president does not sign to promulgate a law, on the day after the completion of that period the bill shall become law as if he had signed it. According to section 106, bills sent back by the president together with his comments shall be sent again to him after the Pyidaungsu Hluttaw accepts his comments and resolves to amend the bill or resolves to approve the bill as it is without accepting the president's comments. The president shall then sign the returned bill within seven days. If not, the bill will automatically become law within seven days.

Myanmar has had three constitutions since it gained independence. The first, the 1947 constitution, was modelled on the Westminster system, and the president, as ceremonial head of state, did not enjoy veto powers over the bills issued by parliament. The second, the 1974 constitution, established a one-party system and the president did not need veto legislation since there were no disputes between the executive and the legislature over bills. But the 2008 constitution practises the separation of powers among the executive, legislative and judicial branches of government. It establishes an executive presidency, and the president's veto is one of the common features of such a system. However, under Myanmar's 2008 constitution, the president is not entrusted with such power. National Convention Working Committee chairman Aung Toe and vice chair Aye Maung argued that since the president was elected by the two houses, he should not enjoy veto power or act against the will of parliament.[16] Aung Toe's clarification to the National Convention on this section mentions a similar section in the 1947 constitution and explains that the constitutions of other countries have a similar article. He did not mention, however, the US constitution or other executive presidential systems.[17] President Thein Sein, who did not have veto power and who was also unable to control his party, faced perpetual delays and deficiencies in his legislative agenda.

Section 228(a)

Section 228(a) states that "The Union Government shall implement the administrative resolutions passed occasionally by the Pyidaungsu Hluttaw and report back the actions which have been taken to the Pyidaungsu Hluttaw." The problem here is the lack of an accurate definition of the scope of administrative resolutions. The provision allows direct interference by the Hluttaw in the administrative affairs of the government. A similar provision existed in the one-party 1974 constitution drawn up by the Burma Socialist Programme Party (BSPP). Section 87(c) of the 1974 constitution said that the "cabinet shall carry out Pyithu Hluttaw decisions". But the 1974 constitution established a one-party system, with no separation of powers between the executive and the legislative.

There are three reasons for these problematic sections. First, although the working committee of the National Convention studied the constitutions of other countries, for the letter and the spirit of the new constitution they mostly relied for guidance on the two previous constitutions of Myanmar. The second reason is that the three main officials[18] from the working committee to have authored the basic and detailed principles were former civil servants who only had criminal law experience. There were no constitutional law experts on the committee, as such experts are rare in the Myanmar legal profession. Lastly, everyone thought at the time that it was written that Senior General Than Shwe would become president under the new constitution. Therefore, as already mentioned, none of the committee members or delegates paid attention to the principle of checks and balances.

Thus, when President Thein Sein started his reforms in a situation where there was no internal or international support, the weak organizational structure of the ruling party and the constitutional provisions restricting the president's powers created great difficulties that frustrated his reform efforts.

Notes

1. Clarifications by minister for information Brig-Gen. Kyaw Hsan to UN envoy Mr Gambari, 6 November 2007.
2. SPDC announcement 2/2007, 18 October 2007.
3. SPDC announcement 3/2008, 26 February 2008.
4. Referendum Commission announcement 4/2008, 9 April 2008.
5. The 1947 constitution was a Westminster system and the 1974 constitution was a one-party system with a parliament that carried both executive and legislative powers.
6. Interview with Aye Maung, 2 September 2016.
7. Interview 005.
8. Kyaw Zwa Moe, "Burma's Ex-Dictator and His Invisible Line", *The Irrawaddy*, 22 May 2013.
9. Interview with Khin Aung Myint, 13 November 2016.
10. Soe Thane, *Myanmar's Transformation & U Thein Sein: "An Insider's Account"* (Yangon: Tun Foundation Literature Committee, 2017), p. 17.
11. When the USDA was transformed to the USDP, they did not convene congress to elect central committees and other organs.
12. Interview 026.
13. First party congress records (2012), USDP.
14. Interview with Thein Sein, 8 September 2016.
15. Interview 004.

16. Interview with Aung Toe and Aye Maung, 2 September 2016.
17. National Convention Record, vol. 6, pt. 2, 17 February 2005 to 31 March 2005, National Convention Convening Commission.
18. Aung Toe, Aye Maung and Thaug Nyunt.

3

The Union Solidarity and Development Party

The Origin of *kyant-kai-yay* (Solidarity)

The word *kyant-kai-yay* (solidarity) was first introduced into Myanmar politics in 1958 during the reign of the caretaker government (1958–60) led by General Ne Win. The caretaker government formed an organization under the name Pyidaungsu Myanmar Naing-Ngan Kyant-kai-yay Athin (Union of Myanmar Solidarity Association) in October of that year. The association was formed with Khin Maung Phyu as chair, Colonel Kyaw Soe as vice chair, Colonel Than Sein as secretary and up to twenty-five central executive committee (CEC) members, including some secretaries of ministries, senior civil servants and senior army officers. The motto of the association was "regional development through dutifulness and self-reliance".[1] The association enlarged its CEC to thirty-nine members at its annual conference in 1960, electing Khin Maung Phyu as chair, Brigadier-General Aung Gyi and Paing as vice chairs, Colonel Than Sein as general secretary and San Lwin as treasurer.

In its charter, the association stated its commitment to work for the perpetuation of sovereignty, the enforcement of social ethics, and the restoration of community peace and the rule of law. The charter also stipulated provisions prohibiting solidarity organizations at all levels from association with any organization participating in or discussing party politics.[2] Although the motto of the solidarity association was regional development, its activities were mainly in line with the endeavours of the caretaker government for ensuring community peace and the rule of law. Because of this, the association met with criticism from political parties, which dubbed it a government stooge.

By 1962 the solidarity association had grown to include 1,908 township or ward branches and 10,851 village branches, with a total membership of 1,163,537.[3] The flag of the Union of Myanmar Solidarity Association was dark green with a white circle in the centre. Inside the circle was the picture of a leaping lion. Under the lion was an inscription that read "valour", and above it were two white stars.

There was speculation that Senior General Than Shwe was influenced by the model of the first solidarity association when in 1993 he established the Union Solidarity and Development Association (USDA). However, a former senior leader of the USDA explained that although the senior general took examples from the name and structure of the original solidarity association, he had much greater ambitions for the USDA.[4]

Union Solidarity and Development Association (USDA)

After assuming the chairmanship of the State Law and Order Restoration Council (SLORC) in 1992, Senior General Than Shwe began the process of drafting the future national constitution by convening a National Convention on 9 January 1993. About nine months later, on 15 September, the USDA was founded. In regard to the formation of the USDA, Senior General Than Shwe explained that the association was founded to promote national unity and to prevent an anarchic crisis like the 1988 uprising.[5]

The USDA adopted as its aims "the preservation of the Union of Myanmar, ethnic amity, the perpetuation of sovereignty and territorial integrity, national development, and the emergence of a modern and peaceful nation". Senior General Than Shwe said that "The five aims are not short term goals. These are significant in the future, and will remain unchanged under any future political and economic landscape."[6] He also called the USDA a national front that would join hands with the Tatmadaw (armed forces).[7] His overriding goal was to establish an organization with the same ideology as that of the Tatmadaw. That organization would represent the Tatmadaw in Myanmar's politics, and the Tatmadaw would be able to withdraw from politics. More importantly, with its affiliated political party in power, the Tatmadaw could prevent another political crisis such as those of 1962 and 1988.[8]

Despite the statement by the USDA that it was only a social organization, few believed this. It was described both inside and outside the country as a political body, since the association was headed by military officers and led campaigns against its opponents, particularly the National League for Democracy (NLD), by holding mass rallies in support of government policies. The USDA was in fact taking measures to turn itself into an effective political party for the future. Than Shwe always used "The Party" when he talked about the USDA with his CEC members of the USDA.[9]

Organizational Structure

Initially the USDA was under the leadership of a panel of central patrons and a CEC. The panel of central patrons consisted of the commander in chief of the Defence Services, the deputy commander in chief of the Defence Services, the commander in chief (army), the commander in chief (navy), the commander in chief (air force), the chief of bureau of Military Strategic Studies, the adjutant-general, the quartermaster-general, the chief of staff (army), and all the military regional commanders. The regional commanders also served as the patrons of their respective state and division USDA.

In the early period, the CEC had eight members, with one general secretary and three secretaries. New members were added on 8 April and 23 June 1994. The membership was enlarged to thirteen, with six ministers, six deputy ministers and one mayor.[10] From 1993 to 1999, the USDA was led by the general secretary. But the record for the 1999 plenary meeting shows SLORC secretary 3 Lieutenant General Win Myint as the vice chairman. His successor until 2010 was General Soe Win (prime minister) and then subsequently General Thein Sein (see Table 3.1).

No one was ever appointed as chairman. Senior General Than Shwe did not want the USDA chairman to be seen by the public as the future leader of Myanmar or his successor.[11] Hence, the senior general as a patron was the final decision maker for all the association's major policies. The late General Soe Win said that when he was vice chairman he only

TABLE 3.1
USDA Vice Chairmen (1995–2010)

1. Lt. Gen. Win Myint (secretary 3 of SPDC)	1995–2001	Forced to resign from all military and political posts in 2001
2. Gen. Soe Win (prime minister)	2001–7	Passed away in 2007
3 Gen. Thein Sein (prime minister)	2008–10	

inspected and met with USDA members in the states and regions that the senior general instructed him to do so. He remarked that the USDA vice chairmanship was a post without real political authority.[12] In actual fact, the vice chairman only served as guardian, and the day-to-day work was conducted by the secretariat.[13] The reason Win Myint was appointed as vice chair was to handle the disputes between general secretary Than Aung and CEC members Aung San, Saw Htun and Win Sein.[14]

Key Positions

Although the USDA had a vice chairman, a general secretary, a secretariat and HQ staff, Senior General Than Shwe created another key post to handle operations at the state and regional levels. They were named "Tarwunkhan Wungyi" (minister in charge) of state and regional USDA organizations. These officers were responsible for the real activities of the USDA. The senior general selected his most trusted ministers and deputy ministers as USDA CEC members and later assigned them as ministers in charge for states and divisions. Than Shwe selected the people who had the political and organizational capabilities to lead local USDA organizations. There were many ministers who wanted to work for the USDA but Than Shwe did not accept them.[15] He appointed two or three ministers in charge in the cases of large states or divisions (for example, Shan State and Bago Division; see Table 3.2).

Their responsibilities involved the USDA regional development projects, supervision of organizational activities, the monitoring and countering of local opposition groups—especially NLD activities—the lobbying of religious and social bodies, including members of the Sangha (Buddhist monkhood), and the launching of campaigns in support of government policies. Ministers in charge coordinated with the commanders

TABLE 3.2
USDA CEC Members and the States and Regions They Were Responsible For (2010)

Name	USDA Role	States/Regions
Htay Oo	general secretary	Ayeyawady
Zaw Min	joint general secretary	Magwe
Thaung	secretary	Mandalay
Tin Tut	secretary	Ayeyawady
Kyaw Hsan	secretary	Sagaing
Aung Thaung	secretary	Mandalay
Soe Thar	CEC member	Yangon
Thein Nyunt	CEC member	Ayeyawady
Ohn Myint	CEC member	Mon
Maung Maung Thein	CEC member	Thanintharyi
Thura Aye Myint	CEC member	Sagaing
Aung Min	CEC member	Bago
Thein Aung	CEC member	Kayah
Thura Myint Maung	CEC member	Kayin
Thein Swe	CEC member	Rakhine
Tin Naing Thein	CEC member	Shan
Dr Chan Nyein	CEC member	Sagaing
Khin Maung Myint	CEC member	Sagaing
Khin Aung Myint	CEC member	Mandalay
Aung Thein Lin	CEC member	Yangon
Thura Aung Ko	CEC member	Chin
Maugn Pa	CEC member	Yangon
Than Htay	CEC member	Ayeyawady
Phone Swe	CEC member	Rakhine
Nyan Tun Aung	CEC member	Mandalay

Source: Based on Kyaw Hsan's personal records.

of the respective military commands who were patrons of regional and state USDA branches.

The ministers in charge reported directly to Senior General Than Shwe. USDA members viewed the secretariat and the headquarters as responsible only for managing administrative affairs, having no influence on policy issues. However, one CEC member disagreed with that view and argued that most of the association's policies were discussed and decided at biweekly CEC meetings in which the vice chairman and the general secretary participated. Then only the matters that could not be decided at the said meetings and major policy issues were submitted to the monthly meeting between the CEC and the senior general for his guidance.[16] However, the CEC member admitted there were some instances when ministers and deputy ministers failed to follow policies laid down by headquarters because the vice chairman and general secretary failed to enforce them. Another possible reason was some ministers in charge were senior to the vice chair during their days in the military, and this made the vice chair reluctant to supervise them.[17]

Business Activities

The USDA adopted regional development undertakings as its main organizational task. It needed financial resources to fund these projects and to also look after the welfare of USDA members. Consequently the USDA established its own business, the MyanGonMyint company, under the CEC. MyanGonMyint was involved in many businesses, including gem mining, construction, agriculture and farming, and export and import. For the lower levels of the organization, such as at the state/division, district and township branches, a basic principle of the USDA was self-reliance and dutifulness for self-perpetuation. The funding for the organization at this level therefore was raised by the labours of the members. In the early days, the USDA prohibited, in an instruction dated 23 January 1995, any of its branches from conducting business.[18] However, another instruction communicated on 27 July 1995 said that the association could conduct business under the following guidelines:[19]

(a) Avoid doing any kind of business that would damage the nation and the people.
(b) Avoid competing with local businesses which might harm USDA organizational work.
(c) Avoid businesses that might tarnish the USDA image, member's [sic] moral[s] or were indecent in the public eye (for example: bars or butcher shops).

Initially, the businesses of local associations served only as fundraising for organizational and administrative work. Since the USDA used development projects as a main organizational tool, the organization needed an increasing amount of money to implement development projects for local communities. So USDA organizations at all levels came to compete with local businesses. Ignoring the guiding principles, ministers in charge encouraged this activity because they were competing among themselves as to which state or division was able to conduct the most organizational and development work each year. Ministers in charge gave special privileges such as government licences and contracts to regional associations for their fund raising. As time went on, local leaders set up private businesses using the influence of the association, and this began to affect the morals and behaviour of its members.

At USDA headquarters, a leading economic body was formed with thirteen members to run the businesses of the USDA. Prime Minister General Soe Win was chairman and minister for industry Aung Thaung was secretary. Under this body was a Business Supervisory Group chaired by Aung Thaung.[20] According to an annual report, MyanGonMyint company had by 31 August 2005 spent 10.604 billion kyat and over US$430,000 on regional development projects for the welfare of USDA staff. The USDA also earmarked 2.936 billion kyat for expenditure for 2004–5.[21]

USDA members, state/division branches and government departments also bought shares in MyanGonMyint to support USDA businesses. According to the minutes of the 2001 USDA plenary meeting, MyanGonMyint received 40 million kyat from USDA headquarters, 20 million kyat from the government's Trade Administration Department and Cooperatives Export and Import Enterprise, 238.7 million kyat from state and division USDA branches, 26.5 million kyat from military regional commands and 2.35 million kyat from CEC members, totalling 327.55 million for investment. In 2005, USDA headquarters spent 1.371 billion kyat, and the remaining balance for the year was 69.9 million.[22]

As time went by, state, division, district and township associations took over nearly all the licences of the profitable businesses in their areas and resold them for profit. The USDA's reputation was further tarnished when businesspersons and opportunists joined the association. As units at all levels of the USDA were running businesses, people began to view the association as another crony business organization rather than a social one aimed at helping people and building a modern, developed nation.[23] General Secretary Htay Oo defended the USDA budget and properties claiming they were all documented and audited because of its plan to transform itself into a political party. He claimed that the USDA never used the government budget for its organizational activities. He admitted however that because ministers in charge used their authority and privileges in fundraising activities, people misunderstood the USDA's activities and intentions.[24]

Membership and Organizational Works

One of the priority missions of the USDA at the state and regional levels was to increase its membership. On its first anniversary, 15 September 1994, the association stated that it had already formed 16 state/division associations, 55 district associations, 316 township associations, and 12,161 village associations, with a total of 830,322 members. It predicted a membership of a million by the end of 1994.[25] Seven years later, on 31 July 2001, the USDA had established 17 state/division level associations, 63 district level associations, 320 township level associations and 15,242 village level associations, with a membership of 17,724,890.[26] Sixteen years after its founding, the USDA stated it had 17 state/division level associations, 67 district level associations, 320 township level associations, 62 sub-township level associations, and 15,473 village level associations, with a membership of 25.71 million.[27] This meant that approximately half the population of Myanmar were USDA members. Of the 25.71 million, 9.67 million were farmers, 6.52 million were workers, 6.89 million were students, and 2.63 million were civil servants.[28]

In reality these figures were greatly inflated. The state/division ministers in charge vied with each other in reporting the membership strength of their respective regions to Senior General Than Shwe. As the senior general praised the states and divisions with the largest number of members as successes, the competition was fierce. In some states and regions, villages erected signboards stating that theirs had become a USDA village as all villagers were said to have joined the association. Likewise, some townships were declared NLD-free areas, claiming that the entire population had joined the association and there were no NLD members there. In point of fact, these were gross exaggerations and false claims by some ministers in order to be seen in a favourable light by the senior general. There were people in the USDA leadership who knew of this phenomenon but dared not express their doubts to the senior general.[29]

According to the USDA regulations, persons between the ages of 10 and 18 could be recruited as youth members and those above 18 as adult members. But those aged under 18 years or older than 70 could not play a role in the association's activities, and only added numbers. There were some cases of forced memberships of students and government employees, which provoked ill feeling towards the USDA. The membership figure of 25 million did not mean solid support.[30] Just how firm in fact was the support for the USDA? We need to look back into history to answer this question. After the 1962 coup, the ruling Revolutionary Council established the Burma Socialist Programme Party—BSPP. It ruled Myanmar under a single-party system until 1988. In 1981, BSPP membership was just over 1.5 million, or 4.4 per cent of the population.[31] Hence, compared with earlier figures, the purported membership strength of the USDA was astonishing.

The major weakness of the USDA was that it was not formed by people who shared a common ideological conviction. It was simply an umbrella organization founded under the leadership of the SLORC military government. Many members joined to gain opportunities or out of fear. It was run like a military organization with a top-down command and control system. Consequently, most state/regional, district, township and village leaders used to work only when ordered to or if provided incentives; few had strong convictions or motivation. There were also people who joined in order to win government contracts or business licences and also people using USDA influence in their daily lives. For these reasons the association's organizational work and image were badly tarnished.[32]

Than Shwe may have understood these weaknesses. He made arrangements to nurture strong cadres by opening organizational and ideological courses for the members. From 1993 to 2009, over 24 million members were trained at courses ranging from the level of headquarters down to the village.[33] In the summer of 2006 alone, over 3.3 million members received training in courses conducted at 28,400 locations.[34]

The reality was, however, that the USDA associations at the various levels relied upon the support of the ministers in charge and the regional military commanders as patrons for their organizational work rather than out of any commitment to USDA ideology. The regional commanders and ministers in charge thought they could win public support by providing the material needs of the people through development projects. Because of this practice, ministers used their authority to provide government funds for schools, hospitals and roads and awarded government contracts to local USDA branches that could be resold for a profit. In some cases they asked businessmen to help with donations, which led to accusations of corruption and nepotism on the part of the USDA and not only further tarnished the image of organization but also of the government. As a result of this, when the USDA transformed into the Union Solidarity and Development Party (USDP), it did not enjoy solid support from former USDA members.

This lack of support could be clearly seen in the results of the 2012 by-elections, in which out of forty-five constituencies the USDP won in only two. In his review of the by-elections results, Tin Htut, CEC member and former minister, pointed out that militarism, opportunism and populism had hurt the party badly and there were many members who lacked true conviction in the party ideology. He highlighted the case of a constituency that claimed over 50,000 party members but where the USDP candidate received only 4,000 votes. He also criticized local USDP party leaders for conducting their jobs like government officials rather than true party cadres. They had no will to do any activity without receiving financial support and daily allowances.[35]

From USDA to USDP

"Will the USDA one day become a political party?" This had been a question on everyone's mind since the establishment of the association in 1993. But the USDA leaders had never given any clear indication to either its members or the public. When he was asked at a press conference in Yangon on 6 December 2005 about the possibility of transforming the USDA into a political party, the general secretary Htay Oo said that it might, depending on the political situation and public opinion. This was the only public reference in connection with the possibility.[36] Actually, after the SPDC declared the seven-step road map to democracy in August 2003, the USDA actively participated in each step of the road map and in preparation to become a political party in the future.

After the announcement on 9 February 2008 that elections would be held in 2010, there was speculation that the USDA would become a political party or that a separate political party with the support of the USDA would be set up. Various ideas were advanced by the public and amongst USDA members. At that time, the senior general and other top leaders had already taken the decision to turn it into a political organization,[37] but only very few CEC members knew of this decision. Preparations for the party's organizational structure, policy and vision were initiated under Prime Minister General Soe Win between 2004 and 2007. However, as no party registration law had yet been enacted for the 2010 election, the USDA could not talk openly about transforming itself into a political party.[38]

At the 2009 USDA annual plenary meeting there were expectations that an announcement would be made about the association's future, but no such statement was forthcoming. Instead, the senior general merely urged members in his opening speech to work for the seven-step road map and to combine theory and practice in organizational activities.[39] Later, on 24 April 2010, at a CEC meeting attended by twenty-seven members, it was agreed to transform the USDA into a political party. Only on 1 June 2010 did the USDP apply for registration with the Union Election Commission. Approval was granted on 8 June 2010.[40] Before this, some thought that the USDA would remain a social organization and that an affiliate party would be set up. Htay Oo said this option was considered. The party leaders took a lesson from the fate of the Burma Socialist Programme Party. After the 1988 uprising and the collapse of the one-party system, the BSPP changed its name to the National Unity Party (NUP) and contested in the 1990 election. It was severely defeated by the NLD. The USDA leaders concluded that the BSPP had lost its identity after the name change and had been abandoned by its core supporters.[41]

During the sixteen years since its birth, the USDA attempted to develop human resources and raise cadres who would become core members when it turned itself into a political party. But it failed to introduce intra-party democracy among its members. There were no elected leaders, even at the grass-roots ward/village level. After the 2008 constitution was adopted, the USDA had ample time and resources to introduce intra-party democracy, at least at the grass-roots level, but this was never on the USDA's agenda.

When the USDA formed into a political party it again failed to convene a plenary meeting to elect the central committee and other lower levels of leadership. The only change was the appointment of Thein Sein as chairman by the USDA's CEC. Than Shwe appointed all CEC and Central Committee members of the USDP in the initial stage.[42] Htay Oo said that they worked together in the USDA for many years, knew each other, and that no one objected to Than Shwe's selections.[43] Hence, Thein Sein had to lead a party in which all CEC and Central Committee members were appointees of Senior General Than Shwe, including himself. As chairman of the USDP, he spent all his time preparing for the coming election and was unable to organize or restructure the USDP. After the election, he became the president and relinquished the chairmanship because the constitution did not allow the president to be involved in his own party's activities.

As President Thein Sein did not have time to organize the party before the election, was not able to lead it after the election, and was appointed by Than Shwe, he lacked a mandate from grass-roots party members. Other USDP leaders saw him as first among equals, not as a party leader. Some, like Aung Thaung, who became USDP CEC members in the 1990s, felt they knew more than Thein Sein and had more influence with USDP Hluttaw members, since they provided campaign funds to them. This situation led to great difficulties in the subsequent reform process.

Notes

1. Article by Saw Kyaw Aye (Pabedan), *Hot News*, 11 November 2011.
2. Myanmar Historical Commission, *Myanmar Politics 1958–1962* (Yangon Universities Press, 1991), p. 304.
3. Article by Saw Kyaw Aye (Pabedan), *Hot News*, 11 November 2011.
4. Interview 005.
5. Senior General Than Shwe's speech at the conclusion of USDA executive committee members management course, 7 March 1994.
6. Ibid.
7. Senior General Than Shwe's opening speech at 1994 USDA annual plenary meeting, USDA conference record, September 1994.
8. Interview 004.
9. Interview 069.
10. CEC report on the 1994 USDA special annual plenary conference, USDA conference record, September 1994.
11. Interview 005.
12. Myint Thu, *Mamyawlintthaw Khayeeshay* [The unexpected journey (the biography of General Soe Win)] (Yangon: Pan Wai Wai Sarpay, 2014), p. 39.
13. Interview with Htay Oo, 16 May 2017.
14. Interview 069.
15. Ibid.
16. Interview 005.
17. Ibid.
18. Network for Democracy and Development, *Pyikhinephyoe Thoemahoke Sitanarshin Sanit Ei Dauktinemyar* [USDA or the pillars of the military dictatorship] (2008), p. 17.

19. Ibid.
20. CEC report on the 2005 USDA annual plenary conference, USDA conference record, May 2006.
21. Ibid.
22. Ibid.
23. Interview 004.
24. Interview with Htay Oo, 16 May 2017.
25. CEC report on the 1994 USDA special annual plenary conference, USDA conference record, September 1994.
26. Annual report, 2001 USDA annual plenary conference, USDA conference record, February 2002. Although there were only fourteen states and divisions, the number reached seventeen as Shan State was divided into Eastern, Northern and Southern Shan State and Baga Division was divided into Eastern Bago Division and Western Bago Division.
27. Annual report, USDA annual plenary conference 2009, USDA conference record, January 2010.
28. Annual report, 2009 USDA annual plenary meeting.
29. Interviews 003 and 004.
30. Interview 004.
31. Central Committee's political report, 4th party congress of Burma Socialist Programme Party, 1982.
32. Interview 004.
33. Annual report, USDA annual plenary conference 2009, USDA conference record, January 2010.
34. Senior General Than Shwe's opening speech at the 2006 USDA annual plenary conference, USDA conference record, May 2007.
35. A review of the by-elections by Tin Htut, former minister and member of the USDP secretariat (unpublished).
36. Network for Democracy and Development, *Pyikhinephyoe Thoemahoke Sitanarshin Sanit Ei Dauktinemyar* [USDA or the pillars of the military dictatorship] (2008), p. 5.
37. Interview 005.
38. Interview with Htay Oo, 16 May 2017.
39. Annual report, USDA annual plenary conference 2009, USDA conference record, January 2010.
40. CEC report of USDP first party congress 2012, USDP congress record, September 2013.
41. Interview with Htay Oo, 16 May 2017.
42. Interview 005.
43. Interview with Htay Oo, 16 May 2017.

4

The Myanmar Spring and Aung San Suu Kyi

President Thein Sein delivered his inaugural address at the Pyidaungsu Hluttaw (Union assembly) on 30 March 2011. In his address the president invited individuals and organizations that had criticized the seven-step road map and the constitution to put aside their differences and work together in the national interest. He also urged them to take power through elections and amend the current constitution in accordance with the provisions in it. Moreover, he promised to start a peace process with all ethnic armed groups. He also outlined the following reform agenda:[1]

1. To amend laws that were incompatible with the new constitution.
2. To submit bills to establish the fundamental rights of citizens.
3. To raise the salaries of government personnel and the pensions of retired former personnel.
4. To study and compile laws on the rights of farmers and review existing laws before amending them as necessary.
5. To review existing labour laws.
6. To submit a new Public Health Care and Social Security Law.

7. To introduce bills to promote health and education.
8. To revoke the existing press laws and introduce new bills to protect freedom of expression.
9. To promulgate laws on environmental conservation and amend laws on industry and mining.
10. To promulgate new environmental laws.

On 31 March the president delivered his first speech to his cabinet and outlined his priorities for the new government. These included:

1. Good governance and a clean government.
2. To promote democratic practices in government and society.
3. The rule of law.
4. Efficiency in government and public services.

The president stated that the first five years of the democratization process would be the most important, and if the government and people of Myanmar were able to implement concrete steps, the road to democracy would be smooth.[2] Thein Sein thus set forth his vision of how to build Myanmar as a peaceful, modern and developed democratic state. The terms might be similar to those used by the previous military government, but the president carefully left out the words "disciplined democracy". His intention was to avoid people seeing his democratic reforms as a form of guided democracy.

Based on this vision, he laid down the following three missions for his government:[3]

1. To restore genuine, eternal peace in Myanmar.
2. Economic development so as to end Myanmar's status as a least developed country (LDC).
3. Become a middle-income country by the year 2020.

Reform Agenda

If the reform agenda of President Thein Sein were to be arranged in priority order, it would be in the sequence 2-1-4-3. The second item in the list encapsulates two reasons behind the reform agenda: peace and stability, and socio-economic development. The president always explained that his reforms were simply fulfilling these two public aspirations.[4]

The first item in the list referred to the guiding policy for the reforms. The president vowed that the entire government policy must be people-centred, and he encouraged the participation of civil society organizations (CSOs) in policy development.[5] This was a totally different approach to that of the previous military government, which preferred a top-down approach, seeing CSOs as threatening the stability of the state.

The fourth item in the list represented the reform programmes of the political, economic, administrative and private sectors. The administrative and private sector reforms were part of the economic and social reform of the initial stage but were later separated because the scope of these reforms were too complex to place under socio-economic reform.[6]

The third item in the list represented the three waves or phases of the reform process. The first phase from April 2011 to May 2012, the second phase from May 2012 to August 2014, and the third phase from August 2014 to March 2016. Each phase of the reform process began with a cabinet reshuffle. The first phase was mostly concerned with political and economic reform. The second phase was a continuation of this political and economic reform with the introduction of administrative and private sector reforms. The last phase was to deliver the benefits of the reforms to the people.

Aung San Suu Kyi

The most important part of President Thein Sein's reform agenda was political reform. This was to be the facilitator for the other three reforms. This agenda had two parts. The first part was to bring the individuals and organizations who did not accept the constitution and had boycotted the 2010 election into the political process, as he promised in his inaugural address. The second part was to begin the peace process with the ethnic armed groups.

The most important accomplishment of the first part was the dialogue between President Thein Sein and the leader of the National League for Democracy (NLD), Aung San Suu Kyi. This commenced on 19 August 2011. Prior to this, Aung San Suu Kyi had appeared implacably opposed to the president and the constitution under which he had been elected. While Aung San Suu Kyi was under house arrest, the NLD released the Shwegondine Declaration of 29 April 2009. The declaration hinted that the NLD would participate in the 2010 election if the government unconditionally released all prisoners of conscience, including NLD leaders, amended the provisions of the 2008 constitution that were contrary to democratic norms, and permitted international monitoring of the coming elections. As the demand for constitutional amendment was out of the question for the military government, they assumed the declaration was an attempt by the NLD to encourage international condemnation of the constitution and 2010 election.

In early 2010 there were signs of disagreement within the NLD over the party's position on the elections. The faction led by Win Tin favoured continued adherence to the Shwegondine Declaration, while another faction under the leadership of Khin Maung Swe and Dr Than Nyein supported the idea of making constitutional amendments through the Hluttaw procedures by contesting the coming elections.[7] Some NLD Central Committee members thought that Than Shwe intentionally released Win Tin on 24 September 2008 in order to split the party leadership on the election issue.[8]

At Central Executive Committee (CEC) meetings, NLD chairman Aung Shwe did not take sides and only weighed up the advantages and disadvantages of running in the elections or the consequences of skipping them. Tin Oo, who had been released from house arrest on 14 February 2010, argued against the NLD participating in the elections because, according to the new Political Parties' Registration Law, the party should expel Aung San Suu Kyi and other leaders who served time in prison and that parties were required to pledge to protect and safeguard the 2008 constitution. Tin Oo and Win Tin concluded that the pledge to protect the constitution would mean that the NLD would not be able to amend or abolish the 2008 constitution in the future.[9]

While the dispute was ongoing among CEC members, Aung San Suu Kyi's opinion on the coming election was most important for the NLD. As she was under house arrest, Nyan Win, a CEC member, was the only person able to visit her, in order to discuss her appeal case. The CEC therefore asked Nyan Win to seek Aung San Suu Kyi's opinion on the election, and chairman Aung Shwe pledged to support her decision.[10]

The NLD held a central committee meeting on 29 March 2010. At the meeting, Nyan Win read out a message containing Aung San Suu Kyi's statement on party registration. The most important points of this statement were her rejection of the 2008 constitution, continued adherence to the Shwegondine Declaration, and the rejection of registration under the current Political Party Registration Law. She said that even if the party were to be dissolved by the government, the NLD would remain as a political force in public opinion. Since Aung San Suu Kyi was not allowed to write a letter to the CEC, Nyan Win had to memorize her words and he subsequently wrote them down. The faction that called for registration therefore questioned the reliability of Nyan Win's words. But most of the central committee members supported Aung San Suu Kyi's decision as conveyed by Nyan Win, and the meeting decided against the NLD's registration and participation in the elections.[11]

Meanwhile, the SPDC issued a notification declaring the illegality of all unregistered political parties. Subsequently, dissident CEC members Khin Maung Swe and Dr Than Nyein founded the National Democratic Front (NDF) and duly registered their new party for the elections. In response the NLD announced the expulsion of some CEC members for their actions, including Khin Maung Swe and Dr Than Nyein, as well as thirteen central committee members.[12]

When the NLD announced its boycott of the elections, some No Vote movements appeared in public. Even though some NLD members were involved, the NLD made no overt attempt to call for a No Vote campaign. Aung San Suu Kyi did not make any direct calls for a No Vote either, but she informed the media through Nyan Win that the people had the right to vote or abstain. Moreover, she said that they could abstain if they had no party to support, with the absence of the NLD from the election.[13]

When she was released from house arrest on 13 November 2010, one week after the election, Aung San Suu Kyi said that as the NLD was a champion for democracy, it did not matter whether the government officially acknowledged it or not.[14] Thus, the political deadlock that had existed between the military government and the NLD persisted until President Thein Sein came to power. He needed to overcome this deadlock before he would be able to implement his political reforms.

After inviting, in his inaugural address, those opposed to the constitution to join in nation building efforts, early one morning in July 2011, President Thein Sein met with ministers Soe Thane and Aung Min at the president's farm house. Some members of Myanmar Egress were also present. They discussed possible ways and means to bring the NLD into the political process. After much discussion, the president decided that he would meet with Aung San Suu Kyi to resolve the political deadlock.[15]

Thein Sein summoned minister Aung Kyi and asked him to meet with Aung San Suu Kyi.

Aung Kyi, minister for labour and social welfare, had served as minister for relations with Aung San Suu Kyi under the SPDC in 2007, and had met with her nine times between 2007 and 2011. They had first met on 25 October 2007, but there were no instructions or guidelines for dialogue with her. Senior General Than Shwe only instructed Aung Kyi to study her response and to report back. Vice Senior General Maung Aye only dealt with logistics matters such as the time and place for a meeting. General Shwe Mann also only discussed logistics arrangements with Aung Kyi.[16] As a result of this, Aung Kyi clearly understood that the main purpose for his meeting was to buy time to reduce international pressure in the wake of the so-called Saffron Revolution of September and the subsequent military crackdown. He thought however that he might use the opportunity to reach some sort of agreement with Aung San Suu Kyi. When they met on 25 October, after some small talk about family and books, they exchanged views on the current political and economic situation. Then Aung Kyi told her that the country and people were suffering because of the political deadlock and the armed conflicts, and that therefore both sides needed to work together for the sake of the country. Aung San Suu Kyi agreed, and they drafted and signed a joint statement that said both sides would work together for reconciliation for the sake of the happiness and welfare of the people of Myanmar. The only disagreement between them was that Aung Kyi wanted to use the government term "Reconsolidation" in the English version whilst Aung San Suu Kyi wanted to use "Reconciliation".[17]

Within an hour of the meeting, Aung Kyi reported to Shwe Mann about the dialogue and the agreement with Aung San Suu Kyi. Aung Kyi flew back to Naypyitaw the next day. He hoped the SPDC leaders would be happy about the agreement because this was a tangible result to show the international community. However, when he gave his report, Aung Kyi noticed that Than Shwe was not happy about the agreement, as he made no response on the issue. Aung Kyi never mentioned it again and kept the agreement to himself.[18]

Although Than Shwe did not intend to find common ground with Aung San Suu Kyi, he sent Aung Kyi again for a meeting one week before UN special envoy Ibrahim Gambari visited Myanmar on 3 November 2007. That time, Than Shwe strictly instructed Aung Kyi that he did not need to reach an agreement with Aung San Suu Kyi and that the meeting was just for the sake of a meeting. When Gambari proposed a tripartite meeting with Aung Kyi and Aung San Suu Kyi, Than Shwe rejected the idea. Between 2007 and 2009, Aung Kyi had nine meetings with Aung San Suu Kyi. They discussed a federal system, the 2008 constitution, and sometimes Aung Kyi's books on leadership and management.[19] There was no timetable for the meetings because Than Shwe and SPDC leaders used these meetings as a game to reduce international pressure. Whenever they were asked about progress, they replied that Aung Kyi and Suu Kyi are working to find common ground. The only positive outcome was that Aung Kyi was able to build a relationship with her.

Unlike for his previous meetings with Aung San Suu Kyi, Aung Kyi received clear and precise guidelines in 2011. Thein Sein said that in the interests of the country, Aung Kyi had to find a means to bring her and the NLD into parliamentary politics. Aung Kyi believed he could achieve that, as he had already reached agreement with her for mutual cooperation during their 2007 meeting. When they met on 25 July, Aung Kyi asked Aung San Suu Kyi what was her prerequisite for implementing their previous agreement.[20] Aung San Suu Kyi requested the amendment of the election and political party registration laws, the opening of NLD party township offices, and the recognition of the 1990 election results. After the meeting, they met the press together and expressed the view that the meeting was satisfactory as it was constructive in that they had discussed ways to find common areas of bilateral cooperation in the national interest.[21]

When Aung Kyi reported back to the president, he agreed to all the requests. Thein Sein then asked Aung Kyi to meet with the two Hluttaw Speakers, Shwe Mann and Khin Aung Myint, and the chairman of the Union Election Commission, Tin Aye, to seek their opinions. All three welcomed the president's decision and pledged to cooperate with his initiative. Later, the Election Commission submitted amendments to the election and party registration laws, and Khin Aung Myint publicly acknowledged that the NLD won the 1990 election and that the SLORC had failed to transfer power to the party. Shwe Mann and the lower house speedily passed the amendments on the election and party registration laws.

Aung Kyi met with Aung San Suu Kyi again on 12 August 2011 with a message from the president that he was ready to enter dialogue with her for future cooperation. Aung San Suu Kyi immediately agreed and they issued a joint statement saying that "both sides will cooperate in pursuing stability of the State and national development" and "will cooperate on a reciprocal basis". President Thein Sein and Aung San Suu Kyi met at the President's Office on 19 August 2011. A photograph of the president and Aung San Suu Kyi standing together under the portrait of Myanmar's independence hero and Aung San Suu Kyi's father, General Aung San, sent a strong message of national reconciliation to the people of Myanmar and the international community. Under the previous military government, all images of General Aung San had been removed from offices and bank notes. The new president now not only put General Aung San's photo in his office but also took a photo in front of it with his daughter. People could then believe that there was a genuine dialogue between the two leaders.

But not everyone was happy with this historic meeting. When President Thein Sein's decision to bring Aung San Suu Kyi into parliamentary politics was discussed at a UDSP CEC meeting, conservatives like Aung Thaung (former minister for industry-1), Maung Thaung (former minister for science and technology), and Lun Thi (former minister for energy) strongly objected and said that the meeting will "give a dead tiger new life".[22] Their response may have reflected Senior General Than Shwe's displeasure at Thein Sein's decision.[23] But acting chairman Shwe Mann agreed with Thein Sein and said "don't worry about giving life to a dead tiger. Tigers are controlled with the whip in a circus. I can control her."[24]

President Thein Sein's decision to bring Aung San Suu Kyi and the NLD into parliamentary politics was based on his desire for political stability and an inclusive political reform programme. He understood that without the participation of the NLD in the Hluttaw, Myanmar politics would be as divisive as usual and no progress would be achieved.[25] So he started a dialogue via Aung Kyi and later personally met Aung San Suu Kyi and created the political and legal environment that enabled the NLD to contest in the 2012 election. He sincerely believed that although they had different opinions on the existing constitution, they could work together under it for democratization.

During his first meeting with Aung San Suu Kyi, Thein Sein did not discuss amending the constitution, specifically section 59(f), which bars her from the presidency. He only promised to amend the political party registration law and election law based on Aung San Suu Kyi's requests.[26] He said that if Aung San Suu Kyi wished to amend the constitution, she would have to build trust with the Tatmadaw (armed forces). As chairman of the National Convention Convening Committee, he knew that one objective of the constitution was to build the political space where civilians and the military would be able to work together and build positive civil-military relations. If he forced the Tatmadaw to accept an amendment to 59(f), Aung San Suu Kyi would not able to build trust with them, even if she became president, and that would affect her long-term relationship with them.

President Thein Sein met with Aung San Suu Kyi nine times[27] during his tenure, and also invited her for lunch with his family. They cordially talked about their families, even about her dog. But later, because of her closed relationship with other people in the Hluttaw, she misunderstood Thein Sein, and their relationship became tense.[28] One reason for Aung San Suu Kyi's change of heart was that the two have very different personalities. Thein Sein is reserved and not inclined to impromptu speech or discussion. He prepares thoroughly for every meeting, personally writing points for discussion in a small notepad, and never wavers from the script.[29] US Secretary of State Hillary Clinton makes this point in her memoir and noted that President Thein Sein "looked more like an accountant than a general". He kept his distance from Aung San Suu Kyi after she became a Hluttaw representative, as he did with his USDP representatives. The same applied as a result of Aung San Suu Kyi's role as chair of the Rule of Law Committee and of the Committees on the Development of Yangon University and Yangon General Hospital. Aung San Suu Kyi had fallen into a Shwe Mann trap. Shwe Mann had set up these Hluttaw committees because he knew of her interest in education and health issues, and he arranged visits for her to these institutions. Aung San Suu Kyi conducted hearings at the Hluttaw committees, personally inspected the institutions, held meetings with department heads, and gave instructions to them. These actions were seen as contrary to the separation of powers between the executive and the legislature, but Aung San Suu Kyi did not understand that.

Thein Sein welcomed her contributions and supported most of her work, but when he felt she had crossed the line over the separation of powers he became less cooperative. Aung San Suu Kyi may have felt that Thein Sein was indecisive or unwilling to cooperate with her. Consequently, she came to trust Shwe Mann more and to rely increasingly on his political support. Shwe Mann had no restraints over dealing with Aung San Suu Kyi. He was Speaker of the lower house and acting chairman of the USDP, whilst she was leader of the main opposition. He could meet with her anytime, assign her to any committee she wanted, and cooperate with her on legislative matters. From August 2012 to August 2015, Shwe Mann held thirty-six closed-door meetings with Aung San Suu Kyi,[30] but he never shared what they discussed with other USDP leaders. Shwe Mann cleverly used these opportunities to create a wedge between the president and Aung San Suu Kyi.

Some ministers thought of bringing Aung San Suu Kyi into the cabinet to work together with President Thein Sein for education and health reform. They sounded her out, but Aung San Suu Kyi was not willing to accept a cabinet post. Her one and only ambition was to be president of Myanmar, so they abandoned this option.[31] President Thein Sein did not know about this option. If he had, he would not have agreed with it. His strategy was only to bring her into parliamentary politics and to provide political space for her and the NLD as part of his political reforms. When he brought Aung San Suu Kyi into the political process, Thein Sein hoped she and the NLD would serve as the loyal opposition. He never expected her to align with Shwe Mann and oppose him.[32] The failure of Aung San Suu Kyi to play a constructive and responsible role as leader of the opposition in the Hluttaw was a real setback for President Thein Sein's reforms.

Notes

1. President Thein Sein's speech on 30 March 2011, *Myanma Alinn*, 31 March 2011.
2. President Thein Sein's speech on 31 March 2011, *Myanma Alinn*, 1 April 2011.
3. Document on reform policies and functions (2015), Union Government; Future reform programmes (2015) (unpublished), p. 4.
4. President Thein Sein's State of the Union Address at the Pyidaungsu Hluttaw, 1 March 2012.
5. President Thein Sein's speech to Union ministers and chief ministers of regions and states, 12 May 2012.
6. Interviews with Soe Thane, 15 November 2016, and Tin Naing Thein, 30 April 2017.
7. Aung Shin (Monywa), *Amyotha Democracy Apwegyoke Mattan 1988–2010* [Chronicle of National League for Democracy (1988–2010)] (Yangon: Pyinsagan Literature House, 2016), p. 575.
8. Interviews with Thein Nyunt, 11–12 June 2018.
9. Aung Shin, *Amyotha Democracy Apwegyoke Mattan*, pp. 578, 581.

10. Ibid., p. 584.
11. Ibid., p. 592.
12. Win Tint Tun, *Malin Naing Thae Tae Bamar Pyay* [Burma still in darkness] (Yangon: Yin Myo Sarpay, 2016), p. 319.
13. Aung Shin, *Amyotha Democracy Apwegyoke Mattan*, p. 615.
14. Win Tint Tun, *Malin Naing Thae Tae Bamar Pyay*, pp. 319, 332.
15. Interview with Soe Thane, 15 November 2016.
16. Interview with Aung Kyi, 10 March 2017.
17. Ibid.
18. Under President Thein Sein this agreement became the starting point for dialogue with Aung San Suu Kyi.
19. Interview with Aung Kyi, 10 March 2017.
20. Ibid.
21. *Myanma Alinn*, 26 July 2011.
22. Interviews 021, 026, 027 and 050.
23. Interview 010.
24. Interviews 027, 050 and 070.
25. Interview with Thein Sein, 25 August 2017.
26. Ibid.
27. Soe Thane, *Myanmar's Transformation and U Thein Sein: "An Insider's Account"* (Yangon: Tun Foundation Literature Committee, 2017), p. 322.
28. Interview with Thein Sein, 25 August 2017.
29. Interview 010.
30. Interview 051.
31. Interview 017.
32. Interview 021.

5

The Union Government

Provisions of the Constitution

The 2008 constitution of Myanmar set the parameters of President Thein Sein's reforms. The relevant sections are as follow:

Section 200:
   The Union Government shall comprise the following persons:

   (a) The President;
   (b) Vice-Presidents;
   (c) Ministers of the Union;
   (d) The Attorney General of the Union.

Section 202:
   The President, with the approval of the Pyidaungsu Hluttaw [Union assembly], may:

   (a) designate the Ministries of the Union Government as necessary, and may make changes and additions to the ministries;

(b) designate the number of the Union Ministers as necessary, and may increase or decrease the number.

Section 203:
The President shall be responsible to the Pyidaungsu Hluttaw. The Vice-Presidents shall be responsible to the President and also to the Pyidaungsu Hluttaw through the President.

Session 224:
The Ministries of the Union Government shall, in carrying out the functions of their subordinate governmental departments and organizations, manage, guide, supervise and inspect in accord with the provisions of the Constitution and the existing laws.

Section 232(b)(ii):
In order to appoint Union Ministers, the President shall:
obtain a list of suitable Defence Services personnel nominated by the Commander-in-Chief of the Defence Services for Ministries of Defence, Home Affairs and Border Affairs;

Section 232(i):
If the Union Minister is a representative of a Hluttaw, it shall be deemed that he has resigned from the day he is appointed as a Union Minister.

Section 232(k):
If the Union Minister is a member of any political party, he shall not take part in its party activities during the term of office from the day he is appointed as a Union Minister.

According to section 233, any Union minister may be impeached and removed by the Hluttaw and according to section 235(c) the president may direct any Union minister to resign.

The Formation of Thein Sein's Administration

Thein Sein, who was elected president at the Pyidaungsu Hluttaw session held on 4 February 2011, presented a proposal on 8 February for the formation of a Union government with 34 ministries and 30 Union ministers. During the Pyidaungsu Hluttaw debate over the list of ministries on 9 February, National Democratic Front (NDF) party representative Dr Myat Nyana Soe objected that there were too many ministries and proposed the number should be reduced to 25, but also proposed the establishment of a new Ministry of Ethnic Affairs. In response, Union Solidary and Development Party (USDP) representative Kyaw Hsan argued that the proposed ministries were reasonable and suitable based on the current socio-economic situation of the nation, and asked the parliament to approve the proposal. President Thein Sein also provided clarification of his plan for the formation of 34 ministries and the appointment of 30 Union ministers. He also explained that since every state and regional government had their own ethnic affairs ministers, the Union government should not form a separate Ministry of Ethnic Affairs. At the parliamentary vote, the proposal was approved with 612 *yes* votes, five *no* votes and 12 abstentions.[1] Then Thein Sein assigned the Union ministers to their respective ministries (Table 5.1).

The Thein Sein cabinet was based on the State Peace and Development Council (SPDC) government. Of the 30 ministers, 17 had served as ministers or deputy ministers under the military government. The remaining ministers were the three nominated by the commander in chief of the Defence Services, four senior military officers who had retired from the Tatmadaw (armed forces) just before the 2010 elections, one former ambassador, one retired civil servant, two technocrats and two businessmen. Hence, the Thein Sein administration was dubbed in the country and abroad as a "semi-military government" and criticized as old wine in a new bottle, with little hope of reform.

There were questions as to who selected the new cabinet. Soe Thane, former minister for the President's Office, has written that the cabinet was selected in advance by Senior General Than Shwe without President Thein Sein's input.[2] In actual fact, Than Shwe only laid down guidelines, especially concerning former SPDC ministers who should be left out of the new cabinet. Then Thein Sein, Shwe Mann, Tin Aung Myint Oo and Tin Aye[3] considered possible candidates for Union ministers and chief ministers of regions and states and submitted the names for approval by the two top leaders.[4] Thein Sein also asked his trusted ministers to nominate ten people who should be ministers in the new cabinet. At that time, Than Shwe said that only a third of the current cabinet should be in the new one.[5]

TABLE 5.1
President Thein Sein's First Cabinet
(30 March 2011)

Name	Ministry
Thein Sein	President
Thiha Thura Tin Aung Myint Oo	Vice President
Dr Sai Mauk Kham	Vice President
Lt. Gen. Hla Min	Defence
Lt. Gen. Ko Ko	Home Affairs
Lt. Gen. Thein Htay	Border Affairs and Myanmar Industrial Development[a]
Wanna Maung Lwin	Foreign Affairs
Kyaw Hsan	Information and Culture
Myint Hlaing	Agriculture and Irrigation
Win Tun	Forestry
Hla Tun	Finance and Revenue
Khin Maung Myint	Construction
Tin Naing Thein	National Planning and Economic Development, Livestock and Fisheries
Win Myint[b]	Commerce
Thein Tun	Post and Telecommunication
Aung Kyi	Labour, Social Welfare and Resettlement
Thein Htaik	Mining
Ohn Myint	Cooperatives
Nyan Tun Aung	Transport
Tint San	Hotel and Tourism
Kyaw Swar Khaing	Industry 1
Soe Thane	Industry 2
Aung Min	Railway Transport
Than Htay	Energy
Zaw Min	Electrical Power 1
Khin Maung Soe	Electrical Power 2
Dr Mya Aye	Education
Dr Pe Thet Khin	Health
Thura Myint Maung	Religious Affairs
Aye Myint	Science and Technology
Khin Yi	Immigration and Manpower
Thein Nyunt	President's Office
Soe Maung	President's Office
Dr Tun Shin	Attorney General

Notes: a. Later, Myanmar Industrial Development was abolished by the Hluttaw.
b. Win Myint, Tint San, Dr Mya Aye, Dr Pe Thet Khin and Dr Tun Shin were the only civilian ministers in the first cabinet.

Government Mechanisms Prior to 2011

After the coup of 18 September 1988, the Tatmadaw abolished all administrative and political institutions, including the State Council, the cabinet, the state/division and other sub-national-level people's councils, and the Pyithu Hluttaw (lower house or people's assembly). It then formed the State Law and Order Restoration Council (SLORC) and subsequently the SLORC government. The respective law and order restoration councils were also formed from the state and division level to the village level as administrative and management organizations. The military retained the executive institutions formed under the 1974 constitution while adjusting them to be workable under the new system. The pattern of administrative machinery was not much different from that under the 1974 constitution.

According to the 1974 constitution, the State Council was the highest administrative body, and under it was the government led by the prime minister. Also under the State Council were the fourteen state/division people's councils concerned with regional administrative functions for their respective areas (Figure 5.1). Now the head of the SLORC was the head of state as well as the head of government, and legislative power was wielded by the SLORC (Figure 5.2). The SLORC comprised ten members from Defence Headquarters and nine regional commanders. At the SLORC's inception, real power was held by five of its key members: the chairman, Senior General Saw Maung; his deputy, General Than Shwe; secretary 1, General Khin Nyunt; General Maung Aye; and secretary 2, General Tin Oo (no relation to former general Tin Oo, NLD leader).[6] After the SLORC took over, the staff of the State Council under the BSPP government were reassigned to the SLORC office, and those of the cabinet office were reassigned to the SLORC government office. The staff of the Pyithu Hluttaw were attached to the SLORC office and the government office.

Under the SLORC government, the head of state and head of government was initially Senior General Saw Maung; later it was Senior General Than Shwe. As Senior General Than Shwe served as the chairman of the SLORC (rebranded in 1998 as the SPDC) from 1992 to 2011, his working style had a great influence on his subordinates.

As under the BSPP government, cabinet meetings were held every Thursday, but there were no debates or open discussions on policy issues. Cabinet meeting were simply to approve cabinet submissions or

FIGURE 5.1
State Institutions under the 2008 Constitution

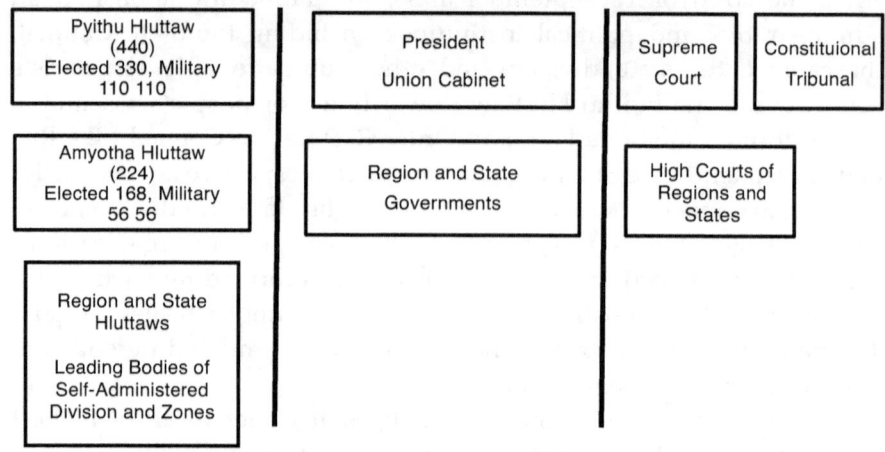

FIGURE 5.2
Structure of the USDP Government at the Union Level (ca. August 2015)

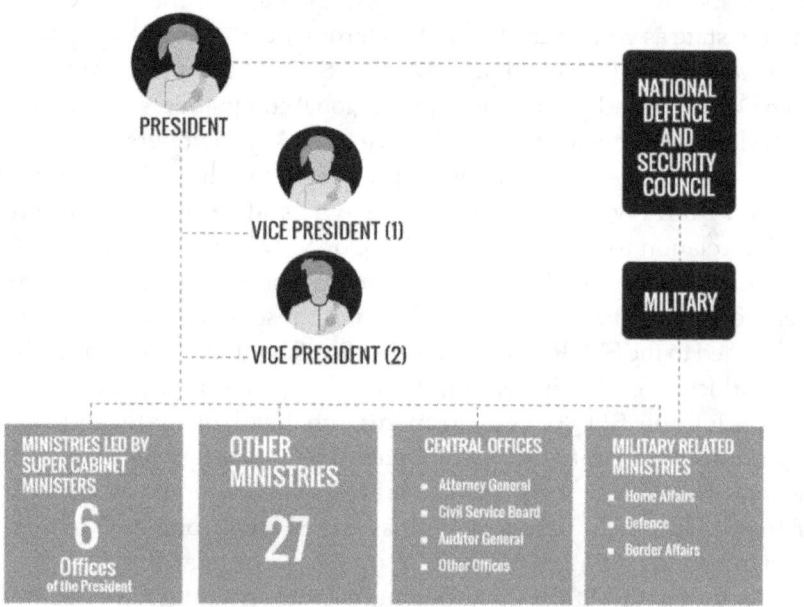

Source: Reproduced with permission from Su Mon Thazin Aung and Matthew Arnold, *Managing Change: Executive Policymaking in Myanmar* (Asia Foundation, 2018).

memorandums. Senior General Than Shwe held specific meetings with ministers responsible for economic affairs every Wednesday and decided all economic policy issues before the cabinet meeting.[7] Other ministers also reported directly to the senior general and sought his approval on important policy issues before submitting them to cabinet. Hence, there was no collective responsibility in cabinet. It merely formalized decisions already taken by the senior general.

For states and divisions, military commanders of the regional commands were appointed as chairmen of the respective state/division peace and development councils, responsible for regional administrative affairs. The state/division peace and development councils acted as the regional governments, with the commander as the chief minister or prime minister of the state/division. State/division-level heads of government departments had to implement the instructions of the chairman of the state/division SLORC/SPDC as well as those from ministers concerned with particular affairs.[8]

The relationships between SLORC/SPDC government ministers and regional commanders were quite complex, as there were no clear guidelines or regulations. When the SLORC was formed, all the regional commanders were council members. But most of the cabinet members were not council members, so regional commanders were more powerful than ministers, apart from the defence minister. The latter post was held by Senior General Saw Maung and later by Senior General Than Shwe. However, when Than Shwe became chairman in 1992, he promoted all the powerful regional commanders as lieutenant generals and appointed them as ministers. He removed them from active military duty and replaced them as regional commanders with division commanders who were loyal to him. Therefore, as the former regional commanders were members of the SLORC as well as ministers, they were senior to the newly appointed regional commanders. So in order to balance their power, Than Shwe issued a notification that recognized the regional commanders as ministers responsible for their states/divisions, and they were given power to oversee all government departments. They could inspect departments and issue instructions to them regardless of their minister's policy. Sometimes they directly contacted the minister concerned to coordinate development projects. This system was practised until the SPDC was dissolved in 2011. Except for a very few civilian ministers, most of the ministers were senior to the regional commanders during their military days, but according to government protocol, regional commanders outranked the ministers. However, the working relationship was based on mutual respect and brotherhood developed from the Defence Services Academy tradition.[9]

Two additional factors that added to the complex functioning of the government were the roles of secretary 1 of the SLORC/SPDC and the commanders of the Special Operation Bureaus. Special Operation Bureaus are responsible for supervising military operations in regional commands. In 1988 there were only two bureaus, but Than Shwe gradually expanded the number and by 2011 there were six bureaus under Army Command, and each bureau had two or three regional military commands under their supervision.

Chiefs of Special Operation Bureaus, who had the rank of lieutenant general, not only supervised military operations but also oversaw the implementation of SPDC political and economic policies at state and divisional levels. Senior General Than Shwe used them as whips to state/region SPDCs, and they reported directly to Than Shwe. Sometimes they would directly coordinate with ministers, and ministers had to fulfil their instructions based on their inspection tours, even though some instructions were contrary to government rules and regulations.

From 1988 to 2003, General Khin Nyunt served as secretary 1 of the SLORC/SPDC as well as chief of military intelligence. He took the role of prime minister and coordinated various ministries and state/region SLORC/SPDCs. He had many responsibilities, apart from the defence, budget and trade portfolios.[10] Matters of defence and the budget were under Than Shwe, and the Trade Council came under Maung Aye. Khin Nyunt also used military intelligence units as his auxiliary administrative organizations. They provided political and economic information to him, arranged his inspection tours, and mobilized local businessmen to support Khin Nyunt's development projects. When Khin Nyunt become prime minister in 2003, General Soe Win succeeded as secretary 1, but because of Khin Nyunt's influence and seniority there was no rivalry between the prime minster and secretary 1. After Khin Nyunt's downfall, Soe Win became prime minister and General Thein Sein succeeded as secretary 1. Their division of labour and relations went well, and Soe Win oversaw most of the development projects and the state and division SPDC. When Prime Minister Soe Win passed away on 12 October 2007, Thein Sein become prime minister and Lt. Gen. Tin Aung Myint Oo succeeded him as secretary 1.

From 2007 to 2011, unlike the case with Thein Sein, Tin Aung Myint Oo as secretary 1 had greater authority over the budget, special development projects and the Trade Council, and he oversaw state and division SPDCs. Ministers sometimes found themselves in a difficult position between the prime minister and the secretary 1 over their ministerial work, especially with respect to economic matters.

Under Than Shwe, a minister's or a commander's personal relationship with the senior general was also an important matter. Normally, if a regional commander, in his capacity as chairman of his respective level SLORC/SPDC, received Than Shwe's approval for a particular development project, ministers had no choice but to try to support the project, even though it might not have been in the ministry budget or long-term plan. Likewise, commanders were reluctant to interfere in the work of a minister in their command area who had a very close relationship with the senior general, although this may not conform to the needs of the region or the people. In some cases the ministries and the division/state SPDCs had to collectively realize the verbal orders of the senior general, such as the nationwide planting of *Jatropha curcas* to produce biofuel. Also, among cabinet members, those ministers who held portfolios related to economics were considered more powerful than those in charge of social welfare functions.[11]

The work processes of the government machinery under the military government depended solely on the wishes or decisions of the head of state and on personal relations with him, and not on rules, regulations or procedures. From 1988, and again from 1992 to 2011, the core executive system was coordinated by just one man. Than Shwe became the most powerful leader and ruled the country without any legal restraint. The tenure of his regime could be considered to be an autocracy. From initiating strategic policy programmes to managing internal core executive relations, the decisions for the appointment or purges of key players and the final arbitration of disagreements among players were determined solely by Senior General Than Shwe.[12] All the ministers and commanders under the military government were familiar with this system, governing their respective regions or institutions under their sole wish, paying little attention to legal procedures, rules or regulations.

Despite some advances, executive governance in Myanmar remained characterized by centralized decision-making, top-down hierarchies and persistent issues around accountability and participation.[13] Those old habits accompanied the new government formed by President Thein Sein in 2011, posing a hindrance to reforms.

Formation of the Government and Administrative Reform

When he delivered his inaugural address to the Pyidaungsu Hluttaw and his first policy speech to the cabinet, the president explained his vision of good governance, clean government and anti-corruption. His speech was quite different from those of previous leaders of the former military government, who avoided such issues in their policy speeches. These two speeches served as the foundation of his administrative reform programme.

Some analysts think that the USDP already had a concrete reform agenda when the party won the 2010 election. This was not the case, for in reality the USDP did not have any concrete reform agenda or even a party manifesto when it was transforming from the Union Solidarity and Development Association (USDA) to a political party in 2010, except to carry out the SPDC's seven-step road map as the vision and mission of the new party. As mentioned in chapter 3, the transformation was rushed through and the party's leaders were not able to prepare a government policy or vision.[14] Htay Oo, the general secretary of the USDA and then of the USDP, rejected the idea that the party had made no preparations for government. He said preparations for the transformation had begun among a core leadership group under the late prime minister General Soe Win (2004–7). There were also preparations for drafting a party organizational structure, policy and vision, but only a very few people knew about it.[15] If this was the case, it had no consequences.

On the evening of 4 March 2010, Brig.-Gen. Kyaw Hsan, minister for information, summoned the general manager of printing and publishing enterprises, Zaw Min Oo, and myself[16] to his office. Since June 2005, we had added to our daily activities the additional responsibility of compiling research papers and articles concerning political and organizational matters for the USDA, as Kyaw Hsan served as head of the USDA education department. Kyaw Hsan explained to us that at the USDA's Central Executive Committee (CEC) meeting that day, the general secretary, Htay Oo,[17] submitted a draft manifesto for the future election campaign. Unfortunately, the three-page draft was too general and too brief for a major political party. As head of the education department, Kyaw Hsan felt responsible for the ideological matters of the USDA. Kyaw Hsan explained to us that in comparison to the NLD's manifesto for the 1990 election, the current manifesto was sub-standard. He had asked the CEC to allow him to compile an alternative draft manifesto. Thein Sein, who chaired the meeting as CEC vice chairman, allowed him to do so.

Kyaw Hsan ordered the two of us to work together with Ko Ko Hlaing (retired lt. col. from the Army Research Department) and Takatho Myat Thu (a seasoned journalist) in recompiling the draft manifesto. This incident demonstrated how an organization with sixteen years of experience as a government-backed social organization could not compile a resourceful manifesto for future political purposes. It appeared that the USDA had failed to heed the senior general's edict to take capacity building of USDA members and preparation for a future political role seriously.

However, most of the USDA leaders believed that the 2010 election would be easily won, since the NLD was likely to boycott the vote unless the government released Aung San Suu Kyi from house arrest. Consequently, they were not interested in the essential organizational work of a political party, especially at the grass-roots level. Only Thein Sein paid attention to these matters, and he was therefore pleased when Kyaw Hsan volunteered to compile a comprehensive draft manifesto.

The Ministry of Information team was engaged in drafting a new manifesto based on Senior General Than Shwe's speeches and the resolutions of USDA annual meetings from the past ten years. They also received some guidelines from Thein Sein on the economy, agriculture, labour and related issues. Based on the draft, they also compiled proposals for the future party's organizational structure and strategy. They raced against time in compiling this draft, which had to be submitted at a CEC meeting on 11 March. The result was not a final or perfect manifesto. It was however much better than the previous draft.

By rights the task of approving such a manifesto should have involved considered debate and negotiation among central committee members and grass-roots organizations. Sadly, the association was not able to do this, as it had not officially declared that it would transform itself into a political party.[18] The party's canvassing campaign for the 2010 election relied heavily on development projects funded by government and private donations. Very few USDP candidates bothered to campaign on the party manifesto or campaign promises. President Thein Sein was among the few candidates who took the manifesto seriously during the campaign, and he used it as a future legislative programme in his inaugural speech. Consequently, some USDP leaders did not see President Thein Sein's reform agenda as a USDP agenda, and Pyithu Hluttaw Speaker Shwe Mann, as acting chairman of the USDP, tried to put forth his own agenda and discredit that of Thein Sein by using the Hluttaw's legislative power.

How did President Thein Sein formulate his reform agenda? Former minister Tin Naing Thein, a minister in the President's Office and a key player in the administrative reforms of the Thein Sein government, explained that the president's ideas were based on key provisions of the constitution.[19] He said that the constitution had four basic principles with regard to the future structure of the state. The first called for the adoption of a Union or federal system; the second, practising of multiparty democracy; the third, separation of the three organs of power; and the fourth, embracing a market economy. The constitution stipulated that the future state's vision should be based on peace and a modern and developed democracy.

Based on that vision, President Thein Sein said his reforms were meant to realize two public aspirations: (i) peace and stability, and (ii) socio-economic development.[20] According to Tin Naing Thein, to realize these aspirations the president implemented political reform for peace and stability, administration, socio-economic and private sector reform for development, and a people-centred approach for democratization.

Some were of the opinion that since the constitution already stipulated a multiparty system, with a federal system and enhanced democracy as strategic objectives, what President Thein Sein did was simply the tactical implementation of Than Shwe's strategy.[21] Others rejected this view. They thought that when the SPDC transferred power to the new government, they only transferred administrative power, without any clear-cut strategy for political reform. The new government spent its first two months in office trying to formulate a suitable reform agenda that could fulfil the people's desire for more freedom in their daily lives and a peaceful transition to democracy.[22]

As President Thein Sein explained his administration's policies in his address to the Union cabinet on 31 March 2011, "Good Governance" and "Clean Government" were the most important missions of his administration. He stressed the importance of transparency, constitutionality, the prioritization of public aspirations, all-inclusiveness, efficiency, and the simplification of the procedures of the Union government and regional/state governments as priorities for good governance.[23]

The second goal of his programme was promoting democratic practices, Thein Sein explained, pointing out that knowledge of democracy and the practising of freedom and rights within a legal framework were vital steps for strengthening democracy. He said every law and procedure should be made with the aim of helping citizens to be able to appropriately exercise their fundamental rights with no hindrance to the fundamental rights of citizens. He urged all ministers to pay serious attention to public opinion.

His third goal, Thein Sein said, was the rule of law, and his fourth was the facilitation of effective government. He gave assurance that his government would cooperate with the legislative branch and he stressed the importance of coordination and collaboration between the Union government and the regional/state governments and among the ministries.

Unlike the military leaders of the previous government, President Thein Sein urged the members of his cabinet to heed criticism and suggestions from the public and the media. He acknowledged the role of the media in the democratization process and urged the media to behave in a responsible and ethical manner. This was in stark contrast with the military government in which he served as prime minister. The president also made clear that he and his government must work for the service of the people and leave behind the authoritative style of the SPDC.

In concluding, he demanded that officials follow sound management and administrative practices while urging members of the cabinet to be free from corruption, the abuse of power and nepotism as this was the cornerstone of clean government. These were taboo issues under the previous military government.

The president acknowledged the need to reform the administrative system in line with the changing political system. He outlined the dos and don'ts for the members of his cabinet who were used to the administrative system of the military junta. He promised the people his government would be different from the single-party socialist government of the 1970s and 80s and the SPDC regime. But very few people foresaw that his speech would begin a bold and far-reaching reform programme.

Unfortunately, when these changes were brought forward, Thein Sein faced many challenges, even from within his own cabinet and from his old comrades in the Hluttaw.

The Consolidation of Presidential Authority

When President Thein Sein established his administration, the working procedures of the government remained much the same as those of the previous SPDC government. During the time of the SPDC, there was a cabinet meeting every Thursday, and until 2004 Senior General Than Shwe chaired these as head of government. Like cabinets in democratic countries, ministers submitted papers and proposals for the cabinet's consideration, but rarely was there active debate or questions from cabinet members except from Vice Senior General Maung Aye, the vice chairman of the SPDC, or the senior general.

Also, during the time of the SPDC government, it was an unwritten rule that ministers should report to Than Shwe to seek his approval on any important matter before cabinet meetings. Cabinet meetings were therefore merely to formalize proposals already approved by the senior general. Than Shwe also met with ministers concerned with the economy every Wednesday or Thursday morning before cabinet meetings.[24] Because of these practices, whenever a minister submitted an important paper or proposal, everyone understood that it had already been approved by Than Shwe and they therefore never raised any questions or objections or had any wish to debate a point of principle. These traditions were carried on after Than Shwe gave up the position of prime minister, and successive prime ministers[25] after him largely avoided making decisions on major policy matters and only decided on day-to-day government functions.[26]

As noted above, in the early days of his term as president, Thein Sein followed the same procedure, but he clearly saw that his administration must function differently from the previous military government. When he met with Union ministers, chief ministers for states and regions, and deputy ministers on 6 April 2011, he urged them to:[27]

1. Use their own initiative in fulfilling their duties and responsibilities.
2. Be accountable.
3. Have regard to the separation of powers between the Union government and the state and regional governments in accordance with the constitution.
4. Liberalize government regulations and procedures, especially in the economics sector.
5. Recognize the desire of the people for change.

6. Decentralize government and encourage bottom-up decision-making in formulating public policies.

President Thein Sein was only able to formulate his reform programme after he was sworn into office, even though he knew he had been selected to be the president by Than Shwe well before the 2010 election.[28] Why had the future president not been able to prepare for his administration? There were several reasons. First of all, Than Shwe did not want to reveal the choice of president until the last possible moment, in order to keep everyone guessing. Secondly, Than Shwe wanted to exert complete control over the political process. If Thein Sein began openly acting as the successor to Than Shwe, he would have faced the wrath of Than Shwe, as General Khin Nyunt and General Shwe Mann had done earlier. Thirdly, this was in keeping with Than Shwe's conception of the democratization process. Than Shwe's priorities for the transition to a democratic government commenced with the promulgation of the new constitution, which guaranteed a political role for the military in the future state, and building necessary infrastructure such as a new capital with a new parliament building, offices, bridges, dams, etc. However, he paid little attention to building the governing institutions of the future state.[29] Because of his lack of understanding of how other countries experienced a transition to democracy, Than Shwe believed a smooth transitional process would be achieved simply by the inauguration of the 2008 constitution and the formation of a USDP-led government.[30] Than Shwe therefore only undertook the preparatory stage by implementing the political, economic and military infrastructures intended to enable a smooth transition to democracy. President Thein Sein was responsible for the institution building that would carry through to the second stage of the democratization process. If the USDP had won the election in 2015, that would have led to a third stage—the consolidation of the democratization process.[31]

For the first two months of its existence the new administration did not lay down any new policies, and merely followed the procedures of the previous government. The president did however appoint nine presidential advisors for political, economic and legal affairs, who were as follow:

A. Political
   1. Ko Ko Hlaing, leader

2. Nay Zin Latt
3. Ye Tint
B. Economics
1. Dr Myint, leader
2. Set Aung
3. Dr Sein Hla Bo
C. Legal
1. Sit Aye, leader
2. Khin Myo Myint
3. Than Kyaw

In August 2013 the president appointed Dr Aung Tun Thet and Dr Zaw Oo as economic advisers and Nyan Naing Win as a legal adviser. One political adviser, Ye Tint, resigned because of ill health. These advisors served as an internal think tank for the president.

At this stage, Thein Sein had not yet used the word "reform" in any of his speeches. Some people claim that the president avoided the term for fear of annoying Senior General Than Shwe. However, former minister Tin Naing Thein rejects this and said that the term "reform" had never been banned by the senior general.[32] He recounted that in the early days the new administration was preoccupied with the national reconciliation process, the formation of Union and state or regional level administrative organs, and the economic liberalization processes. It was not possible to consolidate these programmes into a single framework or to develop new policies simultaneously with these heavy responsibilities. President Thein Sein announced a "second stage of reforms" in May 2012, which focused on the social and economic transformation. Based on his vision, the Framework for Economic and Social Reforms (FESR) was developed in consultation with senior officials of various ministries and departments of the government from May to October 2012. FESR is an essential policy tool of the government to realize the short-term and long-term potential of Myanmar. First, it provides a bridge linking the ongoing programmes of the government to the twenty-year National Comprehensive Development Plan.[33]

During the preparatory stage for the FESR, the president and ministers began to use the term "reform". When the president delivered his State of the Union Address that year he used not only "reform" but also "Myanmar Spring", comparing Myanmar with the so-called Arab Spring that was dominating the world's attention at the time.[34]

The Union Government   73

The first sign of the president's new governing style appeared at a National Workshop on Rural Development and Poverty Alleviation held in Naypyitaw in May 2011. The workshop was attended by international non-governmental organizations and local civil society organizations (CSOs). During the workshop, an action plan for a national poverty alleviation programme was presented and debated. In his opening remarks, Thein Sein pointed out that since seventy per cent of the people of Myanmar live in rural areas, rural development and poverty alleviation would be the main pillar of his economic policy.[35] He also urged participants to discuss five sectors for rural development, such as agriculture, fisheries and livestock, income generating projects, micro finance, and village cooperative societies. After the seminar, a National Plan for Rural Development and Poverty Reduction was drawn up and a Central Committee for Rural Development and Poverty Reduction, headed by the president, was formed. Under this, a working committee was formed to address eight specific areas:

1. Increase agricultural outputs
2. Livestock and fishery
3. Rural production
4. Microcredit
5. Rural cooperative societies
6. Socio-economic improvements (health, education, sports, social security)
7. Rural energy
8. Environment

To express his commitment to rural development and poverty alleviation, rather than leaving the workshop after delivering his opening remarks the president attended for a full day-long session and listened to the differing views of the participants. One of the key players in the administrative reform process, former minister in the President's Office Tin Naing Thein, explained that the president expressed his desire to listen to public opinion before adopting major public policies at this workshop. The president later used the term "People-Centred Policy" for his new approach to decision-making.[36]

After six months in office, the president and some ministers came to understand that their governing style should not be the same as that of the previous military government. They believed that the cabinet should introduce the principle of collective responsibility, and that important issues should not be approved until after open discussion and consultation. Moreover, there should be a sharing of administrative power between the Union government and the regional/state governments, as well as respect for and observation of the fundamental rights of citizens as stipulated in the constitution.[37] Consequently, the president began to issue directives to ministries to implement people-centred policies. According to these directives, ministers had to hold executive committee meetings with all department heads at their ministries to discuss and decide all major policies. They must also conduct workshops where CSOs and other stakeholders would be invited to attend to discuss the issues before implementing any major public policies.

During this time, the government worked closely with the United Nations Development Program (UNDP) to carry out administrative reform. Until September 2012, the UNDP's cooperation with the government of Myanmar was restricted by a 1992 Executive Board decision at the insistence of the US government. As a result of President Thein Sein's political reform, after the revoking of the previous decision by the Executive Board, UNDP Myanmar developed a new comprehensive country programme in 2012 that comprised local governance, the rule of law and access to justice, public administration reform, parliamentary support and public policy.[38] The government also studied the cabinets of Western democracies in order to find a suitable model for Myanmar. They later decided to study the cabinet committee system of the United Kingdom, and former British prime minister Tony Blair assisted these efforts.[39]

After Thein Sein had determined the new governing model, he needed to change the mindsets of ministers who are very familiar with the old system and its procedures. Some ministers who had served under the previous military government were reluctant to change or modify the senior general's policies because they thought they owed their loyalty and positions to Than Shwe, not to Thein Sein.[40] After a year in office, having won support from the international community and the public for his reforms, President Thein Sein felt he had enough political capital to consolidate his power. He had to replace or move aside some ministers who were not in tune with his reform policies. He also wanted to bring more technocrats into the cabinet as deputy ministers.

One-Year Anniversary

With the eventual implementation of a far-reaching reform agenda, President Thein Sein delivered his second State of the Union Address on 1 March 2012. He reviewed his first year as president in six parts. First was a general review of the reform process. He proudly called Myanmar's transition to democracy the "Myanmar Spring", saying this was a remarkable change for Myanmar and also historic for the next generation. As in his inaugural speech, he acknowledged again that people still doubted his government and he pledged to prove his words with deeds. He said the world was watching Myanmar and asked people to work together for a stable and smooth transition to democracy. He also warned that the process of building a democratic nation was only just beginning and that there was still much to be done. Second, he talked about peace and stability for the country. He explained that for political stability he was working for an all-inclusive political process. Without mentioning Aung San Suu Kyi, 88 Generation Students or exiled opposition activists, Thein Sein said that all the democratic forces were joining the political process and working in the interests of nation building.

Thirdly, he spoke about his peace initiative and the three-step approach for long-lasting peace in Myanmar. He emotionally quoted the young soldiers from ethnic armed groups who said they wanted to handle laptops instead of automatic rifles. Even though he avoided the term "federal" in this speech, he said he understood the suffering of the ethnic peoples and was working to heal all their sorrows. He also recognized the need for self-determination and equal rights for ethnic minorities, and said that the majority Bamar were also one of the ethnic groups in the country and not a ruling class. Fourth, he emphasized economic development and said rural development and poverty alleviation would be his number one priority. He promised to expand mobile phone penetration, reduce motor vehicle prices, stabilize a single foreign exchange rate regime and promote the private sector. He also set out his plans for tax reform and a system of universal health insurance. He said his national development strategy would be founded on an environmentally, socially and economically sustainable basis.

In the fifth part of his speech, the president discussed the unity of his government and denied there were divisions between reformers and hardliners. He said all cabinet members were working as a team for the reform process and were taking the utmost effort to serve the public interest. He acknowledged that corruption was the biggest threat to the country's economic development and promised to end it while establishing the rule of law in the country. He also hinted that he planned for more administrative reform, starting from the village level up to the Union government level, and he promised to remove red tape from government regulations. Lastly, he talked about the role of civil society organizations in a democratic society and pledged to protect and promote the basic rights of all citizens.

When he delivered his inaugural speech in 2011, President Thein Sein was very cautious in discussing his reform programme. He understood the sensitivity of the former senior general, and half of his speech was a tribute to the previous military government. He avoided any direct mention of past mistakes. The only negative thing he mentioned was that Myanmar remained a poor country. He also understood the public's mistrust of the new government and he tried to signal that it would be different from the governments of his predecessors. Now, after a year in office and after having won international and local support, the president reaffirmed his commitment to implementing further reform. He wanted to send the message that Myanmar was "leaving behind the authoritarian military government" and "building a new political system based on democratic norms". He stressed the need for sustainable economic development. He envisaged a country where the basic rights of citizens were protected, where there was unity among different ethnic groups, and where there was eternal peace. He said that Myanmar was in transition to a new era and a new system, and that the society of Myanmar was transforming into a democratic one. In the main, the speech reflected the president's confidence in his political capital and set the tone for future reform.

Cabinet Reshuffles

While President Thein Sein was preparing his reform programme, an unexpected development took place. Vice president 1, Tin Aung Myint Oo,[41] made a trip to Singapore in the last week of April 2012 for a medical check-up. When he returned to Yangon, he entered the monkhood, and on 3 May submitted his resignation to the chairman of the Pyidaungsu Hluttaw. The president visited Yangon to meet with him and requested him to change his decision. Tin Aung Myint Oo however refused to do so. Later, the media reported his resignation but the government refused to confirm it. The people behind this leak were certain ministers and their civilian colleagues who saw the vice president 1 as a hardliner and as an obstacle to Thein Sein's reform programme.

When the president understood that Tin Aung Myint Oo would not change his decision, on 4 July the government announced his resignation and requested the Union Parliament to elect a new vice president. On 15 August, the commander in chief of the navy, Admiral Nyan Tun, was sworn in as the new vice president 2.[42] The decision to choose a military leader to succeed Tin Aung Myint Oo was in line with the fact that the previous vice president had been nominated by the Tatmadaw representatives in the Hluttaw. Many observers saw the resignation of the vice president and the appointment of Admiral Nyan Tun—who was viewed as a moderate—as signalling an important change in the power balance between the reformers and hardliners in government.[43] There was also speculation that President Thein Sein might soon remove other top officials and reshuffle the cabinet.

In August the president introduced measures for liberalization and national reconciliation. Prior to the 2012 anniversary of the 8888 uprising, he sent railway minister Aung Min and other ministers to meet 88 Generation Students leaders and donated funds for the commemoration of the 8888 anniversary. As the 8888 uprising was against the military-backed socialist government, the anniversary celebrations were seen as a protest against continued military rule. Previously, the authorities had always tried to suppress these demonstrations. The president's decision to acknowledge the anniversary therefore had a great impact on public opinion and won him support from former student political activists. Later, on 20 August, the government announced the abolition of the pre-publication censorship that had existed since 1964. Then, seven days later, the government announced the removal of nearly two thousand names from the list of Myanmar exiles who were denied the right to return to the country, thereby allowing many exiled opposition members to return.

Then the day of the much-awaited cabinet reshuffle arrived. Between 27 August and 7 September, the president created new ministers for the President's Office, twenty ministers were reshuffled, two resigned, and twenty deputy ministers were appointed (Table 5.1).[44] Many of the newcomers had technocrat backgrounds, and Myanmar saw the appointment of its second female minister in history.[45] People viewed the reshuffle as strengthening the position of the president and the reform-minded ministers. Indeed, the reshuffle created new momentum for the reform programme, but the resignation of Tin Aung Myint Oo as vice president 1 and the creation of President's Office ministers, or so called super ministers, created unforeseen consequences for Thein Sein's cabinet.

Reformers and Hardliners

When President Thein Sein began to implement the reform agenda he had laid out in his inaugural address, people started to speculate as to who were the reformers and who were the hardliners or conservatives in the Union government.[46] It became the talk of the town after six months. Later, the president attempted to stop this issue, which was affecting the unity of his cabinet, in his 2012 State of the Union address:

> Widespread speculation over a split in the government between a reformist faction and a hardline faction are not true. Except from some different opinions based on individual characters, habits and ways of doing things, all cabinets members support the government's policy.[47]

Who was responsible for starting the issue of reformers versus hardliners? Many cabinet members, including myself, believe some members of Myanmar Egress raised this idea during the early days of the Thein Sein administration.[48] Founded in 2006 as an NGO, Egress focused on a peaceful transition to democracy in Myanmar. Members of Egress, including some foreign scholars, had not only access to the previous ruling military government but also to some exile groups, especially former student leaders on the Myanmar-Thailand border. The mother of one of the founders of Egress, Dr Nay Win Maung, had served for many years as a lecturer at the Defence Services Academy, and many senior military officers—including Thein Sein—had been her students. This created a connection, and Nay Win Maung's idea of accepting the new constitution and starting reform under it made a positive impression on military leaders. Under the military government, there was unofficial communication between some ministers who were also senior USDA leaders and Egress.

Aung Min, minister for railways under the military regime was the first person to deal extensively with Myanmar Egress. Aung Min's first engagement with Egress came from his desire to find a means for a peaceful transition to democracy under the 2008 constitution. Aung Min studied the constitution and found that although it provided the foundation for multiparty democracy and federalism, he knew nothing about these principles.[49] During this period, Egress approached Htay Oo, general secretary of the USDA and minister for agriculture and irrigation, to provide some training for USDA members. Although Htay Oo met with Nay Win Maung and other Egress members, the USDA never officially cooperated with Egress. However, they implemented their own training for USDA members in political and international affairs.[50]

Aung Min contacted Egress and was impressed with their pragmatic ideas concerning Myanmar's transition to democracy. He collected and submitted Egress policy papers to then prime minister and vice chairman of the USDA, General Thein Sein.[51] After Thein Sein became president, communication with Egress gained momentum. The president not only received Egress policy papers but personally met with Egress members such as Nay Win Maung, Hla Maung Shwe, Kyaw Yin Hlaing and Tin Maung Than. Later, one or two individuals from Egress took all the credit for the Myanmar Spring and boasted that all the president's speeches and policies came from Egress. They even claimed they had made recommendations to the president about the cabinet reshuffle.[52] Even though Egress enjoyed some access to the president because of ministers Aung Min and Soe Thane, the president always sought advice from different sources, including foreign scholars and diplomats. But the self-promotion and arrogant behaviour of a very few Egress members created tension between other cabinet members and Egress.[53]

When President Thein Sein started the reform process, Aung Min and Nay Win Maung categorized all cabinet ministers into three groups: reformers, hardliners and neutralists.[54] Early in 2012, Aung Min told diplomats that the cabinet was composed of 10 per cent reformers, 45 per cent hardliners and 45 per cent neutrals. He further asserted that the reformers were working hard to overcome resistance from the hardliners. He also said that most of the ministers could not change their mindsets, they were therefore unwilling or unable to participate in the reform process.[55]

Aung Min arranged meetings between Nay Win Maung and some ministers thought to be key players for the future of the reform process. From these meetings they tried to judge the political leanings of those involved and to decide whether or not they were reformers. Many felt insulted by these meetings in which Nay Win Maung asked questions and in some cases Egress members bluntly asked ministers whether or not they were supporters of reform.[56] Most of the ministers thought that using the terms "reformers" and "hardliners" was Aung Min and Egress's method to exert pressure on others who took a different view on government policy.[57]

For Aung Min and Egress, vice president 1 Thiha Thura Tin Aung Myint Oo was the leader of the hardliners.[58] The opinions of Aung Min and Egress influenced local and international observers and they interpreted the retirement of the vice president in July 2012 and the subsequent August cabinet reshuffle as a victory of the reformers led by ministers Soe Thane and Aung Min. Aung Min even declared on many occasions that political and economic reforms gained momentum after Tin Aung Myint Oo's retirement.[59]

It was a mistake to label Tin Aung Myint Oo as a hardliner. He was known for his quick temper and his sometimes very arrogant manner of dealing with subordinates, but he also worked hard and had an extraordinary memory for facts and figures.[60] He could work long hours and had the ability to pick out the salient points of complex issues. Before important meetings such as those of the budget committee, he thoroughly studied each ministry's budget proposals and questioned the ministers concerned on every project or spending item. If a minister could not give a satisfactory answer, he certainly suffered Tin Aung Myint Oo's wrath.[61]

When military intelligence chief General Khin Nyunt was removed in 2014, Senior General Than Shwe tasked Prime Minister General Soe Win and SPDC secretary 2 Lieutenant General Tin Aung Myint Oo with economic and development projects.[62] As he was quartermaster general, Tin Aung Myint Oo was responsible for the military-owned business group, Myanmar Economic Cooperation (MEC).

After Prime Minister General Soe Win passed away in 2007, secretary 1 General Thein Sein became prime minister and Tin Aung Myint Oo was promoted to secretary 1. Unlike his predecessor General Soe Win, General Thein Sein was not responsible for the economy and major development projects. Tin Aung Myint Oo took over all these responsibilities, including the government budget and the powerful Trade Council.[63] Prime Minister General Thein Sein's responsibility was to supervise the governmental machinery and the organizational work of the USDA. Than Shwe ordered Thein Sein to travel across the country and meet with the public, to check on the progress of development projects and to organize USDA activities.

Thein Sein was happy with this arrangement, as the economic sector was marred with corruption, nepotism and conflict among various interest groups. With hindsight, he understood that Than Shwe wanted to keep him away from these economic issues because he was considering Thein Sein for an important future task such as the next president under the new constitution.[64] As secretary 1, Tin Aung Myint Oo was also responsible for the drafting of new laws concerning the future institutions, such as the Pyithu Hluttaw Law, the Amyotha Hluttaw Laws, the Union Government Law, and others.

When the new government was formed under President Thein Sein, Vice President 1 Tin Aung Myint Oo was the only cabinet member who knew the details of existing economic policies, development projects and budget procedures. As vice president 1, Tin Aung Myint Oo was responsible for the budgets of the Union, region and state governments as well as for security, administrative and development projects. During the SPDC period, all ministers who met with Than Shwe had to report to him before and after their meetings because the secretary 1 was like a chief of staff to the SPDC chairman, Than Shwe. The senior general mostly accepted Tin Aung Myint's recommendations on economic and development issues, and Tin Aung Myint Oo was among the very few officers who had the courage to speak his mind to Than Shwe and Maung Aye.[65] He naturally wished to continue this practice under President Thein Sein,[66] and he also wanted to keep some of the SPDC's economic policies and development projects that he believed to be of merit and still relevant to the new situation.[67]

Consequently, he clashed with Shwe Mann, the Speaker of the Pyithu Hluttaw, over the 2012–13 budget. Shwe Mann wanted to cut funding for ongoing development projects, mostly irrigation dams and some infrastructure projects. He encouraged members of the Hluttaw Public Accounts Committee to criticize these projects in their reports. Tin Aung Myint Oo was very angry about this, as Shwe Man had also been a ranking member of the SPDC and had never raised objections to these projects during special development project meetings chaired by Senior General Than Shwe. He remarked that people who always kowtowed to the senior general were now indirectly attacking him for cheap popularity and called them *thar ku* (opportunists). [68]

The heated arguments with Shwe Mann over the drafting of the 2012–13 budget led to a meeting with the big six (the president, the two vice presidents, the Speakers of the lower and upper chambers, the commander in chief of the armed forces, and the chairman of the Union Election Commission) to settle the dispute. At the meeting, Tin Aung Myint Oo expressed his desire to quit as he had already finished his task of preparing the 2012–13 budget, saying he had no will to stay in office in the prevailing political environment.[69] He also informed some of his close friends in cabinet of his intention to soon resign.[70]

Another reason for his resignation was that the president relied increasingly on Soe Thane and Aung Min for political and economic issues. In some cases the president accepted recommendations made by Tin Aung Mying Oo but changed his mind after meeting with Soe Thane and Aung Min. These two ministers never consulted Tin Aung Myint Oo on policy issues nor talked about their meetings with the president. As a consequence, Tin Aung Myint Oo became frustrated after six months in the new government and informed close friends that he would resign after the 2012–13 budget was approved by parliament.[71]

There were other theories about Tin Aung Myint Oo's resignation. According to one of these, Shwe Mann saw Tin Aung Myint Oo as a potential rival for the presidency after the end of Thein Sein's term, as Tin Aung Myint Oo had a mastery of administrative and economic matters. So, by attacking the SPDC's economic policies and development projects and linking them with corruption and mismanagement, Shwe Mann discredited Tin Aung Myint Oo who had supervised them. Thus, Tin Aung Myint Oo felt under pressure and decided to resign to avoid potential scrutiny from the public and the Hluttaw. With his resignation Shwe Mann not only removed a potential rival but also weakened the Thein Sein cabinet, "Killing two birds with one stone".[72] Another theory posits a link with the suspension of the Myitsone dam project. Tin Aung Myint Oo was a focal individual for the deal with the Chinese government, and when President Thein Sein abruptly suspended the project without consulting him, it was claimed that he took responsibility for it and resigned.[73]

It is difficult to label Tin Aung Myint Oo as either a hardliner or a reformer. He may have preferred a more conservative approach in political and economic reforms, but in some cases, such as in dealing with the legislature, he was more moderate than some of his colleagues. For example, he always encouraged ministers to answer questions in the Hluttaw themselves instead of sending deputy ministers to question and answer sessions. He also acknowledged that since the president and vice presidents are elected by the Union Hluttaw, they were accountable to the legislative body. When the president and some cabinet members complained about the Hluttaw, he replied that the executive should respect the legislative role in the system of checks and balance.[74]

Amongst members of the cabinet there was an assumption that reforms would be more effective if Tin Aung Myint Oo was involved because of his knowledge and experience. With his involvement, the president could play "good cop bad cop" with Tin Aung Myint Oo and thereby exert more control over ministries and state/regional governments. After his resignation, the vice presidents were sidelined and ministers from the President's Office had a free hand to involve themselves in the affairs of other ministries. Further, the Union government was less effectively able to control state/regional chief ministers.[75] And, moreover, the president lost the only person who could effectively deal with the lower house Speaker Shwe Mann.

The categorization of President Thein Sein's cabinet members as reformers or hardliners reflected a tendency to see politics in Myanmar as a battle between "them" and "us". In reality there were no hardliners in the cabinet, nor any hard-line faction. Everyone accepted that the country required change and therefore supported the president's reform agenda. However, there doubtless were differences of opinion on some policy issues. But at the end of any policy discussion, all those involved accepted the president's decision and did their utmost to implement the reform agenda. Instead of encouraging open and active debate among cabinet members, portraying minsters who had different opinions from those of Aung Min and Soe Thane as hardliners not only harmed cabinet unity but also prevented the president from hearing conflicting opinions as to how to take the reform process forward.

Ministers in the President's Office

The most important aspect of the 2012 cabinet reshuffle was the appointment of four new ministers in the President's Office. When President Thein Sein formed the new government in 2012, there were two ministers in the President's Office, Thein Nyunt and Soe Maung. Thein Nyunt, minister-1, served as chairman of the Naypyitaw Council and was also the mayor of Naypyitaw, the new capital of Myanmar. He was also responsible for the administration of the President's Office and the presidential residence. Soe

Maung, minister-2, was responsible for public complaints. Thein Nyunt was a former minister under Than Shwe and responsible for the Naypyitaw project, and Soe Maung was the former advocate general of the Tatmadaw. Both were known to have been selected by Than Shwe as ministers in the President's Office. Thein Sein liked and trusted Thein Nyunt. He was not satisfied however with Soe Maung, but kept him because of Than Shwe. Thein Sein received many complaints about Soe Maung's handling of public complaints.

The 2012 cabinet reshuffle saw four additional ministers appointed as follows:

(a) Soe Thane, former minister for industry, as minister-3, in charge of economic reform, trade and investment. He also served as chairman of the Myanmar Investment Commission (MIC).[76]
(b) Aung Min, former minister for rail transportation, as minister-4, responsible for political reform and the peace process.
(c) Hla Tun, former minister for finance and revenue, as minister-5, tasked with administrative reform and ethnic affairs.
(d) Tin Naing Thein, former minister for national planning and economic development, as minister-6, assigned to look after private sector development.

The new ministers acted as coordinating ministers under the president. Additionally, Soe Thane chaired the Cabinet Committee on Economic Affairs and Hla Tun chaired the Cabinet Committee on Administrative, Peasants and Labour Affairs.[77]

The president's idea of appointing new ministers to the President's Office was to use his trusted aids as enablers of the reform process. This was an adaptation of the Army High Command procedure of assigning chiefs of Special Operation Bureaus (SOBs), who coordinated the operations of military regional command headquarters on behalf of the commander in chief.[78] Additionally, the president hoped to use them as buffers against the Shwe Mann–led Pyithu Hluttaw.[79]

The newly appointed ministers were dubbed "super ministers".[80] Minister Soe Thane however rejected the term. He argued instead that since they were ministers without portfolios they did not have any authority over the budget or administrative matters of the ministries. He said, "We just made necessary coordination for the realization of the president's reform policies. The responsibility of my cabinet committee was the scrutinizing of the proposals from each ministry before they were presented at the cabinet meetings. Whatever came, the president's decision was final."[81] Minister Aung Min also said he never interfered with the functions of other ministries and that he worked solely for peace and political reform.[82]

There were some in government who did not accept the comparison between ministers in the President's Office and chiefs of the Special Operation Bureaus, since SOB chiefs hold the rank of lieutenant general and regional commanders are major generals, one rank below SOB chiefs. But ministers in the President's Office were members of the Union government and of the same status as other Union ministers. Although not a single minister opposed the appointments and all respected the president's decision, some felt President's Office ministers interfered in their responsibilities. In some cases, especially for matters that went through the Economic Affairs Committee, ministers felt they had lost their right to present directly to the president on important issues.[83] Although they acknowledged that Soe Thane and Aung Min were progressive, some questioned their competency during their tenures, respectively, as minister for industry 2 and minister for railway transportation.[84] As the president delegated his power to the ministers in his office, especially Soe Thane and Aung Min, they were described as "Vice Presidents in all but name".[85]

When President Thein Sein submitted his nominations for President's Office ministers to the Pyidaungsu Hluttaw, the members, particularly the Shwe Mann–controlled members, opposed them, since many former ministers who were chairmen of Pyithu Hluttaw committees had a personal dislike of Soe Thane. The president therefore sent Vice President Nyan Htun to explain the role of the new ministers to the two legislative Speakers, Khin Aung Myint and Shwe Mann. Khin Aung Myint readily agreed to support the president's nominations and promised to win support from Amyotha Hluttaw (upper house or house of nationalities) members. Shwe Mann initially had reservations but later agreed to support the proposals.[86]

Though the president assigned each minister specific sectors they should coordinate, there were overlaps when they actually conducted their duties. For example, Soe Thane who was responsible for the economy also advised the president on international relations and on the politics and performance of other ministries. Tin Naing Thein who was responsible for private sector development also actively involved himself in administrative reform, including the decentralization of Union government responsibilities, implementation of a people-centred development policy, and the liberalization of government regulations relevant to promoting private sector development.

The most contentious matter surrounding the appointment of President's Office ministers however was not in relation to policy issues but was to do with personal issues. The most controversial minister was Soe Thane. Soe Thane took over the chairmanship of the Myanmar Investment Commission from Tin Naing Thein[87] on 1 September 2012.[88] He also served as chairman of the Cabinet Economic Affairs Committee. As chair of the Economic Affairs Committee and the MIC, Soe Thane had a great influence over the economic policy of the new government. He was involved in the privatization of state-owned buildings and land, especially when investors requested particular buildings or land. As earlier privatization measures under the former military government were marred by corruption and nepotism, many ministers were reluctant for the privatization of government assets. But Soe Thane wanted to facilitate purchases of state-owned assets in order to bring in foreign investment as quickly as possible. To overcome resistance from the ministries concerned, he proposed to the president that ministries should transfer some of their assets to the MIC so that the MIC could transfer these to investors. The president agreed with the proposal.[89]

After the new policy was introduced, however, a decision by the MIC to allow the sale of the former Secretariat building and the former High Court building—of note for their colonial architecture—faced strong opposition from the public. Local media questioned the privatization of such state-owned buildings, claiming the MIC had sold off the properties below market value. President Thein Sein subsequently bowed to public opinion and appointed Finance and Revenue Minister Win Shein as MIC chair. Although the president separated the Economic Affairs Committee and the MIC, Soe Thane continued to have an indirect influence on MIC decisions, since these decisions had to be submitted to the cabinet through the Economic Affairs Committee.[90] Soe Thane's main intention was to facilitate foreign and local investment, but some ministers thought he was more interested in big projects and privatization than macroeconomic policy reform.[91]

Among the President's Office ministers, Soe Thane and Aung Min were closer to the president than the others. Aung Min, responsible for the peace process, travelled a lot for meetings with ethnic armed organizations (EAOs) and was largely away from the president. Soe Thane, on the other hand, met the president nearly every day and discussed not only economic issues but also matters of politics, foreign policy and governmental affairs. Because of his access to the president and his rapid follow up, diplomats, businessmen and technocrats approached Soe Thane to present their opinions and advice on the reform programme, and his office became the busiest of a minister in Naypyitaw.[92]

Soe Thane played an important role in the rapprochement with the United States and the European Union by serving as a track two channel. President Obama's historic visit to Myanmar on 19 November 2012 and President Thein Sein's first meeting with Secretary Clinton on 13 July 2012 at Siem Reap, Cambodia, were initially negotiated by Soe Thane.[93]

Because of his access to the president and his outspokenness about other ministers, businessmen and officials, Soe Thane naturally had many detractors. They accused him of manipulating government policies, removing ministers who disagreed with him, and isolating the president, among other things, but there is little evidence to support these accusations. While it is true that Soe Thane was the most important advisor to President Thein Sein, the president had other advisors and sources of information. When it came to the cabinet reshuffle, the president alone decided who would be replaced or removed. While there were two or three other ministers that Thein Sein considered replacing, he decided not to do so because of their past contributions to the nation and the government.[94]

Soe Thane was a progressive minister who doubtless desired to see the president's reform programme succeed and who seized every opportunity to move it forward. The problem was his modus operandi. He did not try to build consensus among his colleagues but instead bulldozed his way over others. And as a key player in economic reform, he was praised by those who benefitted under the reforms and hated by those who lost opportunities they had enjoyed under the previous government.

There are differences of opinion over the appointments of President's Office ministers. But the president had to strengthen his power after a year in office, having received strong support from the public and the international community. As the original cabinet was seen as Than Shwe's cabinet, now that the president had amassed political capital through his popular reform programmes he needed to consolidate his authority by reshuffling the cabinet, appointing trusted individuals as President's Office ministers and many technocrats as deputy ministers. These were logical decisions to move forward his reform programme. Instead of assigning specific tasks to each minister, however, the president allotted them broad powers not only to coordinate but also to supervise other ministries. This diminished the roles of the two vice presidents in their constitutionally mandated responsibilities and affected the unity of the cabinet as a whole. Also, by making appointments to the President's Office based more on loyalty than competence and by creating "super ministers", President Thein Sein became known as something of an "imperial president".[95]

Vice Presidents

Unlike most countries, Myanmar has two vice presidents, a unique feature of its constitution. According to article 60, the president is elected by an electoral college known as the Pyidaungsu Hluttaw—composed of the Pyithu Hluttaw and the Amyotha Hluttaw—rather than by popular vote. In both houses, the military holds twenty-five per cent of the seats.

The election of the president commences with the nomination of vice presidential candidates by three electoral groups: elected members of the upper house, elected members of the lower house, and military representatives from both houses sitting together. Each group selects a vice president from either a member of parliament or a non-member of parliament. The Pyidaungsu Hluttaw then elects the president from among the three vice presidential nominations. The two runners-up become vice president 1 and vice president 2, in line with the number of votes each receives.

Instead of the two legislative assemblies or political parties submitting their presidential candidates and voting on them, the Myanmar constitution provides military representatives who are nominated by the commander in chief the right to nominate their own candidate. With this unique presidential election system, a military candidate is ensured of becoming a vice president and therefore a member of the National Defence and Security Council. Additionally, the military is guaranteed to have three important ministers in the Union government.[96] This ensures that the Tatmadaw—which already is allocated twenty-five per cent of the seats in the two legislative bodies—also enjoys an important role in the executive, thus fulfilling a mandate promulgated amongst the basic principles of the constitution.[97]

The general election in November 2010 was followed by the formation of multiparty legislative bodies at both the Union and state/regional levels. The two legislative bodies at the Union level held their first session on 31 January 2011. Both houses elected members, and the military representatives duly nominated vice presidential nominees and submitted these to the Union Parliament on 1 February. The nominee from the lower house was former general and former prime minister of the SPDC government Thein Sein (USDP), from the upper house, ethnic Shan Dr Sai Mauk Hkam (USDP), and from the military members, former general and secretary 1 of the SPDC, Thiha Thura Tin Aung Myint Oo.[98] All of the candidates were thus members of the Union Solidarity and Development Party, the largest party in the two houses of the legislature.

When the Union Parliament met on 4 February and voted for the president, Thein Sein won a majority and become the first president of the Union of Myanmar since 1988. Thiha Thura Tin Aung Myint Oo and Dr Sai Mauk Hkam became vice presidents 1 and 2 respectively. As noted previously, when Tin Aung Myint Oo retired in July 2012, military representatives duly elected the commander in chief of the navy, Admiral Nyan Thu, as vice president.[99]

Though Myanmar has two mandated vice presidents, there are no specific responsibilities for them according to the constitution. Rather, section 203 merely states "The Vice-Presidents shall be responsible to the President and also to the Pyidaungsu Hluttaw through the President." Vice presidents are not even sure to replace the president if he or she vacates the post for any reason. Section 73(a) of the constitution stipulates that "One of the two Vice-Presidents who has won the second highest votes in the Presidential election shall serve as Acting President if the seat of the President falls vacant due to his resignation, death, permanent disability or any other cause." Subsequently, the elected representatives or military members of the group whose vice president became president shall elect another vice president in his or her stead. Next, the Pyidaungsu Hluttaw would once again vote to elect the president from among the three vice presidents. Hence, the vice presidents lack the political influence of a designated successor to the head of state, and their role depends on the trust that the president has put in them in assigning official responsibilities.

In the early days of the new government, as discussed above, Vice President 1 Tin Aung Myint Oo was responsible for the security and administrative portfolios and for coordinating Union ministries and regional/state governments. Vice President 2 Dr Sai Mauk Hkam, an ethnic Shan, with his background as a doctor, was responsible for health, education, culture and social affairs. Since he lacked experience in administrative and legal issues, he took time to familiarize himself with the government's regulations and procedures.[100] When Tin Aung Myint Oo retired in July 2012, Sai Mauk Hkam became vice president 1, but the security and administrative portfolios were assigned by the president to newly appointed Vice President 2 Nyan Tun, former commander in chief of the navy.

The two vice presidents had limited personal relations with the president, the Union ministers, or with chief ministers of regional and state governments, since nearly all of these individuals were former army officers.[101] Moreover, neither of the two had much knowledge or experience of the development projects and economic policies of the previous SPDC government.[102] As a result, for cabinet functions the president had to work directly with President's Office ministers or Union ministers.[103] President Thein Sein did not intentionally sideline the vice presidents. However, this was the result, as he felt more comfortable dealing with ministers who shared the same background and who had worked together with him for a long time. Also, he was accustomed to the military government's tradition by which Senior General Than Shwe dealt directly with his ministers.[104] The president sometimes however assigned a special task to one of the vice presidents, such as leading organizational work for the ASEAN Chairmanship (2014) and the Southeast Asian Games (2013). The vice presidents successfully carried out these tasks.[105]

The responsibilities assigned to the vice presidents under the Thein Sein presidency can be divided into two general categories. The first concerned national ceremonies and prominent occasions such as Independence Day, the ASEAN summit and related meetings. The vice presidents were appointed as chairs of the organizing or working committees for these events. This followed the custom of the SPDC, which assigned the secretary 1 and secretary 2 to such responsibilities. The second category was the chairmanship of the national-level policy committees. Vice president 1 was assigned to the peace, education and health committees while vice president 2 was assigned to natural disaster management, energy, water resources and land use policy, etc. This was in keeping with the SPDC tradition.

Although the second responsibility was based on the SPDC model, unlike the secretaries 1 and 2, the vice presidents did not have the full authority or political power to supervise or coordinate Union ministries and regional/state governments. For example, Vice President 2 Nyan Tun was chairman of the Committee on National Energy Policy but he had no authority to supervise the Ministry of Energy. Likewise, the vice president 2 headed the working group on media relations but the minister for information dealt directly with the president's staff or ministers Soe Thane and Aung Min, who relayed the president's instructions to the Ministry of Information and who seldom reported to the vice president 2 on current issues. In another case, while Vice President 1 Dr Sai Mauk Hkam was chairman of the working committee for peace, Minister for the President's Office Aung Min directly dealt with the president, with ethnic armed organization leaders, and ran the Myanmar Peace Centre. Thus, Sai Mauk Hkam's role was merely that of hosting dinners for visiting EAO leaders and presenting them with gifts—he was excluded from the president's private meetings with the leaders.[106]

In the early days of his administration, Thein Sein followed the SPDC tradition of holding a political and security briefing every morning. During the SPDC days, from 2007 onwards these briefings were chaired by Shwe Mann and attended by Prime Minister Thein Sein, Secretary 1 Tin Aung Myint Oo and some ministers. From 2011 the briefings were chaired by the president and attended by the two vice presidents, the Speakers from both houses of the Union legislature and some important ministers.[107] Later, the two Speakers did not attend the briefings because of their legislative duties, which were separate from the executive branch.[108] The president then only met with ministers in his office, and the vice presidents were no longer invited.

When relations between the executive and legislative branches became tense in late 2012, some ministers advised Thein Sein to use the vice presidents more effectively in the cabinet. At first the president invited them again to the security and political briefings, but he stopped doing so after three months because he felt more comfortable dealing with close associates, especially while Shwe Mann's cliques continually threatened him.[109] He used President's Office ministers to coordinate other ministries on his behalf. They were his people and he could pressure them and drive them hard, but he could not or did not want to do the same to the vice presidents.

Usually, using the President's Office ministers yielded good results, but sometimes this was counterproductive. For example, in late 2012 the president launched an administrative reform programme in an attempt to reduce red tape and make government procedures more efficient, but, because of a lack of coordination among various ministries, very little was achieved. Subsequently, the president formed a Public Services Performance Appraisal Task Force and appointed President's Officer minister 6, Tin Naing Thein, as chair. That task force was composed of deputy ministers from various ministries and some prominent scholars. It achieved good results in a short time. Passport and visa controls were relaxed, government regulations were streamlined, a bottom-up approach in public policy was encouraged, complaints from the public were entertained, the performance of each ministry was reviewed, and public awareness of the administrative reforms was promoted and feedback invited.

Some ministers however felt that the task force was interfering in their responsibilities and they complained to Tin Aye, who was a classmate of Thein Sein's at the Defence Services Academy and chairman of the Union Election Commission.[110] Tin Aye in turn complained to the president that activities of the task force were damaging cabinet unity. After the president passed on these complaints to the task force, it reduced its activities and avoided further reform of government regulation. The main job of the task force became receiving public complaints and passing these on to the relevant ministries. The task force was thus no longer relevant to administrative reform. If one of the vice presidents had led the task force, they could have avoided misunderstanding and complaints from the other ministers. The vice presidents also felt they had been bypassed in formulating government policies, and they shared their frustrations with some ministers.[111]

With hindsight, had the president assigned more responsibilities to the vice presidents and brought them into more decision-making processes, there might have been greater unity among cabinet members and consequently more could have been achieved.

The Government Office, the President's Office and the Executive Office of the President

After the military took power on 18 September 1988, they formed a cabinet office and the SLORC[112] office for carrying out government functions. Since the head of state and head of government Senior General Than Shwe was also commander in chief of the Tatmadaw, the Office of the Commander in Chief (Army) Operations Department handled most of his instructions and the day-to-day work. The cabinet office and the SLORC office only handled regular office work and papers. When General Khin Nyunt, General Soe Win and General Thein Sein were prime ministers, the cabinet office was more active in the daily work of government. However, the Operations Department remained in direct contact with ministries and state and division Law and Order Restoration Councils because Than Shwe was still chairman of the SLORC.

When the new government was formed under the 2008 constitution, three offices—the Office of the Union Government (cabinet office), the Office of the President, and the Staff Office of the President—were created. Of these, the Government Office was formed by SPDC law (15/2010) and staffed mainly by personnel from the SPDC-era Government Office. The President's Office was also formed of staff from the SDPC office, whilst the Staff Office of the President was newly raised with staff from various ministries, including the Ministry of Defence.

The Government Office was led by a director general and was responsible for representing the Union Government in supervising and cooperating with Union ministries and regional/state governments. The director general was also cabinet secretary and served additionally as secretary of the National Defence and Security Council in accord with the Union Government Law. The President's Office was also led by a director general and was responsible for the functions of the president with which he was entrusted by the constitution. The Staff Office of the President was led by a deputy director general and was responsible for the personal affairs of the president.[113] However, Thein Sein assigned the Staff Office to handle urgent issues when he needed to contact a relevant minister and in dealing with the Hluttaw, such as writing letters to the Speakers and sending his remarks on bills. Sometimes the president asked the Staff Office to seek opinions from the legal advisory team.

The division of labour between the Government Office and the President's Office is based on the constitution. In chapter 5, "Executive", under the "Powers and Functions of the President", sections 202 to 215 set out the duties and functions of the President's Office. These include the formation of ministries, granting amnesties, addressing the Hluttaw, sending messages, issuing decrees, taking military action against foreign invasion, and signing bills. Also in chapter 5, under the "Executive Powers of the Union Government", sections 216 to 228 list the duties and functions of the Government Office.[114] These include distributing duties among the ministries, approving national plans, ensuring the peace and stability of the state and the rule of law, presenting and allocating budgets, and supervising and coordinating the Union ministries and regional/state governments.

Although the division of labour was clearly defined in the constitution, in practice there were conflicts between the three offices. Access to the president by office holders and their influence over government policies were based on their personal relations with the president. The president had a personal staff officer (PSO) and a Staff Office for his personal affairs, and the President's Office to deal with official matters. But the PSO and Staff Office had direct access to the president, and ministers would directly contact them, especially for urgent or important issues. Sometimes the president would also use them to issue instructions to ministers. This was an old habit brought over from the SPDC era. The Operations Department of the commander in chief of the army served as direct access to Than Shwe as SPDC chairman and commander in chief of the Tatmadaw. Also, at the personal level, head of Staff Office Ye Min and PSO Ko Ko Kyaw had closer relations with the president than did the director general of the President's Office Hla Tun or the director general of the Government Office Zaw Than Thin.[115] That led to a situation whereby Ye Min and Ko Ko Kyaw were involved not only with liaison between the president and ministers but also in policy issues. For example, presidential letters to the Hluttaw were composed mainly by the Staff Office rather than the President's Office. Although Ye Min did his best to consult with legal advisors and officials, the lack of coordination or discussion in cabinet led to some misunderstandings between the president and the Hluttaw. There were also conflicts between Ye Min and Ko Ko Kyaw over access to the president.[116]

There were also conflicts over the division of labour between the President's Office and the Government Office. According to the constitution, the Government Office is responsible for economic issues such as development projects under government ministries. But the President's Office, with its access to the president, superseded the Government Office and took control of these issues. For example, if a businessman wanting to invest in state-owned buildings or land sent an application directly to the president rather that the ministry concerned, the President's Office would review it[117] and submit it to the president with their recommendation. If the president agreed, the President's Office would send the application along with the president's remarks to the ministry concerned and the ministry would deal with the businessman to conclude a formal agreement. If a final agreement was reached, the ministry would submit it to the Government Office for cabinet approval. In this manner, the Government Office merely handled the paperwork and was bypassed in the formal process by the President's Office. Since the personnel of the President's Office did not know about government rules and regulations, sometimes their recommendations were contrary to existing regulations and procedures.[118]

Some ministers exploited this situation and asked their business friends to submit proposals directly to the President's Office in order to avoid responsibility and accountability. Meanwhile they worked behind the scene by approaching the President's Office or Minister Soe Thane to seek approval for their friends.[119] Should a project go wrong, the minister simply needed to say that it was submitted directly to the president and that they had no knowledge of it until the President's Office sent its approval, and thus the president was said to have been responsible.

It is normal in any government that close advisors to leaders compete for access and influence over presidential decisions. As Myanmar had just begun the transition to a new political and administrative system, the competition and machinations among the president's inner circle greatly damaged his image.

Notes

1. Pyidaungsu Hluttaw records, 9 February 2011.
2. Soe Thane, *Myanmar's Transformation & U Thein Sein "An Insider's Account"* (Yangon: Tun Foundation Literature Committee, 2017), p. 20.
3. They are the most senior members of the SPDC after chairman Than Shwe and vice chairman Maung Aye.
4. Interview 011.
5. Interview 019.
6. Su Mon Thazin Aung and Matthew Arnold, *Managing Change: Executive Policymaking in Myanmar* (Asia Foundation, 2018).
7. Interview 006.

8. As there were no military command headquarters in Chin State or in Magway or Sagaing Divisions, the SPDC appointed the senior officers for the job. But the administration of Shan State was divided into Shan State (East), Shan State (North) and Shan State (South) under the commanders of the respective military commands.
9. Interview 022.
10. Interview with Khin Nyunt, 11 November 2016.
11. Su Mon Thazin Aung, "Governing the Transition: Policy Coordination Mechanisms in the Myanmar Core Executive, 2011–2016" (PhD dissertation, University of Hong Kong, 2017), p. 66.
12. Ibid., p. 80.
13. UNDP, *Democratic Governance in Myanmar: Situation Analysis* (December 2013).
14. Interview 030.
15. Interview with Htay Oo, 16 May 2017.
16. I was the director general of the Information and Public Relation Department under the Ministry of Information.
17. Htay Oo was minister for agriculture and irrigation as well as general secretary of the USDA.
18. The USDA officially registered as a political party only on 1 June 2010 after the political party registration law was adopted by the SPDC.
19. Interview with Tin Naing Thein, 9 March 2017.
20. President Thein Sein, State of the Union Speech, 1 March 2012.
21. Interview 019.
22. Interview 010.
23. President Thein Sein, speech delivered on 31 March 2011.
24. Their ministries are those responsible for foreign currency earnings, such as the ministries of Energy, Mining, Forestry, Trade, Finance, Fisheries and Livestock, Industry 1, Industry 2, Agriculture, and Telecommunication. The senior general, aware of the financial disaster that brought down the former BSPP government in 1988, closely monitored the foreign exchange reserve situation as well as government revenue. Interview 031.
25. General Khin Nyunt (2003–4), General Soe Win (2004–7), General Thein Sein (2007–11).
26. Interview 031.
27. President Thein Sein, speech delivered on 6 April 2011.
28. According to President Thein Sein, he was informed by Senior General Than Shwe in March 2010.
29. Interview 010.
30. Ibid.
31. Interview 019.

32. Interview with Tin Naing Thein, 30 April 2017.
33. *Framework for Economic and Social Reforms Policy Priorities for 2012–15 towards the Long-Term Goals of the National Comprehensive Development Plan* (Government of Myanmar, 14 January 2013).
34. Interview with Tin Naing Thein, 30 April 2017.
35. President Thein Sein, speech deliverd on 20 May 2011.
36. Interview with Tin Naing Thein, 9 March 2017.
37. Interview 006.
38. UNDP, *Democratic Governance in Myanmar: Situation Analysis* (2013).
39. Interview with Tin Naing Thein, 10 March 2017.
40. Interview 018.
41. The constitution mandates two vice presidents. Tin Aung Myint Oo was vice president 1 and Dr Sai Mauk Kham was vice president 2, in accordance with the votes they received in the selection process.
42. Vice president 2, Dr Sai Mauk Kham, succeeded as vice president 1.
43. International Crisis Group, *Myanmar: Storm Clouds on the Horizon*, Asia Report N°238 (Brussels, 2012).
44. Ibid.
45. Dr Myat Myat Ohn Khin was appointed as social welfare minister. Four female deputy ministers were also appointed.
46. Aung Min and Soe Thane were considered to be reformers and Kyaw Hsan was seen as a hardliner.
47. President Thein Sein, State of the Union Speech, 1 March 2012.
48. Interview 019.
49. Interview with Aung Min, 7 March 2017.
50. Interview 027.
51. Interview with Aung Min, 7 March 2017.
52. Interview 027.
53. Interview 037.
54. Interview 019.
55. Interview with Aung Min, 7 March 2017.
56. Interview 019.
57. Interview 020.
58. Ibid.
59. Interview 017.
60. Interview 031.
61. Interview 007.
62. Interview 025.
63. The Trade Council was responsible for all export and import policies. It was chaired by vice chairman Senior General Maung Aye from 1992 to 2007.
64. Interview with President Thein Sein, 25 August 2017.

65. Interview 027.
66. Interview 017.
67. Interview 025.
68. Ibid.
69. Ibid.
70. Interview 030.
71. Interview 025.
72. Interviews 027 and 033.
73. Interview 027.
74. Interview 025.
75. Interview 024.
76. He transferred the MIC chairmanship to the minister for finance and revenue Win Shein in 2013.
77. There are five cabinet committees: Foreign Policy; Security, Stability and Rule of Law; Education, Health and Human Resources; Economic Affairs; Ethnic Public Affairs and Administrative Affairs. The Security and Education committees are chaired by two vice presidents.
78. Interviews 023 and 029.
79. Interview 010. Article 71 A(5) gives that the president may be impeached for inefficiently discharging his duties as assigned by law. Lower house members often quoted this and threatened impeachment during the political crisis over the constitutional court in March 2012.
80. International Crisis Group, *Myanmar: Storm Clouds*.
81. Interview with Soe Thane, 15 November 2016.
82. Interview with Aung Min, 13 March 2017.
83. Interview 027.
84. Interview 025.
85. International Crisis Group, *Myanmar: Storm Clouds*.
86. Interview with Nyan Htun, 6 April 2017.
87. Minister for National Planning and Economic Development.
88. Soe Thane held this post until 3 May 2013.
89. Interview 020.
90. Interview 039.
91. Interview 020.
92. Interview 021.
93. Interview 010.
94. Interview with President Thein Sein, 8 July 2017.
95. International Crisis Group, *Myanmar: Storm Clouds*.
96. According to section 232(b) of the constitution, the commander in chief is to propose a list of three individuals to the president to head the ministries of Defence, Home Affairs and Border Affairs.

97. According to section 6(f) of the constitution, "enabling the Defence Services to be able to participate in the National political leadership role of the State".
98. Dr Sai Mauk Hkam was the only civilian. Two were members of the ruling military council the SPDC.
99. Vice president 2 Dr Sai Mauk Hkam became vice president 1 and Nyan Tun served as vice president 2.
100. Interview 032. Before 2010, Sai Mauk Hkam owned a private hospital in Lashio, the Northern Shan State capital, and had no experience of public service.
101. There were only two Union ministers from the navy and air force: Union Minister in the President's Office Soe Thane (navy) and Union Minister for Communications Myat Hein (air force). Among all the chief ministers, Kachin has a civilian and Kayah has a former air force officer.
102. Army regional commanders jointly served as chairs of the division/state development councils and took on the civilian administrative duties. Such duties however were never assigned to naval or air force commanders.
103. Interview 032.
104. Interview 019.
105. Interview 038.
106. The president held informal meetings with ethnic leaders at his farmhouse, mostly attended by Aung Min, Soe Thane and myself.
107. Normally these were ministers from the ministries of Home Affairs, Defence, Border Affairs, Foreign Affairs, Immigration, Information and Finance. Who was invited was dependent on the current situation.
108. Later, the two Speakers only attended the Defence and Security Council meetings, held once a fortnight.
109. Interview 019.
110. When Senior General Than Shwe transferred power to the new government, he suggested that Thein Sein, Shwe Mann, Tin Aung Myint Oo, Tin Aye and the new commander in chief Senior General Min Aung Hlaing should unite and work together on major policy issues. Tin Aye was also a classmate of the president's in the military academy.
111. Interviews 015 and 019.
112. In 1997 the SLORC changed its name to the State Peace and Development Council (SPDC).
113. Each of the two vice presidents has his own staff office led by a deputy director general.
114. Interview 032.
115. Interview 059. Ye Min served with Thein Sein when he was a regimental commander. Ko Ko Kyaw served with him when he was a regional commander. Hla Tun, however, only served as a staff officer when Thein Sein was general

staff officer grade one at the commander in chief's office. Zaw Than Thin had never served previously under Thein Sein.
116. Interview 058.
117. Sometimes President's Office minister Soe Thane was involved in the review process.
118. Interview 032.
119. Ibid.

President Thein Sein and his first Cabinet (31 March 2011). Photo: Ministry of Information

President Thein Sein and the National Defence and Security Council (31 March 2011). At the photo session, Shwe Mann was assigned an ordinary chair while the two vice presidents were assigned special chairs. Shwe Mann was very angry and believed this was done intentionally to insult him. Actually, the President's Office only had three special chairs, and the arrangement had already been decided by the SPDC.
Photo: Ministry of Information

Big Six Political dialogue: President Thein Sein, Speaker Shwe Mann, Speaker Khin Aung Myint, Commander in Chief Senior General Min Aung Hlaing, Aung San Suu Kyi and Dr Aye Maung (Rakhine ethnic politician to represent ethnic parties) on 8 April 2015. They discussed free and fair elections, the peace process and constitutional amendments.
Photo: Ministry of Information.

President Thein Sein and President Obama during Mr Obama's first visit to Myanmar, on 19 November 2012.

Photos: Ministry of Information

President Thein Sein met Aung San Suu Kyi on 14 August 2011. This meeting opened the door for Aung San Suu Kyi and her NLD party to enter *hluttaws*, but some ruling USDP party leaders criticized Thein Sein's decision.

President Thein Sein and Aung San Suu Kyi at the Presidential Palace.
Photo: Ministry of Information

President Thein Sein and members of Egress after the president decided to meet with Aung San Suu Kyi (July 2011). Photo: Hla Maung Swee

President Thein Sein, Commander in Chief Senior General Min Aung Hlaing and Aung San Suu Kyi at the Presidential Palace. Photo: Ministry of Information

President Thein Sein and leaders of the Karen National Union during their informal meeting on the peace process. Photo: Ye Htut

President and First Lady waiting to vote on election day, 8 November 2015.
Photo: Ministry of Information

Transition of power on 30 March 2015. This was the first peaceful tranfer of power from one elected government to another since Myanmar gained independence in 1948.

Meetings with local people were the happiest moments for President Thein Sein during his turbulent presidency.

Photos: Ye Htut

President Thein Sein
and Speaker Shwe Mann
at the Presidential Palace.
Photo: Ministry of Information

President Thein Sein and Aung San
Suu Kyi met on 2 December after the
NLD election victory in November.
Photo: Ministry of Information

Shwe Mann and Aung
San Suu Kyi during one of
their press conferences.
Photo: J Maung Maung

6

The Government and the Parliament

Structure of the Parliament (Hluttaw)

According to the constitution, there are two houses in the Union (federal, or *pyidaungsu*) level legislature, the Pyithu Hluttaw (lower house or people's assembly) and the Amyotha Hluttaw (upper house or house of nationalities). The Pyithu Hluttaw is elected on the basis of one member for each township. The Amyotha Hluttaw has an equal number of representatives elected from each of the country's fourteen regions and states. Each region and state also has its own parliament.

The Pyithu Hluttaw has 440 members, 330 of whom are elected from constituencies and 110 appointed by the Tatmadaw (armed forces). The military members are nominated by the commander in chief of the armed forces. The Amyotha Hluttaw has 168 elected members, 12 from each region and state and 56 from the military. The Pyidaungsu Hluttaw (Union assembly) is the two *hluttaw* combined (Pyithu and Amyotha Hluttaw). The term of all *hluttaw* is five years.

The Pyidaungsu Hluttaw

Like their counterparts in other countries, Myanmar's *hluttaw* are the constitutional legislative bodies. In addition, the Pyidaungsu Hluttaw serves as an electoral college. As the president is elected by the Pyidaungsu Hluttaw, the constitution states that the president shall be responsible to the Pyidaungsu Hluttaw.[1] This stipulation is in contrast with the basic principles of the Union, which say "The three branches of sovereign power, namely legislative power, executive power and judicial power, are separated to the extent possible, and exert reciprocal control, check and balance among themselves."[2] This is very similar to section 71 of the previous one-party state constitution (1974), which states that the "State Council [the highest executive, led by the president] is responsible to the Pyithu Hluttaw".

There are unique provisions in the Myanmar constitution concerning the functions of the Pyidaungsu Hluttaw. Nations that practise a bicameral legislative system also have joint sessions of the two houses with responsibilities for specific functions such as a declaration of war or an address by the president or foreign leaders. Myanmar's constitution however assigns many powers to the Pyidaungsu Hluttaw as a separate legislative body. The Pyidaungsu Hluttaw has its own Speaker and Deputy Speaker who rotate between the lower house and the upper house. The Speaker and Deputy Speaker of the Amyotha Hluttaw serve as the Speaker and Deputy Speaker of the Pyidaungsu Hluttaw for the first thirty months of each electoral term and the Pyithu Hluttaw Speakers serve for the second thirty months.[3]

The Pyidaungsu Hluttaw is not only responsible for the election of the president but also for the approval of the president's cabinet appointees;[4] submitting, discussing and resolving bills; discussing and resolving remarks made by the president concerning bills approved by the Pyidaungsu Hluttaw; submitting proposals (resolutions); and raising questions to the union executive.[5]

Additionally, bills relating to national plans, the annual budget or taxation are only discussed and adopted in the Pyidaungsu Hluttaw.[6] If the lower and upper houses disagree over the contents of a draft bill, the issue will be discussed and decided by the Pyidaungsu Hluttaw.[7] Instead of reaching a compromise between the two houses, a dispute is resolved by the Pyidaungsu Hluttaw, with each member having one vote. This favours the power of the Pyithu Hluttaw, which has 330 elected members, over the Amyotha Hluttaw, which has only 168 elected members. In such a situation the Hluttaws are transformed from a bicameral to a unicameral legislature and the essence of bicameral system disappears from the legislative function.[8]

Zar Ta Lem of the Chin National Party has pointed out that the fact of the Pyidaungsu Hluttaw being a separate *hluttaw* means Myanmar has three *hluttaw* instead of the two of a normal bicameral system.[9] The Amyotha Hluttaw—with an equal number of representatives from all regions and states despite their great differences in size—is intended to protect the rights of regions and states in the manner of the US Senate. However, it is only able to partially fulfil this mission because of the dominant role of the Pyidaungsu Hluttaw.

Khin Aung Myint, the Speaker of the Amyotha Hluttaw between 2011 and 2016, has complained that whenever the Pyidaungsu Hluttaw decided on a draft bill the Amyotha Hluttaw version was always defeated, and thus the Amyotha Hluttaw only has a nominal role to preserve the rights of the states and regions. He felt that the Amyotha Hluttaw should have been provided with special privileges like the US Senate or be given more seats to balance the Pyithu Hluttaw. He stated that during his tenure he tried very hard to maintain the institutional role of the upper house.[10]

A constitutional provision that gives the Pyidaungsu Hluttaw a dominant role over the executive is section 228(a). According to this section, the Union government must implement administrative resolutions passed by the Pyidaungsu Hluttaw, and to subsequently report back on its response to the Pyidaungsu Hluttaw. During Khin Aung Myint's tenure as Speaker of the Pyidaungsu Hluttaw, he rarely passed resolutions that interfered with executive functions, but Shwe Mann used Pyidaungsu Hluttaw's resolutions frequently to exert pressure on the government. This contributed to a power struggle between President Thein Sein and Shwe Mann.

Thura Shwe Mann

As the Speaker of the Pyithu Hluttaw, Thura Shwe Mann played an important role in the relationship between the executive and legislative branches. His supporters praised him for organizing the Pyithu Hluttaw[11] to fulfil its constitutional function of providing checks and balance. Detractors said he misused the Pyithu Hluttaw for his own ends and undermined President Thein Sein's reforms. Both opinions have a degree of validity.

Shwe Mann is a graduate from intake eleven of the Defence Services Academy and is therefore two years junior to Thein Sein, who is from intake nine. They were from the same cadet company, "Aungzeya", but

Shwe Mann was from platoon eight while Thein Sein was from platoon seven. Soe Thane, a President's Office minister, and Shwe Mann were classmates, but Soe Thane was in the same platoon as the president. Thein Sein and Shwe Mann served together in the 1980s in No. 109 Light Infantry Regiment under the 99th Light Infantry Division. During that time, Thein Sein was deputy commander of the regiment and Shwe Mann was a company commander. Their homes were near to each other and their children played together.[12] Both were appointed regional commanders in 1996 and both were promoted and transferred in 2001 to the Commander in Chief's Office (Army). Thein Sein became adjutant general and Shwe Mann became joint chief of staff of the armed forces (army, navy and air force). After the downfall of General Khin Nyunt in 2004, Shwe Mann became the third-highest-ranking officer in the military and the ruling State Peace and Development Council (SPDC). Even though Shwe Mann was his junior in the academy, Thein Sein paid Shwe Mann all the due respect of a senior officer during those days.[13]

After the new constitution was adopted in 2008, many people thought Shwe Mann would succeed Senior General Than Shwe as commander in chief of the Tatmadaw, as he appeared to be Than Shwe's favourite general. During those days, Than Shwe introduced Shwe Mann to foreign dignitaries as the next commander in chief.[14] Their close relationship began when Shwe Mann was a colonel and the tactical operation commander of the No. 66 Light Infantry Division. When Shwe Mann was appointed as a division commander, Than Shwe sent him to No. 3 Mobile Operation Command in Kachin State, but he later called him back to Yangon and appointed him as commander of No. 11 Light Infantry Division, which was responsible for the security of Yangon and as a reserve division of the Commander in Chief's Office (Army), a strategically important elite command. When he was promoted to regional commander, Than Shwe sent him to the South West Command with responsibility for the Ayeyawady delta region. While serving as regional commander he was also chairman of the Ayeyawady division Peace and Development Council. As Than Shwe had also served as commander of the South West Command in the early 1980s, he only appointed his favourite commanders to this position. During those days, Than Shwe made unannounced visits to Ayeyawady region many times. These were mostly day trips. Than Shwe would be driven from Yangon to Nyaungdone, half way between Yangon and Pathein, the regional capital of Ayeyawady division. There he would meet with

Shwe Mann to discuss the development of the delta region, particularly agriculture. Than Shwe liked Shwe Mann's knowledge of economic issues and praised his implementation of regional development projects. Shwe Mann showed deep respect for Than Shwe and Than Shwe appreciated Shwe Mann's manner.[15]

When the SPDC set the date of the general election for November 2010, Senor General Than Shwe ordered General Thein Sein and members of the current cabinet to resign from the army in March or April and join the Union Solidarity and Development Party (USDP). After that, all the lieutenant generals in the Commander in Chief's Office (Army), except for Hla Htay Win, Myint Aung, Ko Ko and Min Aung Hlaing, were informed by Than Shwe that they would have to retire and contest the forthcoming election under the USDP. Shwe Mann remained in the military during this period, and some of the younger lieutenant generals who were in their fifties complained to him about their forced retirement. Shwe Mann consoled them and urged them to work for the USDP and to win the election.[16] At that time he believed he would become commander in chief of the Tatmadaw or president after the election. However, in August he was also summoned by Than Shwe and informed he would also have to resign from the army and contest the election.[17]

Thus, all the SPDC members except Than Shwe and Maung Aye had to retire from the military and stand in the election. Than Shwe also decided that Thein Sein would become president and that Shwe Mann would serve as Speaker of the Pyithu Hluttaw. Than Shwe said that as Thein Sein had served as secretary 2, secretary 1 and prime minister, and was familiar with international affairs, he should be president for the first five years and that Shwe Mann should deal with legislative matters. He asked them to work together, and then Shwe Mann would succeed Thein Sein in 2016.[18]

Senior General Than Shwe's decision to retire from office surprised many people, as did his decision to bypass Shwe Mann for the presidency.[19] Although Than Shwe was the only person to make these decisions, Shwe Mann and his backers blamed Thein Sein.[20]

Senior General Than Shwe had groomed Shwe Mann for a long time and assigned him increasingly greater responsibilities. After the so-called Saffron Revolution in 2007, Shwe Mann chaired daily political and security coordination meetings. Thein Sein, as prime minister, and Tin Aung Myint Oo, as a secretary 1, attended these meetings along with the ministers for home affairs, foreign affairs, information, industry, labour, culture, and science and technology. Other ministers were also present if they felt Shwe Mann's approval was required or if Shwe Mann had summoned them for a particular issue. Most political, security and administrative issues were decided at these meetings. Shwe Mann always sought other people's opinions before he reached decisions, and he sometimes submitted matters for Than Shwe's approval.[21]

However, by 2009 Than Shwe came to feel that Shwe Mann was making important decisions without seeking his approval. His growing ire was indicated when Than Shwe cancelled the rice export policy decided by Shwe Mann, as he thought it was made in the interests of the company of Shwe Mann's eldest son.[22] Than Shwe confided to his most trusted ministers that Shwe Mann was avoiding him and failing to seek his guidance on important issues discussed at political and security meetings.[23] One minister with whom Than Shwe confided warned Shwe Mann about the changing opinion of the senior general and urged him to report all important issues to Than Shwe in order to avoid any misunderstanding. Shwe Mann merely replied that Than Shwe had delegated such authority to him and he was acting in the country's best interest. He said he would report to the senior general on important issues that were beyond his responsibility but not on everything, insisting he would not behave like an adjutant officer.[24]

There is no doubt that the selection of Thein Sein for the presidency was made by Senior General Than Shwe. However, there are two versions of how Shwe Mann became to be selected as the Speaker of the Pyithu Hluttaw. One is that when Than Shwe consulted Maung Aye, Maung Aye proposed that Shwe Mann should retire along with himself and the senior general. However, Than Shwe wanted to appoint him as Speaker because of his contributions in the past. A second version is the reverse, that Than Shwe planned to bring Shwe Mann with them into retirement and that Maung Aye argued to give him the Speaker's post.[25]

A former USDP Central Executive Committee member said that because of his son's business empire and his own vaunting ambitions, Shwe Mann was sidelined by Than Shwe.[26] Than Shwe tested Shwe Mann by giving him power and then judged how he behaved with the new authority. Shwe Mann failed the test. Thein Sein, however, contends that Senior General Than Shwe had already decided to appoint former prime minister (2004–7) General Soe Win as president, but after Soe Win's unexpected death he began to consider Thein Sein.[27] Shwe Mann was reportedly in tears when he heard about Than Shwe's choice of the more malleable, soft-spoken

Thein Sein for the top job, and he immediately called two of his sons to explain the decision.[28] The following day he informed his office staff and he later drove without the usual escorts to test the response from the rank and file about his retirement. He found that many soldiers felt sorry for him and were disappointed about his retirement, so he believed he still enjoyed support from the troops.[29]

When the USDA was transformed into the USDP, Thein Sein was appointed chairman and Shwe Mann was appointed as patron, with no real role in the party. Shwe Mann became angry at this and proclaimed "Kabar Makyay".[30] He complained to Senior General Than Shwe and insisted he be appointed a party vice chairman. Than Shwe refused initially but later changed his mind and appointed Shwe Mann and Tin Aye (another lieutenant general) as vice chairmen of the USDP and Htay Oo as general secretary.[31] When Thein Sein was elected president, Shwe Mann become acting chairman and tried to steal power from him, as the president could no longer participate in party activities because of the constitutional restrictions on such activities.

One can imagine the feelings of Shwe Mann, who had been groomed as Than Shwe's successor and then denied preferment at the last moment. When government media stated that "President Thein Sein had the people's mandate", Shwe Mann angrily commented, "There is no mandate. All are appointed [by Than Shwe]. I was appointed and so was the president."[32] Later, Shwe Mann openly said that "even the president is not elected by the people. We are selected by our superior and assigned these duties. We could not have refused."[33]

After he became Speaker of the lower house, Shwe Mann considered how to check and balance the executive as well as how to enhance his own future political role. As a harbinger of things to come, when I visited his home on 9 April 2011, he told me that the chairman of the National People's Congress (NPC) was the third-highest official in the Chinese Communist Party, and the NPC supervised the government (State Council). He indicated that he would do the same. When the Hluttaw held its first session from 31 January to 30 March 2011, the members' sole concerns were the election of the president and the formation of the executive and judicial branches. These sessions were predetermined by the SPDC, and Shwe Mann had merely to implement them, and he could not act independently. On 30 March, when the new government was sworn in, the SPDC was officially dissolved and the Hluttaw adjourned. With Than

Shwe's retirement from the military and politics, Shwe Mann had an opportunity to play a power game with Thein Sein.

There was one unintended incident that rubbed salt into the wounds of Shwe Mann. On 31 March, at a photo taking session for the new government at the Presidential Palace, Shwe Mann and Khin Aung Myint were invited to participate in the National Defence and Security Council photo. There, the president and the two vice presidents sat on special chairs, but Shwe Mann had to sit on an ordinary chair. Since Vice President 1 Tin Aung Myint Oo was junior to Shwe Mann in the military and Vice President Sai Mauk Hkam was a civilian doctor from the USDP, Shwe Mann took this as a personal insult.[34] From then on Shwe Mann began to promote his and the Pyithu Hluttaw's role in public. Although Khin Aung Myint was Speaker of the Pyidaungsu Hluttaw, Shwe Mann received more publicity. His first political move was on 24 June 2011, when he met with businessmen and members of the Yangon regional *hluttaw*. He said that since *hluttaw* members were elected by the people and the Pyidaungsu Hluttaw elected the president and vice presidents, considered and approved the members of the cabinet, the judiciary and other Union level organizations, the various *hluttaw* were the only state institutions that enjoyed the peoples' mandate. He also said that according to section 228 of the constitution, the Union government must implement administrative resolutions passed occasionally by the Pyidaungsu Hluttaw.[35]

With these words, Shwe Mann indicated that legislative bodies were superior to executive bodies. This was a clear break from the constitution, which states that "The three branches of sovereign power namely, legislative power, executive power and judicial power, are separated, to the extent possible, and exert reciprocal control, check and balance among themselves".[36] Also during that meeting, Shwe Mann started referring to the president as head of government instead of head of state, as stipulated in section 58 of the constitution.[37] By this he meant that he only saw the president as first among equals. Later he expanded his definition of the government as a combination of the legislative, executive and judicial branches, stressing that the public should not think of only the executive branch as the government.[38]

When the second session of the Pyithu Hluttaw commenced in August 2011, Shwe Mann behaved like the third-highest-ranking official, as during the SPDC's time. Although the legislature and executive were separated, when he travelled across the country with ministers and deputy ministers—

as he did in the SPDC days—he gave on-site instructions to ministers, deputy ministers and local administrators during public meetings. Many of his instructions were contrary to the president's economic, social and development policies. This put ministers and deputy ministers in a difficult position. President Thein Sein did not like Shwe Mann's interference in government policies, but he avoided a direct confrontation. He only instructed ministers not to commit to anything that was against government policy. Thus began a struggle between the legislature and the executive that derailed many reform programmes.

After the 2012 by-election, Aung San Suu Kyi became a Hluttaw member. Since Shwe Mann had said "Don't worry about giving life to a dead tiger. Tigers are controlled by the whip in a circus. I can control her",[39] USDP members thought he would control her for the sake of the USDP's interests. Instead, he used her for his own political ends—as a counterweight against President Thein Sein. Shwe Mann held joint press conferences with her and mentioned that they worked together as partners for national reconciliation and that they met often to exchange opinions on legislative and political affairs.[40] Hluttaw sources say that between July 2012 and August 2015 the two had thirty-six closed-door meetings[41]—no one knew what they discussed. Shwe Mann said he cooperated with Aung San Suu Kyi for the sake of the country, but some of his colleagues did not accept this and accused him of pursuing his own interests.[42] The closed-door meetings created suspicion, not only within the government but also amongst USDP leaders in the Hluttaw. Shwe Mann never explained what they discussed or what they agreed. It seems that the two had agreement on a future political strategy, but neither the USDP or NLD CEC members were informed.[43]

Although Shwe Mann was credited with promoting the capacities of the Hluttaw and its members, there were questions over how much his feelings about losing the presidency influenced his decisions. From the time he became chief of staff of the Tatmadaw he had prepared for the position of commander in chief of the armed forces or commander in chief of the army. But Than Shwe and Maung Aye never gave up their positions, and Shwe Mann missed out on those opportunities. After the 2010 election he also missed out on the presidency because of Than Shwe selecting Thein Sein. So when he became Speaker of the Pyithu Hluttaw in 2011 he felt bitter towards both Than Shwe and Thein Sein.[44] Shwe Mann also believed he had the greater ability than Thein Sein to be the head of state.

Even after Thein Sein became president, Shwe Mann asked Thein Sein to consult him before making any major decisions with cabinet members.[45] When Thein Sein refused, Shwe Mann felt the president had disregarded the Hluttaw Speaker's role in state affairs.[46] Shwe Mann later said that as the president was not the chairman of the SPDC, as Than Shwe had been, the president could not order the Hluttaw to do his will.[47]

When Than Shwe informed Thein Sein and Shwe Mann about his decision, he explained that Thein Sein had served as prime minister and had international exposure, therefore Thein Sein should serve as president in the first term. As Speaker, Shwe Mann was to maintain stability in the first Hluttaw and would become president in the second term.[48] But in early 2012, Thein Sein was very popular because of his political reforms, and Shwe Mann became concerned that Thein Sein might alter the arrangement and seek a second term. Thein Sein understood that, and he reaffirmed to Shwe Mann in 2012 and 2013 that he would not seek a second term.[49] Thein Sein also explained that he could not say this publicly in order to avoid becoming a lame duck president. But Shwe Mann was not convinced and he openly said he would contest for the presidency in 2015.[50] On 24 October 2013, Shwe Mann told the media that President Thein Sein had previously confirmed that he would not seek a second term and that he believed the president would keep his promise. The president saw Shwe Mann's proclamation of their confidential agreement as a dirty political trick. He instructed me to inform the press that we were surprised by Shwe Mann's comments and that the president would inform the public about important decisions himself rather than through a third person.[51] Thein Sein had already decided at that time that even if the USDP won the election he would not seek a second term. He always told Shwe Mann and the USDP leaders that the most important issue was to win the election in 2020, for without an election victory neither Shwe Mann nor any another USDP leader could be president. USDP members should therefore avoid rivalry among themselves.

Unlike Thein Sein, Shwe Mann is a smooth operator in politics. He sounded much more like the politician he had become rather than the feared general he had once been.[52] He was able to establish cordial relations with non-USDP MPs. MPs from ethnic minorities were especially surprised by his warm-hearted treatment of them.[53] He treated all MPs equally, regardless of their ethnicity or party affiliation. He patiently guided ethnic minority MPs who had difficulties with language and took a lot of time during question and answer sessions to explain things to them. For that reason, other parties respected him.[54] He also used financial support for MPs as a means to win them over. When the Hluttaws started in 2011, the salaries of MPs was 300,000 kyat, with a 5,000 kyat daily allowance. But MPs complained that that was not enough to perform their legislative duties. When Shwe Mann became Speaker of the Pyidaungsu Hluttaw, he proposed to raise MPs salaries to a million kyat with a daily allowance of 10,000 kyat, and to raise the remuneration of state and regional MPs proportionately. When he proposed this to party leaders in the Hluttaw, all except the New National Democracy Party (NNDP) leader Thein Nyunt welcomed it. Even Aung San Suu Kyi said that two thirds of her NLD party members were poor and that they needed a pay increase.[55] Thein Nyunt pointed out that it was unethical for MPs to raise salaries for themselves in the current term. He reminded MPs that when the Myanmar parliament of 1958–60 decided on a pay increase, they did it only for incoming MPs after the 1960 election. He also said it would cost an extra 9,145 million kyat annually for the 1,349 MPs from the Union, regional and state *hluttaw*, and it would be a burden on the national budget.[56]

Shwe Mann also introduced in 2013, against the objection of the president, a constituency development fund for small public works and development projects in the 330 electoral constituencies. This fund cost the Union budget an extra 33 billion kyat annually, as each electoral constituency received a 100 million kyat. This development fund was popular with MPs as it offered new opportunities for winning the support of their constituents. International and local NGOs warned about possible corruption resulting from these projects, and some MPs expressed concerns about using these funds for campaigning in the 2015 election.[57]

Shwe Mann also used his legislative powers to maximum effect in other ways. During the first session of the Hluttaw in 2011, the USDP formed a steering committee that reviewed all questions from the USDP and other parties to recommend which would be allowed and who would answer each of them. After the first session concluded, Shwe Mann abolished the committee and from then on it was he as Speaker alone who would decide which questions required answers.[58] This allowed Shwe Mann to reward or punish MPs by allowing or prohibiting their questions. It also enabled him to assign MPs to submit resolutions or questions in order to harass or attack the Thein Sein government.[59] Some USDP leaders asked Shwe Mann to stop sabotaging the government, since both the legislature and the executive were from the same party. His action, they believed, would hurt the image of the party. But their requests were to no avail.[60]

Shwe Mann invited MPs who tried to submit resolutions, questions or bills that were contrary to his policies to his office and pressured them to change their position or cut a deal with them. Thein Nyunt, chairman of NNDP, had such an experience with Shwe Mann. Thein Nyunt informed Shwe Mann that he would not make a deal but sought open debate in the Hluttaw chamber on his resolutions and bills. Once Deputy Speaker Nanda Kyaw Swar, as instructed by Shwe Mann, urged Thein Nyunt to submit a prison reform bill, but he refused to do so.[61] Political commentator Sithu Aung Myint wrote that Shwe Mann pressured MP Aung Zin to change a resolution on introducing a proportional representative electoral system before the 26 July 2014 Hluttaw debate.[62] Dr Soe Yin admitted that when Shwe Mann decided to do something, he prepared a plan of action with his closest supporters in advance. Then he invited other party leaders, whips and some MPs to seek their agreement. If someone refused, he used all means to reach agreement. Even Aung San Suu Kyi, who opposed Shwe Mann's proposal initially, eventually had to agree with him. After that, Shwe Mann presented his initiatives as consensus decisions to the Hluttaw.[63] Finally, as a result of Shwe Mann's manipulations, not only USDP MPs but also most of the other MPs fell under his influence.[64]

Shwe Mann also responded strongly to MPs who objected to or questioned his actions in the Hluttaw. Sometimes he reprimanded them in Hluttaw sessions, or sometimes he asked Hluttaw staff to find means for legal action against them. One MP who faced Shwe Mann's wrath personally visited his office and apologized.[65] When Shwe Mann abruptly ended the Hluttaw debate on a proportional representative electoral system without taking a vote, two MPs, Ye Tun and Aung Zin, strongly criticized Shwe Mann's decision. Consequently, Shwe Mann asked their party leaders to reprimand them.[66] Ethnic Shan Party MP Ye Tun later pointed out that one failure of the Hluttaw was that it was too sensitive of criticism.[67]

Shwe Mann even used unconstitutional means during his tenure as Speaker. Although sections 86(b) and 129(b) of the constitution clearly state that the Speaker shall not vote unless the assembly is equally divided, during Pyidaungsu Hluttaw debates on constitutional amendments and Pyithu Hluttaw debates on the impeachment of the Constitutional Tribunal, he voted although his vote was not required to break a tie.[68] Sithu Aung Myint pointed out that Shwe Mann failed to abide by Hluttaw laws during the debate on the proportional representation system.⁶⁹ Former Speaker of the Amyotha Hluttaw Khin Aung Myint agreed with these allegations and said that Shwe Mann had committed many violations of Hluttaw rules and regulations.⁷⁰

One ethnic MP concluded that Shwe Mann conducted his duties effectively in early sessions of the Hluttaw but that his later decisions on political and economic issues were marred by his personal interests. As Shwe Mann became more concerned about the presidency and in promoting his own image, he made mistakes in legislative matters. Khin Aung Myint was better qualified as a Speaker than Shwe Mann.⁷¹ Dr Soe Yin said that Shwe Mann was a very effective Speaker and did a good job in raising the competence of the Hluttaw and of MPs, but he failed to tame his personal interests, and this led to his fall from the acting chairmanship of the USDP.⁷²

Shwe Mann claimed he only sought to achieve three missions of the legislative body: representation, legislation, and check and balance. He insisted that he never interfered in government responsibilities in his personal interest, but only worked in the interest of the nation and the people, including his cooperation with Aung San Suu Kyi. He said he suffered a lot because of his national reconciliation policy.⁷³

Shwe Mann not only controlled and manipulated MPs, he also worked hard to win support from the local media. Unlike President Thein Sein, he had the chance to meet with reporters every day at the Hluttaw. He gave interviews in his office and his staff leaked important news to the media. His youngest son, Toe Naing Man, who was also the youngest member of the Pyithu Hluttaw Legal Affairs and Special Issues Assessment Commission, primarily handled media relations for him. Toe Naing Mann also owned the *Street View* weekly journal. He frequently visited the Hluttaw press room and gave information off the record, including about Senior General Than Shwe's retirement from politics, relations between Thein Sein and Shwe Mann, and Shwe Mann's cooperation with Aung San Suu Kyi. Occasionally he prepared questions for Shwe Mann's press conferences and gave them to his journalist friends. Some journalists had a very friendly relationship with him and called him by his nick name "Ko Nyi". He also invited them for dinner.⁷⁴

Shwe Mann cleverly portrayed himself as being in a political alliance with Aung San Suu Kyi, and for this won support from the media and political commentators. They avoided scrutinizing Shwe Man's legislative agenda and the business activities of his sons. Consequently, there was more sympathy for Shwe Mann and the Hluttaw in disputes between the executive and the legislature. When 36 journalists were asked, "Is media reluctant to make a critical review on Shwe Mann's legislative actions and his sons' business empire because of his relationship with Aung San Suu Kyi?", 11 strongly agreed, 17 somewhat agreed, 5 disagreed and 3 refused to answer.[75]

No one will deny that Shwe Mann worked hard to promote the competence of the Hluttaw members and develop the Hluttaw as a strong and independent institution. But neither can anyone dispute that he used the legislature as a power base for the political and economic interests of his family.[76] Toe Naing Mann admitted that when Shwe Mann entered politics, family members (Shwe Mann, Khin Lay Thet [his wife], Aung Thet Mann and Toe Naing Mann) discussed and agreed a political strategy for Shwe Mann. They also agreed to transform the USDP in accord with Shwe Mann's vision.[77] Between his sons, Toe Naing Mann was more active in politics, and once Shwe Mann's wife said that Shwe Mann was grooming his son as Lee Kuan Yew had done for his son Lee Hsien Loong.[78] He appointed Toe Naing Mann as a member of the Legal Affairs and Special Issues Assessment Commission although he was only in his early thirties[79] and had no political or legal experience. Toe Naing Mann actively participated, not only in the commission but also in USDP organizational activities. When he explained Shwe Mann's policies as acting USDP chairman and Hluttaw Speaker, he said "we" instead of "he", and remarked that all strategies and policies were discussed and approved among family members, including his father-in-law and businessman Khin Shwe.[80] Shwe Mann's eldest son, Aung Thet Mann, was more active in business, but he kept a low profile after Shwe Mann became Speaker of the Pyithu Hluttaw.[81] No one knows the details of the business empires of his sons, but Toe Naing Mann said up to 2014 that they paid 60 million kyat in tax and employed nearly six thousand people.[82]

With his political ambitions, wealth and manipulation of MPs and the media, Shwe Mann became a thorn in President Thein Sein's side after 2012.

Union Solidarity and Development Party (USDP) Hluttaw Members

The USDP won 259 of the 325 elected seats in the Pyithu Hluttaw[83] and 129 of the 168 seats in the Amyotha Hluttaw in the 2010 elections. So with

388 out of the 493 seats of the two Hluttaws, the USDP played the leading role in the election of the president and the formation of the new union government and other institutions, including the Supreme Court. But though it had won the election, the USDP was neither unified nor coherent.

Problems started with the selection of USDP candidates for the 2010 elections. The selection of candidates for state and regional *hluttaw* took place through negotiations among the ministers in charge for the respective states and divisions and the commanders of military commands (patrons of state/division USDPs). For Union level *hluttaw*, Thein Sein, Shwe Mann and Tin Aung Myint Oo collectively selected the candidates after consulting with the state/division ministers in charge.[84]

Though it was formed as a social association, the USDA already had a plan to transform itself into a political party. In this regard it undertook reviews of its members as possible future *hluttaw* candidates four years before the election. The term "local benefactor" was then used instead of "Hluttaw candidate". Each minister in charge had to make a list of local benefactors in his respective state and region. They selected individuals based on their abilities and experience in regional development undertakings.[85] However, many of these possible candidates were not hardcore members of the USDA. They were just well-known people because of their social or business activities. They supported USDA development projects because the USDA was the military government's sponsored association. They were never involved in USDA organizational work.[86] Later, added to these lists were retired civil servants and military officers who enjoyed local support in their native townships. The possible candidates for the Pyithu Hluttaw and the Amyotha Hluttaw could be categorized as ministers and deputy ministers of the military government, senior military officers retired in 2010, retired civil servants, prominent members of local communities, and hardcore USDA members who had participated since the 1990s.

These candidates campaigned more on their contributions to regional development undertakings than the ideology and campaign manifesto of the party. Ministers, deputy ministers and senior military officers used their own money and donations from their business associates. Local candidates had to spend their own money or use funds provided by the minister in charge of the campaign.

As the USDA was turned into a political party just six months before the elections, it was not able to provide campaign funds or tactical assistance to candidates. Some candidates from the military or civil service, or those who were prominent persons, had never been involved in USDA organizational affairs and were not familiar with USDP doctrines or its manifesto.[87] Most of the USDP candidates had little loyalty to the party and paid more attention to their own interests.[88] Sometime their loyalty was with the minister in charge who recommended them as candidates and provided them financial support for the campaign.

Another issue concerned ministers and deputy ministers serving under the military government before the election. Senior General Than Shwe never indicated who would be ministers and deputy ministers in the coming government, even at the time of the 2010 elections. Only after the election did Than Shwe lay down guidelines, and then Thein Sein, Shwe Mann, Tin Aung Myint Oo and Tin Aye[89] considered possible candidates for Union ministers and chief ministers of regions and states and sought approval from Than Shwe and Maung Aye. The cabinet list was kept secret and was recorded only in a handwritten form by Thein Sein. Even at the time the list was submitted to parliament it was still a handwritten document.[90] The list submitted by Thein Sein included only seventeen of the thirty-three ministers of the SPDC government. Some were left out to organize party work in parliament,[91] and some because of their age or unsatisfactory performances as judged by Than Shwe.

Unfortunately, ministers with high expectations of the continuation of their jobs and deputy ministers who hoped for a ministerial job in the new government could not easily accept Than Shwe's decision. Some blamed Thein Sein, as he proposed the cabinet list to Than Shwe and Maung Aye. Actually, Than Shwe did not consider human nature and the bruised egos of those not shown preferment. When warned about the feelings of these individuals, Than Shwe replied that they had all been comrades in the Tatmadaw and they should be able to work together in the new government.[92]

After the second session of the Hluttaw began on 22 August 2011, cracks started to appear between new cabinet members and some former ministers and deputy ministers. New ministers had to abandon old government practices according to the president's economic and administrative reforms. They could not maintain cosy relationships with their former colleagues and could no longer offer special favours to them. Sometimes they had to change the policies of former ministers. Former ministers failed to comprehend the new situation.[93] Even Shwe Mann's family members thought that the government intentionally restricted their businesses after 2012.[94] USDP MPs complained that the government neglected the party and that ministers disrespected former ministers and failed to provide development assistance to their constituencies. For budget meetings, ministers sent only lower ranking civil servants, which annoyed the former ministers who had experience in government affairs.[95] Some former ministers said the government had abandoned the party, and they directed their anger at the new ministers responsible for economic policy.[96]

New ministers failed to understand the new system of checks and balance.[97] They saw questions from the Hluttaw, especially from former ministers and civil servants, as interference in their responsibilities.[98] They thought that while they worked hard for reform, which would promote the USDP image, former ministers were only thinking of their personal and business interests.

Shwe Mann cleverly used these opportunities for his political ends. By abolishing the party steering committee that controlled the questions and resolutions from USDP MPs, Shwe Mann was able to control the motions from them. Then, during the Pyithu Hluttaw second session in August 2011, Shwe Mann created nineteen ad hoc committees.[99] Of the 320 elected members in the Pyithu Hluttaw, only 26 were not members of any committee. Some MPs were members of two or three committees.[100] All committee chairmen except one were former ministers or deputy ministers. Shwe Mann called these committees mini *hluttaw*, and recognized them as Union-level organizations with the same status as government ministries.[101] The government viewed this action by Shwe Mann as forming a shadow government to compete with the president's executive power.

USDP members of these committees were more vocal in criticizing the policies of the Thein Sein government than opposition parties were. Instead of discussions among party leaders, Shwe Mann allowed open criticism in the Hluttaw to discredit President Thein Sein, but this also damaged the party's unity and image.[102] Later, Shwe Mann not only disregarded the government but also the Amyotha Hluttaw in legislative matters.[103] Shwe Mann rejected allegations that these committees were intended to control the government, and he claimed the commission and committees were formed in accord with sections 114 and 115 of the constitution to serve the interests of the people and the nation.[104]

Others said that the forming of these committees was Than Shwe's idea as he wanted experienced former ministers to guide the new cabinet ministers through the Hluttaw committees.[105] President Thein Sein said there was no discussion of such an arrangement at the time of the transfer of power from the SDPC to the new government. These committees were formed only after Shwe Mann sought agreement from Khin Aung Myint during the second session of the Hluttaw.[106] In 2012 Than Shwe encouraged his trusted former ministers who chaired these committees to openly criticize Thein Sein's government because he believed Thein Sein's reforms were too liberal and he wanted to rein in his popularity.[107] Than Shwe never tried to stop the power struggle between Thein Sein and Shwe Mann. He may have wanted to ensure neither of his successors could become a supreme leader as he had been.

Shwe Mann always pointed out that USDP chairman Thein Sein could not deal with elected MPs, as the constitution barred him from taking part in party activities. When the USDP held its first party congress in October 2012, acting chairman Shwe Mann tried to take the chairmanship, but CEC members and chief ministers of regions and states opposed him. To prove he was still in charge of the party, President Thein Sein visited the party congress on the morning of 12 October 2012 before the congress officially opened. He made a short speech and chatted with delegates.[108] Toe Naing Mann claimed that the current party leadership was selected by Than Shwe, and it was his father who transformed the USDP central committee democratically at the party congress.[109]

Although Thein Sein was re-elected as chairman of the USDP he had no influence over the election of the central committee. Shwe Mann talked a lot about intra-party democracy, but the election for the central committee was not by secret ballot. It was tightly controlled by Shwe Mann.[110] Shwe Mann said that as acting chairman he alone had responsibility to reorganize the party.[111] He proposed that all chairmen of the Hluttaw, retired civil servants who were current MPs and some MPs who actively participated in legislative affairs be selected as central committee members. This policy barred many USDP regional, state and district members who joined the USDA after 1993 from becoming central committee members. There was criticism of and opposition to this policy because many of the new central committee members joined the USDP just before the 2010 election. But Shwe Mann countered that this policy was in the party's interest and that members must sacrifice individual interests for the sake of the party.[112]

When the central committee elected a new central executive committee, out of 44 members only 10 were from the current cabinet, including the president. Of 14 chief ministers of regions and states, only 6 were elected to the CEC, and of the 295 central committee members, 118 were MPs.[113] These MPs, especially former civil servants, became hardcore supporters of Shwe Mann in the Hluttaw. After the 2012 party congress, Shwe Mann conducted legislative affairs through his supporters without consulting senior party leaders. He merely informed them after he made decisions. Shwe Mann used the party machine to control the Hluttaw,[114] and the Hluttaw became a pawn in Shwe Mann's struggle against Thein Sein.

Notes

1. Section 203 of the constitution.
2. Section 11(a) of the constitution.
3. Section 76 of the constitution.
4. Section 232 of the constitution.
5. Section 80 of the constitution.
6. Section 100 of the constitution.
7. Section 95 of the constitution.
8. Yash Ghai, *The 2008 Myanmar Constitution: Analysis and Assessment*, p. 21. http://www.burmalibrary.org/docs6/2008_Myanmar_constitution--analysis_and_assessment-Yash_Ghai.pdf (accessed 4 December 2018).
9. Pyithu Hluttaw record, 28 January 2016.
10. Interview with Khin Aung Myint, 13 November 2016.
11. Many thought initially that a USDP-controlled Hluttaw would be merely a rubber stamp Hluttaw.
12. Interview with Thein Sein, 25 August 2017.
13. Soe Thane, *Myanmar's Transformation & U Thein Sein: "An Insider's Account"* (Yangon: Tun Foundation Literature Committee, 2017), p. 314.
14. Interview 027.
15. The relationship between Than Shwe and Shwe Mann as recounted to me by Shwe Mann's son, Toe Naing Mann, during his visit to my office on 19 August 2010.
16. Interview 043.
17. Senior General Than Shwe and Vice Senior General Maung Aye remained in the military and retired in March 2011. Senior General Min Aung Hlaing then succeeded Than Shwe as commander in chief (armed forces).
18. Interview 043.
19. On 10 November 2011, three days after the election, Information Minister Kyaw Hsan told me that Shwe Mann would not be president.
20. Soe Thane, *Myanmar's Transformation*, p. 19.

21. I accompanied Minister Kyaw Hsan to these meetings from 2007 to 2009.
22. Interview 020.
23. Interview 027.
24. Ibid.
25. These stories started to appear in 2013 when Shwe Mann openly allied with Suu Kyi and against Thein Sein. The first version was told by supporters of Maung Aye and the second by Than Shwe supporters. Actually, both leaders wanted to avoid responsibility for selecting Shwe Mann as Speaker of the lower house.
26. Interview 044.
27. Interview with Thein Sein, 21 November 2017.
28. Aung Zaw, *From General to Politician: A Conversation with Shwe Mann* (Irrawaddy, 2013).
29. Recounted to me by Toe Naing Mann on 19 August 2010.
30. Interview 033. *Kabar makyay* (ကမ္ဘာမကြေ) means never forget and forgive in Myanmar.
31. Interview 026.
32. Interview with Zaw Myint Pe, 15 November 2016.
33. Shwe Mann's answer to the Irrawaddy news agency at a book launch event on 14 June 2018.
34. Interview 050.
35. Chronicle of Pyithu Hluttaw Speaker Shwe Mann, Pyithu Hluttaw, February 2014. pp. 14, 15.
36. Section 11(1).
37. Chronicle of Pyithu Hluttaw Speaker Shwe Mann, Pyithu Hluttaw, February 2014. p. 18.
38. Ibid., p. 205.
39. Interviews 027 and 050.
40. Joint press conference of Shwe Mann and Aung San Suu Kyi, 26 March 2014.
41. Interview 051.
42. Thura Shwe Mann, *Thu Kyuntaw nint Myanma Naingan Ayee* [She herself, I myself, and Myanmar affairs] (Yangon: Pann Swe Mon Sarpay, 2018), p. 10.
43. Interview 050.
44. Interviews 003 and 011.
45. Interview 014.
46. When I became Union minister, I paid a courtesy call to his office. He pointed to a phone on his desk and angrily said, "President never call and consult me".
47. Remark by Shwe Mann at a book launch event on 14 June 2018.
48. Interview 043.
49. Interview with Thein Sein, 1 March 2017 and 26 August 2017.

50. Shwe Mann, RFA interview, 10 June 2013.
51. My interviews with DVB news on 28 October 2013 and *Yangon Time* journal on 31 October 2013.
52. Aung Zaw, *From General to Politician: A Conversation with Shwe Mann* (Irrawaddy, 2013).
53. These feelings were expressed by ethnic party members of the Pyithu Hluttaw during the last session of the Hluttaw on 28 January 2016.
54. Interview with Ye Tun, 15 September 2018.
55. Interview with Thein Nyunt, 12 June 2018.
56. Thein Nyunt discussion in the Pyidaungsu Hluttaw, 22 January 2015.
57. "Vote-Buying Fears over MP Funds Plan", *Myanmar Times*, 15 December 2013.
58. Interview 019.
59. Interview 004.
60. Interview with Tin Htut, 10 September 2016.
61. Interview with Thein Nyunt, 12 June 2018.
62. *Mizzima* newspaper, 30 July 2014.
63. Interview with Dr Soe Yin, 18 November 2018.
64. Interview 053.
65. Interview 055.
66. Interview with Aung Zin, 11 November 2018.
67. Hluttaw record, 28 January 2016.
68. Shwe Bawlone, "Shwe Mann Three Mistakes", *Messenger Journal*, 13 July 2015.
69. Sithu Aung Myint, "Who is Dishonest? Aung Zin, Shwe Mann or Hluttaw Office ?", *Mizzima*, 30 July 2014.
70. Interview with Khin Aung Myint, 13 November 2016.
71. Interview 055.
72. Interview with Dr Soe Yin, 18 November 2018.
73. Interview with Shwe Mann, 15 November 2016.
74. Interview 056.
75. This survey was conducted by the author on 5 and 6 October 2018.
76. Interview with Dr Soe Yin, 18 November 2018.
77. Interview with Toe Naing Mann, *Messenger Journal*, 17 August 2015.
78. Interview 014.
79. He is thought to have been born in 1978.
80. Interview with Toe Naing Mann, *Messenger Journal*, 17 August 2015.
81. Interview 057.
82. Interview with Toe Naing Mann, *Messenger Journal*, 17 August 2015.
83. Because of security concerns, no election was held in five townships.
84. Interview 011.
85. Interview with Htay Oo, 16 May 2017.
86. Interview 050.

87. Ibid.
88. Interview 011.
89. They were the most senior members of the SPDC after chairman Than Shwe and vice chairman Maung Aye.
90. Interviews 010 and 026.
91. Interview 050.
92. Ibid.
93. Interview 010.
94. Interview with Toe Naing Mann, *Messenger Journal*, 17 August 2015.
95. Interviews 004 and 009. And interview with Aye Mauk, *Messenger*, 2 December 2013.
96. Interview 050.
97. Interview with Thein Zaw, 27 March 2018.
98. Interview 050.
99. When the first Hluttaw ended in January 2016 it had twenty-one ad hoc committees and one commission for legal affairs and assessment of special issues.
100. Myanmar Consolidated Media, *The Parliaments of Myanmar* (Yangon: Zin Yandanar Saw, 2013).
101. Speeches by Shwe Mann on International Day of Democracy, 15 September 2011 at Naypyitaw and 26 March 2012 at Mandalay.
102. Interviews 007 and 050.
103. Interview with Khin Aung Myint, 13 November 2016.
104. *Kyaymon*, 25 November 2011.
105. Interview 043.
106. Interview with Thein Sein, 21 November 2017.
107. Interview 010.
108. This visit was questioned by the NLD in the Hluttaw and by the media, which accused the president of violating the constitution. Subsequently, Thein Sein kept away from the party and lost all contact with central committee members.
109. Interview with Toe Naing Mann, *Messenger Journal*, 17 August 2015.
110. The party congress elected 222 central committee members and 73 alternate members.
111. Speech by Shwe Mann to the USDP congress, 16 October 2012.
112. Ibid.
113. USDP party congress record (2012).
114. Interview 050.

7

Shwe Mann's Checkmates

The greatest impact on the Myanmar Spring was the rivalry between President Thein Sein and the Speaker of the lower house Shwe Mann. On the surface this was seen as a rivalry between the executive and the legislative branches. In reality it was a consequence of Shwe Mann's attempt to control the USDP and to sideline the president. Shwe Mann believed that Thein Sein was of lesser ability than himself and that he had been denied his rightful position of the presidency by Senior General Than Shwe. From the first day, he sought to use the parliament as a tool to impose his policies on the government.[1] Six major incidents took place between 2011 and 2016 in which Shwe Mann tried to weaken the president and undermine his power.

2012–13 Budget

The first incident was the 2012–13 budget. On 7 February 2012, Shwe Mann delivered a speech as the Speaker of the Pyithu Hluttaw (lower house or people's assembly) at a rare meeting of the Pyidaungsu Hluttaw (Union assembly). Unusually, instead of speaking from his seat like other representatives, he mounted the rostrum from which he addressed the joint assembly. Rather astonishingly, Shwe Mann failed to consult with the president or the cabinet in advance of this address, which mainly concerned the government's economic policy.

The immediate issues Shwe Mann dealt with in detail were the raising of the salaries of civil servants and the suspension of development projects[2] carried over from the previous military government. He announced three issues that the Union Parliament should demand the government to comply with. Of these, the following two had an immediate impact on the government.[3]

1. The government should increase civil servants' salaries in the coming 2012–13 budget.
2. The Pyidaungsu Hluttaw should thoroughly scrutinize government development projects and suspend or reject those thought to be unnecessary.

Shwe Mann urged the Pyidaungsu Hluttaw members to consider a resolution based on his suggestions. That was Shwe Mann's political trick. If he had made this proposal in the Pyithu Hluttaw, the resolution would have been nonbinding. However, if the Pyidaungsu Hluttaw adopted such a resolution, the government was bound to implement it and to duly report back to the Hluttaw.[4]

The government had already submitted its annual budget on 31 January, prior to Shwe Mann's speech. Furthermore, various ministers had already discussed with Hluttaw committees details of the budget before it was submitted to the Hluttaw. Vice President 1 Tin Aung Myint Oo had supervised this process, and the Hluttaw team was led by USDP CEC and former minister for national planning Soe Tha.[5] Therefore, a mechanism was already in place whereby the cabinet and the party leaders could make necessary adjustments to the budget and national development plans. At that critical juncture, Shwe Mann made these demands at the Pyidaungsu Hluttaw as if he was the leader of the opposition party. For the government, this was like a stab in the back. As the third-highest official of the Tatmadaw (armed forces), Shwe Mann had attended all the meetings of the special projects implementation committee, which were chaired by SPDC chairman Senior General Than Shwe. He had supported and sometimes supervised these projects,[6] which had now been inherited by Thein Sein's administration. In making his attack on the current government development projects, he was indirectly criticizing Than Shwe. The demand to suspend ongoing projects was seen by the president's administration as an irresponsible act.[7]

Although Shwe Mann mentioned corruption and the economic hardships of government employees in his speech, he failed to mention the adverse impact on national economic development resulting from nepotism and cronyism, including the business empire of his eldest son Aung Thet Mann. Aung Thet Mann set up the Ayer Shwe Wah Company several years earlier. His company was involved in construction, palm oil production and the import and export of chemical fertilizers and agricultural products. When his father, General Thura Shwe Mann, was the regional commander in Irrawaddy Division, Aung Thet Mann received lucrative government contracts to supply fertilizer to farmers throughout the delta region. His company was involved in construction projects in the new administrative capital of Naypyitaw. In 2001, Ayer Shwe Wah had more than thirty thousand acres of wetlands and rice paddy in the delta region. In 2005 it became the first private company to receive permission to export rice to Bangladesh and Singapore.[8]

Shwe Mann boldly advocated reviewing and suspending development projects from the period of the State Peace and Development Council (SPDC), but he was not bold enough to admit his role and responsibilities in these projects.[9] In a statement to the Pyithu Hluttaw on 17 February 2012, Shwe Mann argued that his criticism of the projects left behind by the SPDC had nothing to do with legal action against former SPDC members, as they were already under the protection of section 445 of the constitution.[10] But whenever he had a chance, Shwe Mann criticized infrastructure projects such as roads, bridges and dams built by the SPDC for not benefiting the public. He claimed he was now working in the interest of the people.[11]

Shwe Mann's speech was followed by further harsh attacks on the performance of SPDC-era projects by other USDP MPs. Among them Maung Toe, Aye Mauk, Thurein Zaw and Win Than, who were well-known Shwe Mann men, and the government assumed that Shwe Mann used them to harm the government's image and undermine public support for the new administration.[12] However, Aye Mauk argued that they were offering suggestions in good faith in the public interest and not in the interest of the party. He claimed they were also carrying out their constitutional duty to check and balance the executive.[13] Zaw Myint Pe, another of Shwe

Mann's men, boasted that Shwe Mann's speech on 7 February was bold and courageous and that the government had to implement the proposals. He also organized MPs to support Shwe Mann's ideas.[14]

The address by Shwe Mann indicated his decision to use the Hluttaw rather than the party machinery to steer government policies the way he wanted and to exert pressure on the government under section 228 of the constitution. Finance Minister Hla Htun was sent by Thein Sein to the Pyidaungsu Hluttaw, where he explained that if the government implemented Shwe Mann's proposals the budget deficit would be 66 billion kyat, or 12.87 per cent of GDP.[15] Such a deficit would lead to hyperinflation and a consequential increase in poverty. He explained that macroeconomic reforms were necessary before the raising of salaries. But for most of the Hluttaw members, the raising of salaries of civil servants was a popular issue and they supported Shwe Mann's demands.

When President Thein Sein delivered his State of the Union speech on 1 March 2012, he said that since civil servants made up just 3.3 per cent of the population, the government and the Hluttaw must consider the economic interests of the other 96.7 per cent of the population. He warned that the mere discussion of raising civil servant salaries had led immediately to the inflation of commodity prices. He urged Hluttaw members to weigh all the consequences before taking steps to increase the salaries and allowances of civil servants. Subsequently, the Hluttaw agreed to a government plan to provide a one-off 30,000 kyat payment to all civil servants instead of a pay raise. Although the government had to adjust the 2012–13 budget to take account of this bonus, the president was able to limit the damage of Shwe Mann's duplicitous gambit.

The President's Salary

When Shwe Mann realized he had lost the battle over civil servants' salaries, he sent a letter to the Speaker of the Pyidaungsu Hluttaw on 14 March 2012. The letter stated three points that amounted to a demand that parliament conduct an investigation into whether the president's actions were within the framework of the existing laws, including the constitution. The three points were:

1. Should the president, vice presidents and cabinet members continue taking the same salaries as prescribed by the previous SPDC government instead of the higher salary rates under the current law?

2. Was the raising of pensions in July 2011 legal?
3. Was the designation of the newly formed national human rights commission as a Union-level organization legal?

President Thein Sein, in addressing members of the government a year earlier, on 31 March 2011, had said that he and all the cabinets members would continue receiving the salaries at the rates fixed under the SPDC government instead of enjoying the higher salary rates specified under the new law, in consideration of the economic hardships of the people. The president's monthly salary was 1.5 million kyat (US$1,500), but under the new law it would have been 5 million kyat (US$5,000). The demand by Shwe Mann to review whether taking salaries at the lower rates was legal was rather weird, if not ridiculous. The fact of nearly a year having elapsed between the president's announcement of the decision on the matter and the submission of the letter by Shwe Mann raised questions about his intentions.

After assessing Shwe Mann's proposal, the Union Hluttaw formed a committee and decided that the president's action in taking a reduced salary was unlawful. Subsequently, on 28 March 2012, the Speaker of the Union Hluttaw sent a message saying that the president's action was contrary to the constitution. In response the president pointed out examples of leaders of other nations receiving lower salaries on their own volition, depending on the economic situations in their countries, and also mentioned the decision of Prime Minister Nu's cabinet (the nation's first PM) to receive only 50 per cent of the allotted salary figures in 1949 as a fine instance of such behaviour.[16] The Union Parliament did not proceed any further, simply recording the president's explanation in connection with the matter.[17]

Shwe Mann, in taking the matter to the Hluttaw instead of discussing and settling the issue among party leaders, was clearly seeking to pressure President Thein Sein. As it was the duty of the Constitutional Tribunal to decide whether the president's action was constitutional or not, parliamentary interference in the matter appeared to be ultra vires. Nonetheless, Shwe Mann sent a message to the president to the effect that he was constantly watching the latter's actions and considering the possibility of impeachment.[18] Later, the words "impeachment of the president" became popular among MPs. Former minister Soe Thane believes attempts at impeachment had been planned around November 2013 and again in the latter months of 2014.[19] Khin Aung Myint also knew that Pyithu Hluttaw MPs had threatened to impeach the president, and he said to Thein Sein that if that should happen the Amyotha Hluttaw (upper house or house of nationalities, of which he was Speaker) would defend the president.[20]

Amyotha Hluttaw versus Pyithu Hluttaw

After fourteen years of a one-party system and twenty-three years of military government, Myanmar's legislative institutions were totally unknown to the two new Speakers and their members. As the Speaker of the Pyidaungsu Hluttaw, Khin Aung Myint had greater authority than Shwe Mann, reversing their relationship from during the SPDC period. However, after six months Shwe Mann found an opportunity to assert his power over Khin Aung Myint. At the 28 October 2011 Pyidaungsu Hluttaw meeting, Khin Aung Myint proposed to send bills adopted by the Pyidaungsu Hluttaw to the new Constitutional Tribunal if the Hluttaw had doubts about its conformity with the constitution. He explained that before a bill was sent for the president's signature, he wanted to ensure the bill conformed to the constitution. When he asked for the agreement of MPs, the Pyidaungsu Hluttaw unanimously approved his proposal.

Three days later, however, Shwe Mann changed his mind. On 1 November, Shwe Mann informed the Pyithu Hluttaw that there would be an emergency resolution from the Hluttaw Rights Committee. He further explained that after the 28 October Pyidaungsu Hluttaw session, some Pyithu Hluttaw members complained to him that the Pyidaungsu Hluttaw Speaker's decision was not in conformity with the constitution, Hluttaw laws or by-laws. He also said that he had already sent a letter to Speaker Khin Aung Myint informing him that the Pyithu Hluttaw would handle the issue in accord with the rules and regulations.[21] The then secretary of the Hluttaw Rights Committee, Dr Soe Yin, submitted the resolution, which called for repealing the Pyidaungsu Hluttaw Speaker's proposal of 28 October. In the following debate, MPs strongly denounced Khin Aung Myint's decision, which they had previously accepted. Some said his proposal placed the legislative branch under the judicial branch and was therefore contrary to the constitutional concept of the separation of powers.[22] They also said Khin Aung Myint's decision was against the constitution because the Constitutional Tribunal could only review a bill after it was signed by the president and had become law.[23]

In his closing statement, Shwe Mann thanked MPs for their active participation in the debate and said he was proud of the MPs who maintained the integrity and dignity of the Pyithu Hluttaw.[24] After his speech the Pyithu Hluttaw adopted the resolution, which called for the repeal of Khin Aung Myint's proposal. Some MPs also gave interviews to the media and made harsh comments about Khin Aung Myint.

Khin Aung Myint and Amyotha Hluttaw MPs were not aware of this action by the Pyithu Hluttaw and only learned about it from the evening prime-time television news. Although Khin Aung Myint had received Shwe's Mann letter, he thought the Pyithu Hluttaw would form a joint committee to review the issue. He never expected that the Pyithu Hluttaw would debate on and then decide the matter alone.[25]

The next day, 2 November, Speaker Khin Aung Myint defended his decision. He said it was a precautionary measure to ensure that all laws approved by parliament were in accordance with the constitution. He dismissed the objection by the Pyithu Hluttaw, saying the issue could only be discussed in the Pyidaungsu Hluttaw again. He also warned that, as the Speaker of the Pyidaungsu Hluttaw, he could take disciplinary action against Pyithu Hluttaw MPs who made personal attacks on him in interviews; he however tolerated them in this case. He said that if MPs were not satisfied, the best means to resolve the issue was to form a joint committee with MPs from both Hluttaws, and he would accept the committee's recommendation.[26]

Amyotha Hluttaw MPs also submitted an emergency resolution that defended the Speaker's decision. They denounced the one-sided decision of the Pyithu Hluttaw. They pointed out that a decision by the Pyidaungsu Hluttaw could only be amended or repealed by the Pyidaungsu Hluttaw, and the Pyithu Hluttaw had no right to repeal a Pyidaungsu Hluttaw decision.[27] However, some MPs expressed concern over the open confrontation between the two Hluttaws, as it would affect the democratization process. But the Amyotha Hluttaw unanimously approved the resolution that supported Khin Aung Myint's decision and objected to the Pyithu Hluttaw resolution. On 4 November, Khin Waing Kyi, Amyotha Hluttaw MP from Yangon Region Constituency 1, submitted a resolution calling for the formation of a joint committee to review Khin Aung Myint's decision,[28] but the Amyotha Hluttaw MPs were of the opinion that this could only be done by the Pyidaungsu Hluttaw and they rejected her resolution.

The following days were filled with speculation over how to end this dispute. There was some discussion among USDP leaders. Some of them supported Khin Aung Myint[29] but others supported Shwe Mann and blamed Khin Aung Myint for making a rash decision.[30] There were also meetings between Khin Aung Myint and Shwe Mann to solve the impasse. Since there had been no Pyidaungsu Hluttaw meeting since 28 October, everyone waited for the next session to reveal the backroom discussions that had taken place among Khin Aung Myint, Shwe Mann and other USDP leaders.

The next Pyidaungsu Hluttaw session was held on 18 November. Khin Aung Myint formally informed the Pyidaungsu Hluttaw about the official letter received from the Pyithu Hluttaw calling for the repeal of the Pyidaungsu Hluttaw decision of 28 October. He then delivered a lengthy explanation defending his decision, with quotations from the constitution, Hluttaw laws, and parliamentary procedures between 1948 and 1962. He criticized the action by the Pyithu Hluttaw and called for respect for the duties and functions of the Speaker of the Pyidaungsu Hluttaw. Many MPs thought Khin Aung Myint would challenge Shwe Mann, but in the end, and as a surprise to all, Khin Aung Myint said that to maintain the noble tradition of the Pyidaungsu Hluttaw and respect for the Pyithu Hluttaw, he cancelled his decision of 28 October.

This was the result of the discussions among USDP leaders who thought Khin Aung Myint's decision was against the constitution and Hluttaw laws.[31] Khin Aung Myint still thought he was right, and only withdraw his decision in order to avoid confrontation between the two Hluttaws.[32] Khin Aung Myint said he decided to cancel his previous decision because the dispute had intensified between the two Speakers and the two Hluttaws and therefore might cause harm to future legislative programmes.[33]

In actuality it was a test over the authority between the two Speakers, and Shwe Mann won the battle. After this, Khin Aung Myint and the Amyotha Hluttaw were never again able to challenge Shwe Mann.

Proportional Representation (PR) System

Since Myanmar's first legislative elections in 1922, elections have been carried out under the British first-past-the-post (FPTP) system. After the landslide victory of the National League for Democracy (NLD) in the 1990 election, the National Unity Party (NUP)[34] considered introducing a proportional representation (PR) system as a more inclusive approach. During National Convention Sessions between 2004 and 2007, the NUP proposed to use a PR system for future elections. It was submitted to the political parties group and later submitted to a plenary session, but was rejected by the convening committee.[35]

After another NLD landslide victory, in the 2012 by-election,[36] the National Democratic Force (NDF)[37] party considered the PR system as the only means to create a more inclusive parliament in Myanmar. Representatives from the Friends for Democracy group,[38] including NDF chairman Dr Than Nyein, were invited to Australia to study the PR system used there. After this visit, Dr Than Nyein wrote a policy paper on the PR system and submitted it to the NDF Central Executive Committee (CEC). After a long debate the CEC approved the paper, and the Central Committee officially adopted it on 15–16 June 2012.[39] The NDF proposed the PR system to the Friends for Democracy group and they all supported it.

With instructions from Dr Than Nyein, NDF Pyithu Hluttaw MP Aung Zin submitted a resolution on using the PR system in elections to Speaker Shwe Mann on 6 July 2012. The ten-party alliance of the Friends for Democracy group also sent a recommendation on the use of PR to the Union Election Commission (UEC) on 13 July. When the government asked the UEC for its opinion on Aung Zin's proposal, the UEC replied on 20 July that the commission was still reviewing the recommendation from Friends for Democracy and was also seeking the opinion of the Constitutional Tribunal. After receiving this response from the commission, Speaker Shwe Mann did not allow Aung Zin to officially submit his resolution in the Hluttaw.[40]

President Thein Sein met with the Friends for Democracy group on 7 August and listened to their proposal on the PR system, but he made no commitment, as only the Hluttaw could amend the election laws. The UEC invited leaders from fifty-three political parties to discuss the PR issue on 8 April 2013 and did the same with representatives of civil society and international organizations on 26 April. The UEC then informed Khin Aung Myint[41] on 13 May that if the PR system were to be used in the 2015 election, the Pyidaungsu Hluttaw would have to decide the matter in 2013 in order to allow enough time for the UEC to prepare. The UEC published the results of their discussions with the political parties in state newspapers on 15 June 2013. But on 1 July, Khin Aung Myint rejected the UEC notification because the UEC had publicized the notification before the Pyidaungsu Hluttaw had considered the matter, contrary to Hluttaw by-laws.[42]

In 2013 the NDF again tried to discuss proportional representation in the Amyotha Hluttaw, and Speaker Khin Aung Myint allowed them to table a resolution. Khin Aung Myint personally believed that PR was suitable for the Amyotha Hluttaw[43] because of the large constituencies and equal representation by regions and states.[44] Before the Hluttaw debated the resolution, ethnic MPs led by Dr Aye Maung of the Rakhine Nationalities Development Party officially requested a ruling from the Constitutional Tribunal as to whether the PR system would be in conformity with the constitution. The tribunal did not respond to this request, and never stated its reason for not responding. Tribunal chairman Mya Thein was a Shwe Mann appointee after the previous tribunal members had resigned under pressure from the impeachment process, and that may have been the reason for its silence on the PR system (discussed below).[45]

While the Amyotha Hluttaw submission on PR was stalled in the Constitutional Tribunal, Shwe Mann asked Aung Zin to resubmit his resolution on PR. This message was sent through Aung Thein Lin, USDP MP and CEC member.[46] Aung Zin happily submitted his resolution on 20 July 2014, and Shwe Mann allowed a debate on it on 24 July. According to the 24 July Hluttaw Agenda, Aung Zin's motion was "To implement a suitable electoral system for the Pyithu Hluttaw which conforms to Myanmar's situation".[47] It did not mention the PR system, but when Aung Zin read his motion to submit in the Hluttaw, he mentioned in his concluding remarks that the PR system was the only electoral system suitable for a multi-ethnic nation like Myanmar. The Pyithu Hluttaw decided to debate Aung Zin's motion, with 314 *yes* votes and 42 *no*.

Debate on Aung Zin's motion began on 25 July and lasted three days—25, 28 and 29 July. During the debate, USDP and NDF MPs supported PR, and ethnic minority parties opposed the system. Military MPs urged a thorough study before deciding. Twenty-two ethnic minority MPs took leave of absence from the Hluttaw[48] to demonstrate their opposition to the PR system.[49] Originally, Chin, Shan and Rakhine parties supported the PR system during the Friends for Democracy Group discussions. Later they thought a PR system would reduce the number of seats won by ethnic minority parties, and they decided to vote against it.[50] When the 28 July session commenced, NLD MP Khin Htwe Kywe protested that Aung Zin's motion on the day's agenda was different from the versions of the 24th and 25th.[51] She pointed out that in the agenda of the 24th, Aung Zin's resolution did not mention the PR system as a preferred electoral system for the Pyithu Hluttaw, but the agenda for the 28th stated that PR was the preferred electoral system. Shwe Mann responded that that day's version was correct and that the version for the 24th was a typographical mistake by the Hluttaw office. He even played an audio recording of the session of the 24th to prove that Aung Zin mentioned PR in his speech. He then said he would reprimand Hluttaw staff for this mistake and ordered MPs to accept the version of the 28th as the original motion.[52] Shwe Mann failed to explain why he did not correct this mistake on the 24th or 25th. Political commentator Sithu Aung Myint said Shwe Mann may have intentionally removed the reference to the PR system from the version of the 24th in order to avoid objections from MPs, and that Shwe Mann was not honest about the issue.[53] Four years later, Aung Zin admitted that when he submitted his motion to Shwe Mann, he used "PR system" in the headline and also in his speech. Before the motion was officially put on the Hluttaw agenda, Shwe Mann notified Aung Zin that he would change the headline and remove "PR System" in order to avoid strong opposition from MPs. But he allowed Aung Zin to keep his original version in his speech.[54] Before the debate began on 24 July, Aung Thein Lin asked Aung Zin to insert a sentence into his speech requesting for the formation of a committee or commission to study the PR system. Aung Zin did not understand the reason for this request at the time but he later understood it to be a political trick on the part of Shwe Mann.[55]

During the three days of debate, 39 MPs participated—18 supported the motion, 18 opposed it, and 3 were non-committal.[56] NDF, USDP and military MPs were the main supporters of the motion, and the NLD and Rakhine and Shan ethnic parties were against it. On 29 November, Shwe Mann summarized the debate and proposed to form the commission for a new electoral system. Before Shwe Mann sought a Hluttaw vote, Aung San Suu Kyi stood up and asked whether the vote was to support Aung Zin's resolution or Shwe Mann's proposal. Shwe Mann pointed out that although the formation of a commission was not mentioned in the agenda, Aung Zin proposed it in his resolution. Then Shwe Mann played an audio recording to prove it.[57] When Shwe Mann called for the vote, the NLD did not protest, and Aung Zin understood why Shwe Mann had asked him to add the sentence into his speech. Later, Aung San Suu Kyi explained to the media that the NLD did not support Aung Zin's resolution—the party only supported Shwe Mann's proposal to form the commission. Aung Zin countered that Aung San Suu Kyi did not understand the Hluttaw rules and regulations because Shwe Mann called the vote on Aung Zin's resolution, not Shwe Mann's proposal.[58]

A twenty-four-member commission was formed on 31 July 2014, headed by Tin Maung Oo, a USDP MP. The commission took eighty-one days and held nineteen hearings and discussions about the future electoral system.[59] The commission invited international organizations such as the National Democratic Institute, the Institute for Democracy and Electoral Assistance, and the Hanns Seidel Foundation. The commission proposed eight options for a future electoral system. Option 1 was the current FPTP system and option 2 was a PR system. The remaining six were hybrids of the FPTP and the PR systems.[60] Option 8 was proposed by Ye Tun, an MP of the Shan Nationalities Democratic party (SNDP). Ye Tun initially opposed the PR system, but when the commission invited his opinion on the seven options he proposed his own idea for a future electoral system. It was a hybrid of the PR and FPTP systems but would only apply in 165 constituencies (accounting for half of the seats in the Pyithu Hluttaw) located in regions with a Bamar majority. The remaining 165 constituencies—126 of them located in states with ethnic minority majorities—would use the existing FPTP system.[61] Among the eight options, Ye Tun's option 8 found favour among MPs.[62]

The commission submitted its report on 21 October, and thirty-eight MPs debated it. The final day of debate on the commission's report took place on 14 November. During the discussion, the chairman of the commission, Tin Maung Oo, said that the Hluttaw would vote on the eight options separately.[63] Ye Tun was the last MP to speak, and after him, according to Hluttaw procedure, the Speaker would have to take a vote on the commission's report. But while Ye Tun was speaking, Shwe Mann suddenly stopped him. Then Shwe Mann dropped a bombshell. He informed MPs that he had asked the Constitutional Tribunal to review the commission's eight options and the tribunal replied that only option 1, the existing FPTP system, conformed to the constitution; the remaining seven did not. So he decided that the Hluttaw could not select any of the other seven options.[64] Aung Zin, Ye Tun and other supporters of the PR system were surprised but were unable to protest against Shwe Mann's decision.

After the Hluttaw session, Aung Zin and Ye Tun made strong remarks to the media about Shwe Mann's action. Aung Zin said Shwe Mann lacked respect for MPs and bullied them. The next day, Shwe Mann summoned parliamentary leaders from the NDF and SNDP and asked them to control Aung Zin and Ye Tun.[65]

Aung Zin pointed out that instead of following due process for a tribunal ruling, the tribunal replied to Shwe Mann's letter on the same day it received it. This was contrary to the Constitutional Tribunal Law and by-laws.[66] Ye Tun thought Shwe Mann must allow a vote on all eight options, and only after the Hluttaw decided on a new electoral system should the tribunal review its conformity with the constitution.[67] Thein Nyunt, a supporter of the PR system, said the action by Shwe Mann was shameful and damaged the integrity of the Hluttaw. He also said that Mya Thein, the chairman of the tribunal, was an appointee and puppet of Shwe Mann's.[68]

Later, Aung Zin reflected that he had been tricked by Shwe Mann. When Shwe Mann asked him to submit a motion for PR, he sincerely believed Shwe Mann was genuinely trying to find a suitable PR system for Myanmar. He now understood that Shwe Mann had used the PR issue to bargain with Aung San Suu Kyi, who strongly opposed the PR system and saw PR as a threat to an NLD majority in the Hluttaws. He began the PR debate, and when Aung San Suu Kyi and the NLD became concerned about the vote on the commission's report, he cut a deal with them. That is why Aung San Suu Kyi said to her trusted NLD MPs on the morning of 14 November that they should not worry anymore about a PR system.[69] Aung San Suu Kyi believed she owed Shwe Mann, and that is why Shwe Mann played an important role as chairman of the Pyidaungsu Hluttaw Legal Affairs and Special Issues Assessment Commission after the 2015 election, even though he is not an elected member of the Hluttaw.[70]

The Constitutional Tribunal[71]

One feature of the 2008 constitution is the provision for the existence of a Constitutional Tribunal.[72] Section 46 states that "A Constitutional Tribunal shall be set up to interpret the provisions of the Constitution." According to sections 320, 321 and 327, the tribunal should have nine members: three judges selected by the president, three by the Speaker of the lower house, and three by the Speaker of the upper house. The president nominates one judge from among the nine members as chairperson.

According to section 322, the functions and duties of the Constitutional Tribunal of the Union are as follows:

(a) interpreting the provisions under the Constitution.
(b) vetting whether the laws promulgated by the Pyidaungsu Hluttaw, a Regional Hluttaw, a State Hluttaw or a Self-Administered Division Leading Body and a Self-Administered Zone Leading Body are in conformity with the Constitution or not.
(c) vetting whether the measures of the executive authorities of the Union, the Regions, the States, and the Self-Administered Areas are in conformity with the Constitution or not.
(d) deciding Constitutional disputes between the Union and a Region, between the Union and a State, between a Region and a State, among the Regions, among the States, between a Region or a State and a Self-Administered Area and among the Self-Administered Areas.
(e) deciding disputes arising out of the rights and duties of the Union and a Region, a State or a Self-Administered Area in implementing the Union Law by a Region, State or Self-Administered Area.

The first Constitutional Tribunal was approved on 11 February 2011 by the Pyidaungsu Hluttaw. Most of the nominees reportedly were academics and legal experts, although it was headed by a former general who had a legal background as judge advocate general of the Tatmadaw.

In its early days, the Constitutional Tribunal had to review and decide two major cases, both of which were concerned with executive power. The first ruling concerned a dispute between the chief justice and the Ministry of Home Affairs.[73] The Ministry of Home Affairs instructed the Supreme Court of the Union to empower twenty-seven sub-township administrative officers with first-class magistrate's powers as judicial officers. The chief justice believed such an empowerment would confer the power of criminal jurisdiction to the sub-township administrative officers of the General Administration Department and would therefore be contrary to the separation of powers under the constitution. He therefore sought a decision from the tribunal as to whether the instruction was constitutional or not.

The Constitutional Tribunal decided that if the sub-township administrative officers of the General Administration Department of the Ministry of Home Affairs were to be conferred judicial powers, this would be against the constitution.[74] The tribunal stated unequivocally that section 11(a)[75] should be read as a firm guarantee of judicial independence, despite the ambiguity. It argued that section 11(a) could not be read in isolation, but rather in context with section 18(a)[76] and chapter VI, which describe judicial power as only vested in the judiciary. It noted that nowhere does the constitution authorize administrative officers to perform judicial functions. It also explicitly rejected the use of historical arguments. It stated that the situation under the SPDC was "not the same" because the 2008 constitution was not yet in effect.[77]

The second ruling concerned the status of ministers of ethnic affairs.[78] Twenty-three representatives of the Amyotha Hluttaw led by Dr Aye Maung from the Rakhine Nationalities Development Party sought a decision from the tribunal as to whether ethnic affairs ministers had the same status as other ministers of the regional or state governments under the constitution.[79] The government argued that section 262(a)[80] authorized the appointment of an official from the state/regional *hluttaw* to oversee race or ethnic affairs and described the process of appointment, but did not confer ministerial status to these officers. The Constitutional Tribunal found that the ethnic affairs ministers did in fact qualify as ministers under the law. It noted that section 262(f) of the constitution allows the president to appoint the persons selected by the state/regional chief minister "as Ministers" and does not differentiate those appointments from those selected under section 262(a)(iv).[81] It also ruled that the provision of allowances for the ethnic affairs ministers—which were separately defined under sections 5 and 17 of the Law of Emoluments, Allowances and Insignia of Office for Representatives of the Region or State[82]—was unconstitutional.

When the government tried to appeal this decision, the tribunal refused to accept the appeal because according to section 324 of the constitution, decisions of the Constitutional Tribunal of the Union are final and conclusive.[83]

As mentioned in chapter 6, while relationships between ministries and Hluttaw committees were tense, on 18 January 2012 the President's Office directed the Attorney General's Office to seek a decision from the Constitutional Tribunal on the status of Hluttaw committees on behalf of the president. The Attorney General's Office filed its submission on 2 February and the Hluttaw submitted counterarguments on 17 February. On behalf of the Hluttaw, the Deputy Speaker of the Pyithu Hluttaw,

Nanda Kyaw Swar, presented its case on 24 February. On 28 March the tribunal decided that designating Hluttaw commissions and committees as Union-level institutions was not in conformity with the Constitution of the Republic of the Union of Myanmar.

The tribunal noted that chapter IV of the constitution made separate provisions for the formation of legislative committees. Given the separation of powers in the constitution, the tribunal took this to imply that legislative committees were being treated differently and separately from "Union Level Organizations". The tribunal interpreted this to define "Union Level Organizations" as (1) bodies arising out of the 2008 constitution, (2) whose members were appointed by the president, and (3) confirmed by the Pyidaungsu Hluttaw. The tribunal therefore declared that legislative committees were not "Union Level Organizations".[84]

After the tribunal made its ruling, the Speaker of the Pyidaungsu Hluttaw, Khin Aung Myint, ordered the joint bill committee to review the decision. On 24 April 2012, the joint committee disagreed with the tribunal ruling and MPs urged the Speaker to find a means to repeal it.[85]

Hluttaw MPs, in particular ten Pyithu Hluttaw MPs, were incensed by this and denounced the tribunal's decision. They cited section 334(a) of the constitution and urged the impeachment of the chairperson and members of the tribunal.[86] Some even talked of impeaching the president.[87] Some of them felt that requiring the Deputy Speakers of the upper and lower houses to stand in front of the tribunal whilst the verdict was given was a sign of great disrespect to the Hluttaw.[88] After the debate about the joint committee report on 26 April, 191 Pyithu Hluttaw MPs signed a petition asking Shwe Mann to commence the impeachment process.[89] Shwe Mann told them to suspend their motion and he would try to solve the issue.[90] After Aung San Suu Kyi and NLD MPs entered the Hluttaw on 4 July 2012, Shwe Mann appointed her on 7 August 2012 as chair of the Rule of Law and Stability Committee. This was a clever political manoeuver by Shwe Mann. As Suu Kyi was the chairperson of a Hluttaw committee, the tribunal's decision was also perceived to be against her. Thus Shwe Mann automatically won the support of Suu Kyi and the other NLD representatives in his struggle against the tribunal.

After appointing Suu Kyi as chair of the Hluttaw committee, Shwe Mann moved against the tribunal. On 8 August, a day after Aung San Suu Kyi became chair of the Hluttaw committee, 301[91] MPs submitted a second petition to Shwe Mann again calling for impeachment of the

Constitutional Tribunal.[92] On 14 August 2012, he sent an official letter to the president proposing that the tribunal should withdraw its decision and the members resign on their own volition.[93]

The president replied on 20 August that according to the constitution the legislative, judicial and executive pillars were separate, and that he had no authority to order the members of the tribunal to resign. Moreover, the tribunal's decision was final and conclusive in accord with section 324. He then offered an alternative solution, which was to amend the constitution in order to change the status of Hluttaw commissions and committees.[94] The president's recommendation was practical, as Shwe Mann already had the support of a majority of MPs to start the constitutional amendment process. He refused. His refusal, and only calling for impeachment, was a means for the legislative branch to gain power over the executive and judicial branches.[95] That same day, the Constitutional Tribunal held a press conference and made a statement that the tribunal ruling on the Hluttaw Committees was final and could not be withdrawn or amended. Tribunal members pledged to do their duty in accord with the constitution.[96] Shwe Mann also read the president's letter to MPs and said the tribunal had committed a mistake. If it did not withdraw its decision, he would take necessary action against the tribunal in order to defend the integrity of the Hluttaw.[97]

On 24 August, four days after the president's reply, Pyithu Hluttaw MP Win Than submitted an emergency resolution calling the Speaker of the house to explain recent developments relevant to the impeachment of the tribunal. Win Than asked for Shwe Mann's response to the president's reply and questioned whether Shwe Mann had neglected the desire of Hluttaw members to impeach the tribunal.[98] Shwe Mann replied that he could not deny the majority desire of the Hluttaw and that he and Khin Aung Myint had had a meeting with the president the day before. He did not explain the outcome of this meeting but he said that the Amyotha Hluttaw would start action on the tribunal and that MPs should be patient and prepare for the impeachment process.[99]

As Win Than was a close associate of Shwe Mann's, the government saw his emergency proposal as having been arranged by Shwe Mann in order to portray his decision to act against the tribunal as a step to implement the majority view. Win Than admitted that Shwe Mann ordered him to submit the emergency proposal and had provided guidelines on how to write it.[100]

Very few people noticed that Shwe Mann had mentioned that the upper house would start the impeachment process soon. This was a cunning political trick by Shwe Mann. Even though a majority of the Pyithu Hluttaw MPs demanded the impeachment of the Constitutional Tribunal, Shwe Mann arranged for the upper house to start the process. According to the constitution, when one Hluttaw approves an impeachment process, the other Hluttaw will form a committee to investigate the claim.[101] If the Pyithu Hluttaw therefore had been the house to approve the impeachment, the Amyotha Hluttaw's committee would have been the one to investigate the tribunal and Shwe Mann might not have been able to influence the committee's decision. This is why Shwe Mann used all his power to push for an Amyotha Hluttaw resolution on impeachment.

To start the impeachment process in the upper house, Shwe Mann directly tasked upper house member Zaw Myint Pe[102] to initiate it, and he did not consult with upper house Speaker Khin Aung Myint.[103] When Zaw Myint Pe told Khin Aung Myint what Shwe Mann had asked him to do, Khin Aung Myint replied that if the party (USDP) wished to do it, Zaw Myint Pe should act in accordance with Hluttaw rules and regulations. He also informed Zaw Myint Pe that as a Speaker of the Hluttaw, he would be impartial on this issue.[104]

On 28 August 2012, the upper house voted on impeachment of the tribunal. During the debate the chairman of the tribunal, Thein Soe, said that even the president had to accept tribunal rulings,[105] and that trying to impeach the tribunal because of its ruling against the status of Hluttaw committees would harm judicial independence and was against the rule of law.[106] He also pointed out that a parliamentary vote to repeal a tribunal ruling was unprecedented, not only in Myanmar but also in other countries. The Hluttaw would be acting contrary to the constitution, which states that "The three branches of sovereign power namely, legislative power, executive power and judicial power are separated, to the extent possible, and exert reciprocal control, check and balance among themselves."[107]

Within twenty-four hours of the upper house approving the resolution for impeachment, the lower house formed a committee to investigate the tribunal's behaviour. Shwe Mann instructed the investigative committee to report on 5 September, allowing just one week for the investigation. On 6 September, as everyone expected, the investigative committee found that the tribunal had failed to discharge its duties effectively in accord with section 334(a)(5) and recommended that the tribunal was unfit to continue in office.[108]

According to the constitution, the Pyithu Hluttaw should vote on the committee's report, and if not less than two-thirds of the total number of representatives of the Hluttaw pass the resolution, the charge would be substantiated, rendering the tribunal members unfit to continue in office. However, Shwe Mann avoided a vote on the resolution. He declared that since 320 members of the Pyithu Hluttaw[109] had signed the petition for impeachment of the tribunal, that was more than the 286 required to pass a resolution. He therefore decided that the Pyithu Hluttaw had found the tribunal unfit to continue office.

Khin Aung Myint, Speaker of the Amyotha Hluttaw, commented that signing the petition was just an expression of the members' desire and was not a decision as to whether the tribunal was guilty or not. The Hluttaw should therefore still need to pass a formal vote. He later said that Shwe Mann committed many mistakes regarding Hluttaw procedures and regulations because of his subjectivity.[110]

One reason behind Shwe Mann's decision to avoid a secret vote was that some members had begun to doubt the wisdom of impeaching the tribunal. If just 22 members[111] changed their minds, he would not be able to get the 286 votes required to pass the resolution. At the time of collecting signatures for the petition for impeachment, members were emotionally charged and many senior USDP leaders like Aung Thaung[112] openly courted USDP members to support the signature campaign.[113] Not only USDP MPs but also those of other parties sought to punish the tribunal for denying the Hluttaw's rights.[114] Actually, though, the tribunal members primarily used a textual approach in interpreting the constitution.[115] One among those who had second thoughts was Ye Tun of the SNDP, who was an ardent supporter of impeachment in the early stages.[116] Later, he thoroughly studied the 2010 Hluttaw Laws and concluded that instead of impeachment the Hluttaw should amend the respective Hluttaw Laws. He planned to discuss this at a session of the Pyidaungsu Hluttaw on 4 August. Shwe Mann however learned of this and asked Pyidaungsu Hluttaw Speaker Khin Aung Myint to allow only one representative from each party to speak in the debate. Ye Tun was therefore denied the opportunity to present his opinion—though he distributed his draft speech to others and asked them to study it. Later, some representatives who had read Ye Tun's speech went to Shwe Mann and urged him to stop the impeachment process. Shwe Mann declined.[117]

Even Khin Aung Myint could not persuade Shwe Mann.[118] The tribunal members saw the impeachment process like a defendant prosecuting the judge because he lost his case.[119]

After Shwe Mann adopted the resolution, the chairman and all the members of the tribunal submitted their resignations to the president before the Hluttaw submitted their decision to the president. The president accepted the resignations. They resigned because if the president had disagreed with the decision of the Hluttaw and was reluctant to remove them, Shwe Mann would try to impeach the president, and the nation would face a serious political crisis.[120]

The tribunal members were also frustrated by constant pressure from Shwe Mann. Before the tribunal decided on the government's submission, Shwe Mann invited six tribunal members who had been nominated by two Speakers of the houses[121] and pressured them. When the chairman of the tribunal, Thane Soe, learned of this, he warned all members not to bow to political pressure and to respect the constitution. He forbade them from meeting Shwe Mann again, and warned them that they would have to resign from the tribunal if they did so.[122] When the tribunal decided that Hluttaw committees were not Union-level organizations, Shwe Mann and other Hluttaw members became very angry with these six members.[123]

When the tribunal members resigned, Shwe Mann and his supporters celebrated. Some said no one was above the Hluttaw.[124] But international observers had a different opinion. Some saw that the impeachment of the Constitutional Tribunal presented an interesting example of the interplay between jurisprudence and politics. They opined that the Constitutional Tribunal was essentially defunct in the early stage of the reform.[125] They concluded that the tribunal's reasoning in the "Union Level Organizations" case was not patently in breach of the constitution. However, the impeachment proceedings reflected the legislature's desire to protect its hard-won power.[126] Some saw warning signs that the impeachment of the tribunal provided a clear demonstration of the enormous powers of the Hluttaw and that the threat of impeachment could be used to pressure the executive in the future.[127]

After the resignations, the president asked Shwe Mann and Khin Aung Myint to nominate new members in accord with the constitution, but Shwe Mann refused to do so. Instead, Shwe Mann sent a letter to Khin Aung Myint on 31 October 2012 asking him to declare the tribunal ruling invalid. On 2 November the Pyidaungsu Hluttaw duly approved Shwe Mann's request and informed the president that the Constitutional Tribunal ruling was invalid, even though section 324 clearly stated that tribunal rulings shall be final and conclusive.[128]

Next, Shwe Mann sought to amend the Constitutional Tribunal Law (2010) in order to reduce the tribunal's mandate and its independence. A 2012 amendment adopted by the Pyidaungsu Hluttaw on 21 January 2013 greatly reduced the Constitutional Tribunal's mandate, judicial powers and independence. When the amendment bill was presented to the president, he sent it back to the Pyidaungsu Hluttaw with remarks to the effect that the bill did not reflect the tribunal's mandate as stipulated in the constitution. Not surprisingly, when the Pyidaungsu Hluttaw convened and voted on the president's comments, a majority rejected all the comments and adopted the original bill. Since the president has no veto power to stop a bill, he was forced to sign it. However, in his signing statement he declared that, with due respect to the majority view in the Hluttaw, whilst he has signed the law, a future tribunal should review the constitutionality of the amendment bill.[129] When a new tribunal was formed on 25 February 2013, after a three months gap, the Pyidaungsu Hluttaw confirmed U Mya Thein, a retired director-general of the Supreme Court, as chairman of the Constitutional Tribunal. Mya Thein was nominated by Shwe Mann, who seemed to have won a significant victory over President Thein Sein.

In hindsight, Shwe Mann did not start the dispute on the status of the Hluttaw's commissions and committees, but when the tribunal ruled against the Hluttaw he cleverly exploited the emotions of the members of the Pyithu Hluttaw. As the president has no veto power, his only means to check and balance the legislature was the Constitutional Tribunal. With all the members of the tribunal having been impeached and with an amendment act that clearly weakened the tribunal's independence, Shwe Mann was able to impose his policies on the government and undermine Thein Sein on political and economic reform. When he became Speaker of the Pyidaungsu Hluttaw on 31 July 2013,[130] Shwe Mann used the power of the Pyidaungsu Hluttaw to undermine Thein Sein's policies.[131]

The impeachment of the Constitutional Tribunal had a profound impact on Thein Sein. After that, to avoid another constitutional crisis, he no longer submitted any matter for resolution by the tribunal. If he believed some clauses in the bills from the Hluttaw might be unconstitutional, he simply sent his comments and accepted the decisions of the Hluttaw. Sometimes he issued a signing statement or refused to sign a bill and issued a non-signing statement of his opinion for the public record. From September 2012 to March 2014, he refused to sign ten bills and issued six non-signing statements.[132] When his reform policies or bills faced Hluttaw resistance or objections, he did not fight to overcome this. He wanted to avoid another political crisis that could stop the reform programme.[133] He reflected this strategy in his farewell speech, in that he addressed all the challenges by balancing his desire against the existing political reality. He did everything he could to prevent the reform programmes from stalling or losing ground.[134]

Amendments of the Pyithu Hluttaw and Amyotha Hluttaw Laws

The Pyithu Hluttaw Law (2010) and the Amyotha Hluttaw Law (2010) were adopted by the SPDC on 21 October 2010 as part of preparatory arrangements for the 2010 general elections. When the government eventually submitted a resolution on the status of Hluttaw committees to the Constitutional Tribunal, both Hluttaws had tried to amend the Hluttaw Laws to expand their legislatives power. An amendment bill for the Amyotha Hluttaw Law was adopted on 19 March 2012, and an amendment bill for the Pyithu Hluttaw Law was adopted two days later. The Pyidaungsu Hluttaw sent both bills for the president's signature on 23 March.

The president sent back his comments on both amendment bills on 30 March. He commented on the articles that he believed were unconstitutional or that violated the principle of the separation of powers. Out of his ten comments, the most salient points were these:[135]

1. Designating Hluttaw committees as Union-level institutions was contrary to a Constitutional Tribunal ruling.[136]
2. The opening of Hluttaw representative office in all townships was not practical in the current conditions because of the burden this would impose on the state budget.[137]
3. Allowing Hluttaw representatives to coordinate with local authorities on local and national development issues was contrary to the principle of the separation of powers.

4. Providing logistical and security support by local authorities for Hluttaw representatives when they visited their constituencies was also contrary to the principle of the separation of powers.
5. Providing an allowance for free electricity, water, telephone service and transportation (air and train) for Hluttaw members was not suitable, as they already received salaries, a daily allowance and other allowances.
6. Designating Hluttaw representatives as eminent persons of the constituency who local authorities should consult in regard to local development projects was not acceptable and an interference in administrative functions.
7. Setting up Constituency Development Funds from the state budget might lead to corrupt practices and amounted to pork-barrel politics.

The Pyidaungsu Hluttaw did not take immediate action on the president's comments. They were then busy with the campaign to impeach the Constitutional Tribunal. After the Constitutional Tribunal resigned en masse on 6 September 2013, the Pyidaungsu Hluttaw began responding to the president's comments on both of the amendment bills. They discussed, debated and eventually accepted only two comments out of the ten and kept all the important articles that gave administrative and financial power to Hluttaw members in their local constituency affairs.

On 18 November 2012 the Pyidaungsu Hluttaw sent the bill for the president's signature, but as most of his comments had been rejected, Thein Sein refused to sign it, and sent it back again on 23 November. But because of section 106(c) of the constitution, these bills automatically became law.[138]

After these two amendment laws were adopted, Shwe Man became a hero for almost all the Hluttaw members, regardless of their party affiliation. He was seen as the man who gave them administrative and financial power over their local authorities. Like the one-party system under the Burma Socialist Programme Party between 1974 and 1988, Hluttaw representatives were now eminent persons who executive and judicial authorities should respect and from whom they should seek their advice. After that, Thein Sein, though chairman of the ruling USDP, lost control of the party, thus undermining his future legislative programme of economic and administrative reform and the implementation of his programme at the local level.

Amendment of the Pyidaungsu Hluttaw Law (2010)

Shwe Mann assumed the post of Speaker of the Pyidaungsu Hluttaw from Khin Aung Myint on 31 July 2013.[139] As soon as he became Speaker, Shwe Mann began attempting to expand the mandate of the Pyidaungsu Hluttaw. The Pyidaungsu Hluttaw already enjoyed unique power under the constitution and in many ways made the Myanmar Hluttaw unicameral rather than bicameral.[140] Shwe Mann wanted to increase his own powers and sought to use the Pyidaungsu Hluttaw as a mechanism to control Thein Sein's government.

An amendment bill for the Pyidaungsu Hluttaw Law was submitted to both the Amyotha and Pyithu Hluttaw, and the Pyithu Hluttaw agreed with the upper house version. The bill was then sent for the president's signature on 15 November 2013, just over two months after Shwe Mann became Speaker of the Pyidaungsu Hluttaw. The president sent sixteen comments on the amendment bill on 22 November. The president's comments were based on the constitutional principle that states the Pyidaungsu Hluttaw was merely a joint session of the Amyotha Hluttaw and Pyithu Hluttaw, not a separate legislative body.[141] He therefore objected to the articles that granted the Pyidaungsu Hluttaw a separate office headed by a director general and the authority to form committees and commissions. He also commented that the Myanmar Parliamentary Union, headed by the Pyidaungsu Hluttaw to coordinate legislative affairs of regional and state *hluttaw*, was contrary to the constitution, which clearly stated that the legislative power of the Union was shared among the Pyidaungsu Hluttaw, Regional Hluttaw and State Hluttaw,[142] not controlled by the Pyidaungsu Hluttaw.

The amendment bill also extended Pyidaungsu Hluttaw powers to restrict the president's authority over international relations and the economy. The amendment bill sanctioned that all international agreements[143] and all matters relating to mining and hydropower projects[144] must be decided by the Pyidaungsu Hluttaw. The president objected that not only was this contrary to the separation of powers but it also tied his hands on international and economic affairs. Not surprisingly, the Pyidaungsu Hluttaw rejected all of these except for two minor points.

The Hluttaw sent the bill back to the president on 17 January 2014. The president refused to sign it and returned it on 22 January. The government then announced they intended to submit to the Constitutional Tribunal for decision four unsigned laws and four laws to which the president had expressed his reservations.¹⁴⁵ However, the president later aborted this plan as the tribunal's independence had been badly compromised by the amendment bill on the Constitutional Tribunal Law.

After all of these checkmates by Shwe Mann, the president's power and freedom of action had been greatly constrained. There remained however an important question. Why had Shwe Mann, who had clearly expressed an ambition to occupy the presidency, taken the action he had? If Shwe Mann were to become president after 2015, his powers would also be greatly constrained by the laws he had promoted as Speaker. A possible answer is that Shwe Mann accepted that the USDP could not win the 2015 election and that his chance for the presidency was therefore slim. He understood that the military would not agree to amend section 59(f), which prohibited Aung San Suu Kyi from becoming president, but he also understood that the military and NLD members were against his presidency, even though Aung San Suu Kyi might support it. He therefore decided to become Speaker again in a new Hluttaw by allying himself with Aung San Suu Kyi and implementing his own legislative agenda as Speaker.

Shwe Mann, of course, denied he was seeking personal power. He said he was only fulfilling the duties and functions of the Speaker, which were to represent the people, legislate, and to check and balance the executive. He claimed that some people misunderstood him and thought he was interfering in executive functions. He said he had a clear conscience about what he had done as Speaker because he never served one person or one organization but only served the interests of the nation and the people.¹⁴⁶ He even said he was happier as Speaker of the Pyithu Hluttaw than as the third-highest-ranking general in the SPDC government. Saying he always preferred justice and righteousness on each and every issue, while in the past his actions had been circumscribed, now there were no restraints to his ability to fulfil the desires of the people.¹⁴⁷

Notes

1. Interview 010.
2. In 2014, Shwe Mann was able to amend the Pyidaungsu Hluttaw Law and place megaprojects like hydropower under Hluttaw supervision.
3. Speech by Shwe Mann at the Pyidaungsu Hluttaw, 7 February 2012.
4. Section 228.

5. Interview 025.
6. Ibid.
7. Ibid.
8. "Tracking the Tycoons", *Irrawaddy*, September 2008.
9. Interview 020.
10. According to section 445, "No proceeding shall be instituted against the said Councils or any member thereof or any member of the Government, in respect of any act done in the execution of their respective duties."
11. Speech by Shwe Mann at Shwe Pyi Thar Township, Yangon, *Union Daily* [Pyidaungsu Naysin], 7 December 2013.
12. Aye Mauk and Maung Toe were former managing directors of state owned enterprises, Thurain Zaw was a former deputy minister and Win Than was a retired civil servant. All of them were retired military officers.
13. Interview with Aye Mauk, *Messenger*, 2 December 2013.
14. Interview 020.
15. Union minister for finance and revenue Hla Tun's explanation to the Pyidaungsu Hluttaw.
16. *Myanma Alinn*, 29 April 2012.
17. Ibid.
18. According to section 71(a)(ii), the president may be impeached if he breaches the provisions of the constitution.
19. Soe Thane, *Myanmar's Transformation*, p. 175.
20. Interview with Khin Aung Myint, 13 November 2016.
21. Pyithu Hluttaw record, 1 November 2011.
22. When the Pyithu Hluttaw tried to impeach the Constitutional Court, Shwe Mann and his supporters changed their position and said the tribunal was not a judicial court and could not be judicially independent under section 19(a) of the constitution.
23. Ibid. and section 322.
24. Ibid.
25. Amyotha Hluttaw Record, 2 November 2011.
26. "Decision Sparks Hluttaw Row", *Myanmar Times*, 7 November 2011.
27. Amyotha Hluttaw Record, 2 November 2011.
28. "Decision Sparks Hluttaw Row", *Myanmar Times*, 7 November 2011.
29. Interview with Khin Aung Myint, 2 November 2018.
30. Interview with Zaw Myint Pe, 1 November 2018.
31. Ibid.
32. Interview with Ye Tun, 11 and 18 October 2018.
33. Interview with Khin Aung Myint, 2 November 2018.
34. In the 1990 election, the NUP received 21.2 per cent of the popular vote but only won 10 seats. The NLD received 58.7 per cent of the popular vote and

won 392 seats. Another Shan ethnic party, the SNLD, only received 1.7 per cent of the popular vote but won 23 seats, all from ethnic Shan areas.
35. Interview with Htun Yee (NUP), 6 November 2018.
36. The NLD led by Aung San Suu Kyi won 43 out of 45 seats.
37. The NDF was a party that splintered from the NLD in 2010 and contested in the 2010 election.
38. The Friends for Democracy group was a ten-party alliance composed of the National Democratic Force, the Chin National Party, the Phalone Sa Paw Democratic Party (Kayin), the Mon Regional Democracy Party, the Rakhine Nationalities Progressive Party, the Shan Nationalities Democratic Party, the Democratic Party (Myanmar), the Democracy and Peace Party, the Union Democracy Party, and the Unity and Peace Party. None of the last four parties listed won a seat in the Hluttaw.
39. Aung Zin (MP), *Kyuntaw Nint Ahchokya Ko Sar Pyu Sanit* [I myself and proportional representative system] (That Htun Maung, 2016), p. 6.
40. Interview with Aung Zin, 26 October 2018.
41. Khin Aung Myint served as Speaker of the Pyidaungsu Hluttaw at that time.
42. Aung Zin, *Kyuntaw Nint Ahchokya Ko Sar Pyu Sanit*, p. 33.
43. Interview with Khin Aung Myint, 2 November 2018.
44. Twelve MPs from each of the seven regions and seven states.
45. Interview with Khin Aung Myint, 2 November 2018.
46. Interview with Aung Zin, 26 October 2018.
47. Pyithu Hluttaw Record, 24 July 2014.
48. Pyithu Hluttaw Record, 25 July 2014.
49. Interview with Ye Tun, 7 November 2014. Of the twenty-two, thirteen were ethnic Shan MPs.
50. Interview with Ye Tun, 26 November 2018.
51. Pyithu Hluttaw record, 28 July 2014.
52. Ibid.
53. *Mizzima*, 30 July 2014.
54. Interview with Aung Zin, 6 November 2018.
55. Aung Zin, *Kyuntaw Nint Ahchokya Ko Sar Pyu Sanit*, p. 48.
56. Remark by Shwe Mann at the 29 November 2018 Pyuthu Hluttaw session.
57. Aung Zin, *Kyuntaw Nint Ahchokya Ko Sar Pyu Sanit*, p. 70.
58. Ibid., p. 72.
59. Hluttaw Proportional Representative System Review Commission report, 21 October 2014.
60. Ibid.
61. Interview with Ye Tun, 7 November 2018.
62. Aung Zin, *Kyuntaw Nint Ahchokya Ko Sar Pyu Sanit*, p. 93; and interview with Ye Tun, 7 November 2018.

63. Aung Zin, *Kyuntaw Nint Ahchokya Ko Sar Pyu Sanit*, p. 92.
64. Hluttaw Record, 14 November 2014.
65. Aung Zin, *Kyuntaw Nint Ahchokya Ko Sar Pyu Sanit*, p. 96.
66. Ibid., p. 97.
67. Interview with Ye Tun, 7 November 2018.
68. Interview with Thein Nuynt, 11 and 12 June 2018.
69. Interview with Aung Zin, 6 November 2018.
70. Interview with Aung Zin, 26 October 2018. Shwe Mann lost his seat in the 2015 election but Aung San Suu Kyi arranged for his appointment as chairman of the legal affairs commission, which held great influence over legislative issues.
71. For an apolitical account of this issue, see Dominic Jerry Nardi, Jr, "How the Constitutional Tribunal's Jurisprudence Sparked a Crisis", *Constitutionalism and Legal Change in Myanmar*, edited by Andrew Harding (Oxford: Hart, 2018), pp. 174–93. See also Khin Khin Oo, "Judicial Power and the Constitutional Tribunal: Some Suggestions for Better Legislation Relating to the Tribunal and its Role", in the same volume, pp. 194–214.
72. Under the 1947 Constitution, the Supreme Court is authorized to review and make decisions on constitutional issues (section 25). Under the 1974 Constitution, the Pyithu Hluttaw is authorized to interpret the constitution (section 201).
73. Constitutional Tribunal Submission No. 1/2011.
74. Ibid.
75. Section 11 is concerned with the separation of powers.
76. Section 18 is concerned with judicial power.
77. Dominic J. Nardi, "Finding Justice Scalia in Burma: Constitutional Interpretation and the Impeachment of Myanmar's Constitutional Tribunal", *Pacific Rim Law & Policy Journal* 23, no. 3 (2014): 659.
78. According to sections 15, 17 and 161 of the constitution, national races (ethnic groups) that represent at least 0.1 per cent (currently 50,000) of the national population can elect their own representative to the state and regional *hluttaw*. These representatives are appointed as ministers of the "National Races Affairs" in respective state and regional governments to represent their ethnic groups.
79. Constitutional Tribunal Submission No. 2/2011.
80. Section 261 is concerned with the appointment of ministers at the regional and state levels.
81. Nardi, "Finding Justice Scalia in Burma", p. 660.
82. This law was adopted by the SPDC. It designated separate allowances and status to ethnic affairs ministers.
83. Interview with Thein Soe, 9 March 2017; and *Myanma Alinn*, 31 March 2012.

84. Nardi, "Finding Justice Scalia in Burma", p. 665.
85. Pyidaungsu Hluttaw Record, 24 April 2012, pp. 605–11, and 26 April 2012, pp. 620–68.
86. Ibid.
87. International Crisis Group, *Myanmar: Storm Clouds on the Horizon*, Asia Report no. 238 (Brussels, 2012).
88. Ibid.
89. Pyidaungsu Hluttaw Legal Affairs and Special Issues Assessment Commission, Record and Research Group, *Nainggantaw Pweseepone Achekan Upaday Sineyar Khone Yone Noke Htwet Chin Sineyar Laylar Twesheechat* [Review on resignation of Constitutional Tribunal] (Pann Swe Mon Sarpay, 2018), p. 10.
90. Statement on letters between the president and Pyithu Hluttaw Speaker, *Myanma Alinn*, 21 August 2012.
91. Later, more MPs joined and the number reached 320.
92. Pyidaungsu Hluttaw Legal Affairs and Special Issues Assessment Commission, *Nainggantaw Pweseepone Achekan Upaday Sineyar Khone Yone Noke Htwet Chin Sineyar Laylar Twesheechat*, p. 11.
93. Statement on Letters between the president and Pyithu Hluttaw Speaker, *Myanma Alinn*, 21 August 2012; and Pyithu Hluttaw Record, 16 August 2012 – 6 September 2012, p. 810.
94. Ibid.
95. Article by Maung Aye Chan (Havard), *Myanma Alinn*, 17 August 2012.
96. *Myanma Alinn*, 21 August 2012.
97. Pyidaungsu Hluttaw Legal Affairs and Special Issues Assessment Commission, *Nainggantaw Pweseepone Achekan Upaday Sineyar Khone Yone Noke Htwet Chin Sineyar Laylar Twesheechat*, pp. 11 and 17.
98. Pyithu Hluttaw Record, 24 August 2012, p. 317.
99. Ibid., p. 323.
100. Telephone interview with Win Than, 26 December 2017.
101. Section 334.
102. Zaw Myint Pe was former deputy director general of the SPDC office and Amyotha Hluttaw MPs.
103. Interview with Zaw Myint Pe, 15 November 2016.
104. Interview with Khin Aung Myint, 13 November 2016.
105. He mentioned two rulings that stated that government policies were unconstitutional.
106. Constitutional Tribunal website, 29 August 2012, 1:45 p.m. When the new tribunal was formed, the ruling on the status of Hluttaw committees and some other announcements were removed from the site. http://www.myanmarconstitutionaltribunal.org.mm (accessed 3 January 2018).
107. Section 11(a).

108. Section 334(A)(5): "The Chairperson and members of the Constitutional Tribunal of the Union may be impeached [in the event of the] inefficient discharge of [their] duties [as] assigned by law." The investigative committee concluded that in rejecting the status of Hluttaw committees as Union-level organizations, the tribunal had failed to discharge its duty properly.
109. Pyidaungsu Hluttaw Legal Affairs and Special Issues Assessment Commission, *Nainggantaw Pweseepone Achekan Upaday Sineyar Khone Yone Noke Htwet Chin Sineyar Laylar Twesheechat*, p. 24.
110. Interview with Khin Aung Myint, 13 November 2016.
111. On 6 September 2012 there were 307 elected MPs and 101 MPs from the military present. Since the military MPs were against impeachment, Shwe Mann needed 286 elected MPs to support the resolution.
112. Aung Thaung was the former minister for industry 1 and responsible for Mandalay Region USDP organizations.
113. Interview with Khin Aung Myint, 13 November 2016.
114. Interview with Zaw Myint Pe, 15 September 2016.
115. Nardi, "Finding Justice Scalia in Burma", p. 659.
116. *Weekly Eleven*, 25 July 2012.
117. Interview with Ye Tun, 26 December 2017.
118. Interview with Khin Aung Myint, 13 November 2016.
119. Interview with Thein Soe, 9 March 2017.
120. Interview 012.
121. The tribunal has nine members. The president and the two Speakers nominate three each.
122. Interview with Thein Soe, 9 March 2017.
123. Interview 012.
124. One of them was Aung Ko, the former deputy minister for religious affairs and a classmate of Shwe Mann.
125. Nardi, "Finding Justice Scalia in Burma", p. 669.
126. Ibid.
127. International Crisis Group, *Myanmar*.
128. The tribunal ruling on the status of the Hluttaw committee was removed from the tribunal's official website. http://www.myanmarconstitutionaltribunal.org.mm (accessed 3 January 2018).
129. President's letter to the Speaker of the Pyidaungsu Hluttaw, 21 January 2013.
130. The Speaker of the Amyotha Hluttaw and the Speaker of the Pyidaungsu Hluttaw each serve as Speaker of the Pyidaungsu Hluttaw for thirty months.
131. According to section 228, "The Union Government must implement the administrative resolutions passed by the Pyidaungsu Hluttaw and report back."

132. According to section 105, "[If the] President does not sign to promulgate, on the day after the completion of that period, the Bill shall become a law as if he had signed it."
133. Interview with Thein Sein, 18 November 2016.
134. Speech by the president at the Pyidaungsu Hluttaw, 29 January 2016.
135. President's letter to the Speaker of the Pyidaungsu Hluttaw, 30 March 2012.
136. On 28 March 2012, the tribunal decided that designating Hluttaw commissions and committees as Union-level institutions was not in conformity with the Constitution of the Republic of the Union of Myanmar.
137. There are 330 elected members in the Pyithu Hluttaw and 168 elected members in the Amyotha Hluttaw.
138. The president does not have veto power to turn down the bill. According to section 106(c), "If the Bill sent back by the Pyidaungsu Hluttaw is not signed by the President within the prescribed period [seven days], it shall become law as if he had signed it on the last day of the prescribed period."
139. According to the constitution, "The Speaker of the Amyotha Hluttaw shall serve as the Speaker of the Pyidaungsu Hluttaw for 30 months and the Speaker of the Pyithu Hluttaw shall also serve as the Speaker and the Deputy Speaker of the Pyidaungsu Hluttaw for the remaining term."
140. Yash Ghai, *The 2008 Myanmar Constitution: Analysis and Assessment*, p. 21. http://www.burmalibrary.org/docs6/2008_Myanmar_constitution--analysis_and_assessment-Yash_Ghai.pdf (accessed 4 December 2018).
141. Section 12(b): "The Pyidaungsu Hluttaw consisting of two Hluttaws, one Hluttaw elected on the basis of township as well as population, and the other on an equal number of representatives elected from Regions and States."
142. Section 12(b).
143. In the Pyiduangsu Hluttaw Laws (2010), conventions or agreements concerned with war and peace, the demarcation of international borders, national security and defence, or which enact or amend domestic laws need Pyidaungsu Hluttaw approval.
144. In the previous law, these matters did not need Hluttaw approval.
145. Union Government Information Committee, press statement, 27 January 2014. The four unsigned laws were laws on the Pyidaungsu Hluttaw, Pyithu Hluttaw, Amyotha Hluttaw and regional and state *hluttaw*. The four laws returned with a signing statement were the Auditor-General Law, Constitutional Tribunal Law, Anti-Corruption Law, and the Defending and Promotion of Peasantry Law.
146. Interview with Shwe Mann, 15 November 2016.
147. Interview with Shwe Mann, *Pyidaungsu Naysin* [Union Daily], 24 January 2014.

8

Turning Points

During Thein Sein's presidency there were many developments that hindered his reform programme. This chapter covers some of the decisions and actions that deeply affected the reforms. These became seen as turning points in the Thein Sein administration and marked some of its successes and failures.

The Myitsone Hydropower Project

The Myitsone Dam development project was intended to build a large hydroelectric power plant at the confluence of two rivers, the Mali Kha and the N'mai Kha. The two rivers come together to form the Ayeyawady River at a point 42 kilometres north of Myitkyina, the capital of Kachin State. It was to be one of seven dams under the Ayeyawady River Confluence Region Hydropower Project (CRHP) of the State Peace and Development Council (SPDC). According to the national thirty-year electrification strategic plan, on completion the seven dams would have created a total installed capacity of 20,000 megawatts. An eighth dam, Chipwi Nge Hydropower Project, completed in 2013, was installed to provide electricity for the construction projects.

The Ministry of Electric Power (MOEP) and the Japanese Kansai Electric Power Company (KEPO) surveyed the area in 2002 and KEPO established a small weather station at Tang Hpre village near the confluence in 2003. Chinese companies, including the Yunnan Machinery Equipment Import & Export Company and the Kunming Hydropower Institute of Design, surveyed the dam site in 2005.

The MOEP and China Power Investment Cooperation (CPI) signed a memorandum of understanding for Myitsone and the N'mai Kha and Mali Kha Ayeyawady River basin hydropower project on 28 December 2006. In 2007 the Changjiang Survey, Planning, Design and Research Co. (CDC) conducted geological drilling, reservoir inspection and hydrological measuring. CDC also concluded terms of reference for an environmental impact assessment and a feasibility research report in 2008–9. An environmental impact assessment was conducted by Myanmar's Biodiversity and Nature Conservation Association (BANCA) and a Chinese team from January to July 2009.[1]

The total of eight hydropower plants would produce 18,499 megawatts and they were to be completed within fifteen years.[2] Myitsone was the largest dam and was to be located 3.2 kilometres below the confluence of the Mali and the N'Mai. The dam was projected to produce 6,000 megawatts of electricity by 2017. CPI would provide most of the US$2.5 billion investment for the project[3] and would receive 90 per cent of the electricity generated. Myanmar would receive the other 10 per cent. It was also agreed that the government would have a 15 per cent share for land use, Asia World company[4] would have a 5 per cent share and CPI an 80 per cent share. In addition, the Myanmar government would charge a withholding tax and an export tax on electricity exported to China. After a fifty-year period, Myanmar would receive total ownership of the project.

People living near the confluence were the first to object to the construction of the dam. Villagers from Tang Hpre village—located at the Ayeyawady confluence and therefore the first village to be relocated—sent a letter in February 2004 to the Kachin Consultative Assembly, which is composed of Kachin community and religious leaders, expressing their concerns over the environmental and social impact of the dam project. Twelve Kachin community leaders sent a letter to Senior General Than Shwe in May 2007 along similar lines.[5] Also, the Kachin Independence Organization (KIO), which at that time had a ceasefire agreement with the government, sent a letter to Senior General Than Shwe in July 2007 requesting a review of the project. In March 2010 the KIO wrote to the commander of the Army Northern Command warning of possible clashes between army troops who planned to enter an upstream project area and Kachin Independence Army (KIA) troops.[6] The KIO also appealed directly to Chinese president Hu Jintao to suspend the dam project.

The KIO proposed that the site of the Myitsone Dam be moved to a suitable upstream location, and they stated that the KIO had no objection to the other six hydropower projects on the Mali Kha and the N'mai Kha. The KIO again warned however about the possible collapse of the ceasefire agreement because of the Myitsone project and complained that CPI officials refused to cooperate with them.[7]

With the prevailing tight censorship and limitations placed on all possible anti-government movements, anti-Myitsone movements were only active on the Internet. As the government blocked most such websites and blogs, few people inside the country were aware of the growing controversy. But following the 2010 election, the release of Aung San Suu Kyi from house arrest and some relaxation of censorship, local media began testing the waters in early 2011. On the occasion of the eleventh anniversary of the Eleven Media Group in January 2011, the chief executive officer Dr Than Htut Aung warned that the future of Ayeyawady was under threat from a powerful neighbour. Although he avoided mentioning the Myitsone Dam project and China, everyone understood what he meant. After that event, the *Eleven* weekly journal started a campaign against the Myitsone Dam and was soon followed by other media and activist groups. The Anti–Myitsone Dam movement gained momentum when Aung San Suu Kyi issued a "Save the Ayeyawady" statement on 11 August 2011. Although she did not call for the project to be abolished, she expressed concern over the environmental and social impact and urged the Thein Sein government to review the situation with a view to finding a solution that would end concerns over the future of Ayeyawady.

During this period the Ministry of Information began an attempt to counter the growing anti-Myitsone movement. On 5 August, information minister Kyaw Hsan chaired a coordination meeting between the Ministry of Information (MOI) and the MOEP to organize a public awareness campaign on the economic benefits of the Myitsone project. They decided to print articles in the state-owned newspapers based on facts and figures provide by the MOEP. Minister Kyaw Hsan also instructed Soe Win, deputy minister for information, to arrange informal meetings with some activists. As a result, government newspapers printed one article from the MOEP on 9 August and an article from the MOI on 10 August. The MOEP however only provided information on the benefits of the project. And the MOI did not have access to all the relevant information, such as the environmental impact assessment report. The MOI and MOEP also failed to consider the historical and sentimental value of Ayeyawady for the people of Myanmar, especially the ethnic Kachin.[8]

Both articles failed to point out that the environmental impact assessment report stated that it was preliminary and a more detailed assessment and evaluation including social components should follow.[9] Also, neither article informed the public that a 48-kilometre section of the Myitkyina–Putao road and a 64-kilometre section of the Myitkyina–Chibew road would be submerged as a result of building the dam.[10] There were also differences between the government articles and a BANCA report on the relocation of the villages. The government said that only 5 villages and 2,146 people would need to be relocated, but BANCA reported that up to 47 villages and over 8,000 people would need to move.[11]

Local media and civil society organizations (CSOs) strongly condemned the articles and distributed the BANCA report via the Internet. The government lost all credibility in its incompetent defence of the Myitsone Dam. Critics also pointed out that Myanmar would receive only 10 per cent of the electricity produced and that 80 per cent of the country was not yet connected to the national grid. They also questioned the role of Asia World in the project and the fifty-year ownership by the Chinese company instead of thirty years as standard for other build-operate-transfer agreements in Myanmar.

While the government was fighting a defensive campaign to save the Myitsone Dam project, it committed two more public relation blunders. The first occurred at a 12 August press conference organized by the MOI. This conference was intended to be about recent clashes between the Tatmadaw (armed forces) and the KIA in Kachin State, and not about Myitsone. However, after Aung San Suu Kyi's recent release and her call, on 11 August, to review the Myitsone Dam, reporters asked about Myitsone as well as whether SPDC projects were serving the public interest. Minister Kyaw Hsan defended SPDC development projects and praised the benefits of the Myitsone project. He became emotional and said that Suu Kyi and political activists were not the only ones that loved the Ayeyawady, but SPDC leaders too, and he broke down in tears. The press then twisted his words and had a field day reporting that Kyaw Hsan cried over the Myitsone Dam project.[12]

Another disastrous blunder occurred at a meeting on 10 September between ministers and media at the Ministry of Industry. It was meant to be a routine meeting between ministers Soe Thane and Aung Min and the media. Zaw Min, the minister for electric power, arrived at the ministry to invite Soe Thane to a 17 September workshop on Myitsone. Though he was not meant to be part of the meeting with the media, he unfortunately decided to join it. When reporters saw him, they asked questions about the Myitsone project. Zaw Min stated that the project would go ahead despite the public protests, and he labelled the protests the latest Ayeyawady disease. The media and activists saw this as a challenge to them and they strongly denounced Zaw Min's impromptu remarks.[13] After Zaw Min's statement, the anti-Myitsone movement became an anti-government and anti-Chinese campaign, with active support from Aung San Suu Kyi. The 88 Generation Students group commenced a petition campaign for the public to express their opposition to the project. Later Zaw Min regretted his emotional response to aggressive questions from the media. His intention had been only to explain the benefits of the project, but his remarks had a strongly negative impact. His uninvited but well-intentioned intervention created more opposition to the dam project.[14]

In early September, President Thein Sein asked Zaw Min to consider two options for the Myitsone project. The first was to revise the dam design to lessen its impact, even though this would result in a lower electric power output. The second was to suspend the project but continue the other six upstream projects.[15] The Chinese contractors had however already commenced construction and had committed a sizeable investment. Zaw Min conducted a workshop on the Myitsone project on 17 September at Naypyitaw. It was attended by members of the government, the Hluttaw and CSOs. They discussed the possibility of conducting an environmental assessment impact survey, a review of the dam design, and a relocation of the dam site. The participants at the meeting decided to seek a decision from the Hluttaw on the future of the Myitsone project.[16] The president instructed Zaw Min to draft a letter for the Hluttaw, and Zaw Min did so based on discussions at the workshop. The president also asked Thein Zaw, Hluttaw member from Myitkyina and a former minister for telecommunications, to draft another letter. Both versions were based on the workshop conclusions and sought a Hluttaw decision on the Myitsone project.[17] The President however did not send the two draft letters but kept them to himself.

There was no further discussion on Myitsone within the cabinet. At this time the Executive Office of the President had submitted a review of recent demonstrations against the Myitsone project and concluded that opposition groups were trying to use the issue to topple the government. The report offered three options: (a) temporary suspension of the project followed by a review of its environmental and social impacts; (b) a renegotiation with the Chinese of the dam design; or (c) continue the project.[18]

Finally, on 30 September, the president sent a letter to the Pyidaungsu Hluttaw (Union assembly), but not the one that Zaw Min drafted. Neither did he recommend any of the three options from the Executive Office. Instead, the president announced that he would suspend the Myitsone Dam project for his term in office. He said that since the government was elected by the people, it had to respect the desires and concerns of the people. President Thein Sein explained that he made the decision alone on the night of 29 September and drafted the letter himself. He was concerned that further protests in other parts of the country would lead to a political crisis and derail his reform process. His decision was not based on geopolitics or a strategic decision to move away from China.[19] It was based purely on the domestic political situation and the president's desire to avoid a crisis that could harm his political reform process.[20]

People from all walks of life welcomed the president's decision. The international community, especially the West, welcomed it as a sign that Myanmar was moving away from Chinese influence. The president amassed great political capital from this and it created a good opportunity to implement his reform agenda forcefully. However, unexpected consequences made more difficulties for him in the coming years. The first of these, as noted above, was Shwe Mann's concern about the president's growing popularity. With his decisions to build national reconciliation with Aung San Suu Kyi and to suspend the Myitsone Dam project, President Thein Sein was very popular both internationally and domestically. Shwe Mann was worried that Thein Sein might change his mind about serving a single term and prevent Shwe Man from becoming president in 2016—as the SPDC leaders had agreed in 2010. As a consequence, Shwe Mann began to undermine President Thein Sein's authority from early in 2012.[21]

The second consequence was the resulting damage to Myanmar's relations with China. Although the decision was for purely domestic reasons, the West said it was a strategic foreign policy decision. The government did not attempt to clarify the situation. The Chinese began to feel that they were the only loser in Myanmar's democratization process. Some USDP leaders criticized Thein Sein for suspending the project, and discussions between Shwe Mann and Aung San Suu Kyi with Chinese leaders made matters worse.[22] The decision by the president to suspend the project without consulting Chinese leaders and the unfortunate coincidence of announcing the decision on 30 September, the day before Chinese National Day, did not help either. It is not a coincidence that following the suspension of the Myitsone Dam project and improvements in relations with the West, new ethnic armed groups appeared in Northern Myanmar and more heavily armed conflicts in Kachin and Northern Shan State occurred. Nor does it seem to be a coincidence that none of the ethnic armed groups along the Chinese border agreed to join the Nationwide Ceasefire Agreement three years later.

A third negative consequence of the decisions was that some USDP members believed that the president and government took credit for Myitsone without consulting with party Hluttaw members. Later Shwe Mann cleverly used this feeling in his campaign against President Thein Sein and his government.[23]

The National Education Law

In his inaugural speech in March 2011, President Thein Sein said:

> We need more and more human resources of intellectuals and intelligentsia in building a modern, developed democratic nation. In this regard, a fundamental requirement is development of human resources including new generations who will take over State duties. Therefore, we will promote the nation's education standard to meet the international level and encourage human resource development.

He promised to work in cooperation with international organizations, including the UN, INGOs, and NGOs for education reform. During 2012, the Ministry of Education (MOE) and international organizations conducted a Comprehensive Education Sector Review (CESR), publishing their findings and recommendations in early 2013. One recommendation was to draw up a National Education Policy and National Education Law.

A Practical Education Reform Conference was held on 7 October 2013 at Naypyitaw, with President Thein Sein delivering the keynote address. He urged the MOE and all stakeholders to draw up an action plan and he resolved to form a committee to draft the National Education Policy and National Education Law.[24] On 18 October 2013, he formed a 27-member Education Promotion and Implementation Committee (EPIC). It was headed by minister for the President's Office Tin Naing Thein as chair and with minister for education Dr Khin San Ye as vice chair. Under the committee was a 43-member task force of government officials, a 34-member advisory board of scholars and academicians, and a 17-member working group.

At the first meeting of EPIC, minister Tin Naing Thein explained that in accord with the president's guidelines, the process of drawing up the National Education Policy should be a bottom-up approach based on the CESR report. After the policy was approved by all stakeholders, the National Education Law would be drafted based on the policy. He also invited inputs from the public and opened all the meetings to the media. Unlike education seminars held under previous governments, which just convened for one week with invited guests, EPIC's consulting process took nearly a year. According to EPIC procedures, working groups met with stakeholders from across the country and gathered facts and data, then each task force met with working groups, scholars and international experts. After that, each task force finalized their recommendations and discussed them with the advisory board. Once the advisory board agreed, these recommendations were submitted to EPIC.[25]

In the early stages of the EPIC process, the National Network for Education Reform (NNER) and student unions were not involved in meetings, but there were informal channels between EPIC and NNER and the National League for Democracy (NLD). The patron of the advisory board, Than Oo, was a friend of Su Su Lwin (the wife of the first NLD president, Htin Kyaw), a leader of the NLD education network. Dr Thein Lwin of the NNER was also a member of the NLD Central Committee and education network. The NLD gave the NNER financial support as well as human resources. Thein Lwin regularly reported to Aung San Suu Kyi and the NLD Central Executive Committee about NNER activities, and Aung San Suu Kyi supported the NNER education policy.[26] According to Tin Naing Thein, when the framework on the National Education Policy was agreed in EPIC, all stakeholders, including NNER and student unions, would be invited for stakeholder meetings at the national and regional levels.

Early in the process, Aung Min, another President's Office minister responsible for political reform, urged Tin Naing Thein to meet with student leaders. But Tin Naing Thein thought that if student leaders participated in the early EPIC process it would become a political dialogue instead of an academic discussion. So he rejected the idea and decided to invite them later to the stakeholder meetings.[27]

When the Ministry of Education started the CESR process, NNER—a coalition of civil society groups that included student unions, teacher unions, ethnic education groups, faith-based education groups, community-based education groups, education networks of political parties and scholars—also started a series of forums on education reform. Between October 2012 and May 2013, NNER held twenty-five education forums across the country and sought input from the people and CSOs. On 8–9 June 2013 a national education conference was held in Yangon, and 1,274 representatives from all fourteen states and regions attended. Attendees discussed the outcomes of twenty-five education forums and approved education policy for thirteen education sectors.[28] On 13 July 2013, with the help of ministers Soe Thane and Aung Min, representatives of NNER met with the president and presented the basic principles of their draft policy and the policy recommendations. Minister for education Dr Mya Aye and minister Tin Naing Thein were also present. From the NNER side were Dr Thein Lwin, Dr Tin Hlaing, Dr Tant Lwin Maung and Thu Thu Mar. The president had already read the NNER paper and expressed his agreement with its recommendations on critical thinking. He asked NNER to coordinate with the MOE, and also suggested that the NNER paper be sent to the Hluttaw.[29]

A week after meeting with the president, Dr Thein Lwin met with Aung San Suu Kyi and presented NNER's paper. As arranged by Aung San Suu Kyi, a NNER delegation met with the Education Promotion Committee of the Pyithu Hluttaw (lower house or people's assembly) to present their paper in November 2013. Aung San Suu Kyi and Shwe Mann delivered the opening remarks and left the meeting. The NNER delegates continued discussions with chairman Dr Chan Nyein (a former education minister) and committee members. After the meeting, Dr Chan Nyein said to Dr Thein Lwin that the NNER recommendations were good but too idealistic. Thein Lwin could not tell whether this was intended as a complement or whether it meant it would not be feasible to implement the NNER's recommendations at the current time.[30]

Later, Thein Lwin was invited to attend three committee meetings on the education policy. After the parliamentary recess, such invitations were never extended again. When Thein Lwin contacted the committee chairman, Chan Nyein responded that he would no longer need to attend any future meetings. Aung San Suu Kyi did not know about this and later angrily commented to other NNER members that Thein Lwin failed to attend committee meetings, although she had made arrangements for him to do so.[31]

Two weeks before a stakeholders meeting in December 2013, Tin Naing Thein met with members of NNER and teachers and student unions and briefed them about procedures and arrangements for the meeting. After the meeting, students proposed to issue a joint statement, but Tin Naing Thein rejected this suggestion because EPIC had already met with dozens of similar organizations and never released a statement. From then on, Tin Naing Thein was convinced that, unlike NNER, the students were trying to politicize the education reform programme.[32]

When the stakeholders' meeting for Yangon region was held at Yangon University's Diamond Jubilee Hall on 31 December, student leaders attended with NNER and representatives of the teachers union. But on 6 January, students and teachers union representatives walked out of the meeting in a dispute over the role of the teachers union as a stakeholder. From the point of view of the Ministry of Education, teachers were already represented in various working groups and task forces, and teacher unionist should not have been represented separately. But teacher and student unionists disagreed—they walked out of the meeting and never came back. As for the student unionists, they had already decided that their demands would not be met by merely attending meetings and issuing statements.[33] Scholars and teachers from the working groups complained about the rude behaviour of the student unionists and submitted video files as evidence. Dr Yin Yin New blamed Tin Naing Thein for inviting them to an academic discussion.[34] Thein Lwin admitted that the behaviour of the student unionists was inappropriate but he said that it was unintentional and that it came from a lack of maturity and their strong desire to transform the education system.[35]

Although NNER participated in public consultations held by EPIC, there were many disagreements between them. For NNER, the discussions were not real debates on education policy principles but were merely presentations by EPIC working groups.[36] The impasse between EPIC and NNER was over issues of educational freedom, the right of students to select their major subjects at university, and issues related to the inclusion in education of the languages and cultures of ethnic groups. According to Thein Lwin, NNER twice attended stakeholder meetings, but instead of engaging in negotiation, the working groups and task forces strongly defended their drafts and rejected any NNER recommendations.[37] NNER saw EPIC stakeholder meetings as a top-down approach and different from the NNER's approach of participatory policymaking.[38] But the MOE gave a statement that eighteen working groups from EPIC had consulted with over 8,000 politicians, civil servants, scholars, parents, teachers, members of ethnic groups, international organizations and CSOs between 18 October 2013 and 26 February 2014. They also held sixteen regional meetings attended by over 5,600 people to seek sectoral recommendations.[39]

In hindsight, Thein Lwin thought that if the NNER had participated in EPIC working groups or task forces in the initial stages, misunderstanding might have been avoided and it would have been possible to build personal trust between the MOE and NNER. NNER discussions with the president and minister Tin Naing Thein were cordial and displayed mutual respect. Discussions with director generals of the MOE like Zaw Htay, Dr Khine Myae, Dr Aung Min and Than Oo were different. They always opposed NNER proposals. Khine Myae and Aung Min in particular denounced NNEP recommendations as impractical and amateurish.[40]

When regional stakeholder meetings were concluded in February 2014, EPIC planned to hold a national stakeholders conference at Naypyitaw. At that time, Thein Lwin met with the director general of the Education Research Department, Dr Myo Thein Gyi (current education minister under the NLD government), through an intermediary. At that meeting, Myo Thein Gyi informed him that a "National-level Practical Education Reform Conference" was to be held on 5–6 March in Naypyitaw and that about 700 people would be invited. Myo Thein Gyi suggested that NNER send 150 representatives—transportation and accommodation would be provided by the ministry.[41] On 1 March 2014, the NNER working group held a meeting and decided to attend the conference.[42] On 3 March, Myo Thein Gyi phoned to tell NNER that the invitation had been cancelled because his previous invitation had been misunderstood. Angered by EPIC's decision to cancel the invitation, NNER commented that "repeated breaking of promises, cancelling previously agreed arrangements, and spreading false news have caused us to lose all faith in EPIC and the Ministry of Education's process of education reform."[43]

From EPIC came a different version of the story. When EPIC began the education reform process, Aung San Suu Kyi and Dr Chan Nyein visited Tin Naing Thein's office and discussed cooperation between the executive and the legislature on education reform. Tin Naing Thein reported to the president and received approval. He informed Aung San Suu Kyi of this during the Union Day state dinner. When they discussed a national-level conference, Suu Kyi favoured a smaller meeting with about 150 participants, but Tin Naing Thein preferred to invite about 700 people in order to get more diverse opinions from states, regions, ethnic groups and CSOs. Tin Naing Thein then instructed Myo Thein Gyi to coordinate with the Hluttaw Education Committee with regard to the invitations.[44] EPIC also officially informed the Hluttaw committee to invite NNER because NLD members were closely working with NNER and Thein Lwin was an NLD Central Committee member. But on the evening of 4 March, education minister Dr Khin San Ye and Myo Thein Gyi reported to Tin Naing Thein that Myo Thein Gyi had invited the NNER and that their delegation had already arrived in Naypyitaw. Tin Naing Thein asked them to discuss with the Hluttaw committee about arranging seats for NNER in the conference hall and to also transfer fifteen of the seats reserved for the MOE to the NNER. The Hluttaw committee however replied that they had not planned to invite the NNER. When NNER learned that they had only been allocated fifteen seats at the conference, they left.[45] For EPIC, the incident was the result of a misunderstanding between the Hluttaw committee and the NNER. Thein Lwin said that the Hluttaw Education Committee never contacted them about the conference.[46]

The national conference was held from 5 to 7 March and approved the National Education Policy, and the MOE drafted a National Education Law based on it. At the same time, the Pyithu Hluttaw Education Committee also drafted its own version. The MOE version had 14 chapters and 80 articles; the Hluttaw version had 14 chapters and 71 articles. The Pyithu Hluttaw combined the two versions and approved a draft on 23 March 2014. This was an unusually quick process to approve a complex bill just two weeks after the national-level conference. The NNER and students concluded that that the government and Hluttaw had never intended to listen to their input. Thein Lwin said that the Pyithu Hluttaw Education Committee had already drafted the National Education Law prior to the EPIC conference and was not happy that the MOE prepared its own draft through the EPIC process. He felt the NNER was a victim of rivalry between the government and the Hluttaw.[47] Tin Naing Thein also confirmed that Aung San Suu Kyi said the EPIC process to draft a National Education Policy as a first step was a waste of time. She planned to draft an education law in the Hluttaw without public consultation on a national education policy.[48] Although she was not chairperson of the Hluttaw Education Committee, Suu Kyi played a principle role in the Hluttaw's education reform programme.

The NNER strongly opposed the National Education Law and announced it would peacefully campaign against the law until its demands were met.[49] When the law reached the Amyotha Hluttaw (upper house or house of nationalities), the bill committee invited NNER representatives on 30 May to discuss it again, but there were disagreements between the NNER and Hluttaw over academic and administrative freedom of the universities, the role of the student unions, the university entrance system, and ethnic languages and culture in education. At that time, student unions were beginning small protests and they sent their recommendations on the Education Bill to the two houses. Both houses rejected the recommendations of the student unionists.[50]

Later, the upper house approved the Education Bill with 136 amendments to the lower house version. The Pyidaungsu Hluttaw then considered both versions and approved a final bill on 30 September. The law adopted was quite different from the original MOE draft, with 46 per cent of the final bill added by the Hluttaw and only 54 per cent from the MOE version based on the outcomes of the EPIC National Conference.[51]

Student unions began their campaign against the Education Law in early November. On 12 and 13 November they held a national students' conference in Yangon with 500 representatives from various universities and formed a 15-member "Action Committee for Democratic Education (ACDE)". ACDE demanded four-party talks between students, NNER, the government and parliament to reconsider the National Education Law. They vowed to organize a nationwide protest if there was no response from the government within sixty days. On 15 November, student demonstrators marched to Yangon University, forcibly entered the university compound and delivered speeches at the site of the former student union building.[52] On 16 November they marched to Shwedagon Pagoda and held a National Day ceremony at the National Day commemoration statue.[53]

That day, director general Zaw Htay from the MOE met with student union leaders but they failed to reach an agreement. The students then marched to the Yangon regional government building and staged a one-day sit-in strike.

For sixty days the Education Ministry took no other initiative for dialogue while the ACDE sent their representatives to universities to organize a campaign against the National Education Law. President Thein Sein's cabinet had no clear-cut policy for dealing with student protests. Tin Naing Thein and EPIC thought that since the Pyidaungsu Hluttaw alone could amend or remove the Education Law, the students should negotiate with members of parliament. Aung Min saw the student protests as a political issue and was willing to deal with the students. The minister for home affairs Lt. Gen. Ko Ko wanted to crush the protests at an early stage. The president was caught between opposing views and was not able to lay down clear policy guidelines.

After the moratorium expired on 16 January 2014 without an official response, the ACDE announced on 17 January their decision to start a nationwide protest. After this decision by the students, the president sent a letter to Shwe Mann on 19 January urging the Hluttaw to consider the students' demands and to amend the National Education Law if necessary. Shwe Mann responded that should the MOE send an amendment the Hluttaw would consider it, but the Hluttaw would not initiate its own amendment.

On 20 January, a main protest column began marching from Mandalay, Myanmar's second-largest city, towards Yangon. Other columns also started from Monywa, Dawei and Pathein. Although there were only a few dozen students in the march, state and regional governments failed to stop them at this stage because of a lack of clear policy from the central government. On 24 January, the ACDE issued a list of eleven demands:[54]

1. The inclusion of representatives of teachers and students in legislative processes on education policies and laws, by-laws and other related laws.
2. The right to freely establish and operate student and teacher unions and legal recognition for them.
3. Establishment of a National Education Commission and University Coordination Committee mentioned in the approved National Education Law.

4. Self-determination and self-management on educational affairs of individual states/regions and schools.
5. Modifying the current examination and university matriculation system.
6. Modifying teaching methods such that they ensure freedom for thinking and self-studying by students.
7. Inclusion of a provision in the National Education Law that ensures freedom for the practice of ethnic languages and mother-tongue-based multilingual education for ethnic populations and tribes.
8. Inclusive education for all children, including children with disabilities
9. Re-enrollment of students expelled from schools as a result of the student uprisings.
10. An allocation of 20 per cent of the national budget for education.
11. Regulating free compulsory education up to the middle school rather than primary school level.

When the main protest column started from Mandalay with about sixty students, there were two opinions on how to deal with the protest march. Home affairs minister Lt. Gen Ko Ko, the Mandalay chief minister and some cabinet members wanted to arrest the leaders before they could gather more support along the road. Aung Min asked for a dialogue with the students. The president vacillated between the two opinions. Even though he knew the protest had a political agenda other than education reform, the president did not want to be remembered as the person who used force to stop a student protest. On 27 January, Thein Sein allowed Aung Min to negotiate with ACDE leaders whilst the protest column was stopped by police near Taung Thar.[55] Aung Min met with ten student leaders from the ACDE on 28 January at Naypyitaw and they agreed to hold four-party talks between the government, Hluttaw, NNER and ACDE on 1 February at Yangon. The students also agreed to stop their protest march when the negotiations began in Yangon. But, the same day, the ACDE issued another nine points of preconditions for the 1 February meeting, including free media coverage during the four-party talks. Aung Min agreed to all the demands.

At about this time, Aung San Suu Kyi barred Thein Lwin and other NLD Central Committee members from attending the four-party talks as NNER representatives. When Thein Lwin insisted on attending he was expelled from the Central Committee. Aung San Suu Kyi said that Thein Lwin had a conflict of interest between the NNER and the NLD.[56]

During their negotiation on 1 February at Yangon University, in the presence of local media, students cleverly used the occasion for their propaganda purposes. Nearly four-dozen students participated in the discussion, clapping and shouting slogans when their leaders talked. Aung Min, who conducted many official and unofficial meetings with ethnic armed organizations (EAOs) during the peace process, had difficulty dealing with the students. EAOs are well organized and have a clear mandate for negotiation with the government. The students were disorganized, rude and had no clear mandate among themselves. No one among them could give an assurance that the remaining students in the protest columns would accept the decisions reached at the meeting. Aung Min and his friends from the Myanmar Peace Center were frustrated.[57] They stopped the meeting and arranged to meet again on 3 March at Naypyitaw. Aung Min also informed ACDE leaders that he would arrange accommodation for them at the City Council's guest house.

But Aung Min, in his usual working style, only reported to the president and failed to coordinate with other ministries about the ACDE leaders' visit to Naypyitaw. Thein Nyunt, another President's Office minister and also mayor of Naypyitaw, was very conservative and had always been suspicious of CSOs and activists. He had strictly ordered officials at the City Council's guest house that no activists were allowed to stay there without permission from him. Aung Min failed to consult Thein Nyunt about the student leaders' visit. So when the ACDE delegation arrived at Naypyitaw on the evening of 2 March, they could not get rooms, as Thein Nyunt had not given his permission. The students had to sleep in their cars and the ACDE leaders believed the government had done this intentionally in order to harass them. Tensions were high when the meeting commenced on the morning of 3 March. The students demanded that instead of fifteen representatives from each party, they wanted the whole of their delegation (forty-five people) to attend. After much discussion the meeting was postponed until 12 February. The students then decided to resume their protest march to Yangon, and Aung Min was not able to stop them. As a result, the president lost confidence in Aung Min's approach.

On 5 February the government issued a statement promising to amend the National Education Bill and asked for public cooperation with the government and Hluttaw. It also warned that the student protests were illegal and had been instigated by political organizations. On 7 February the Ministry of Education called on parents to recall their children from the protest march, as the ministry was preparing to amend the Education Law. On 9 February the government issued another statement calling on the students to stop the protest marches as they had agreed on 28 January.

Surprisingly, Shwe Mann had largely remained silent during this dispute and had not made any public statement. Although the National Education Law was initiated at the Pyithu Hluttaw, he arranged that the amendment law had to be submitted to the Amyotha Hluttaw. That way he could avoid negotiating with the students at the Hluttaw, which he saw as problematic and as having little prospect of reaching agreement. Aung San Suu Kyi, who was very active in the drafting process, was also silent during the subsequent dispute. Aung San Suu Kyi was apparently concerned the student protests could spoil the coming elections in November 2015.[58]

On 9 February, deputy minister for education Thant Shin and ACDE representatives met and agreed a framework for future discussions on 11 February. The president assigned Hla Htun, another President's Office minister, to lead the government team. The four-party talks resumed on the 11th and reached agreement on ten of the ACDE's demands. It was also agreed to draft amendments to the National Education Law based on the students' demands. However, the ACDE leaders could not stop the protest marches as they had agreed and only promised to explain the agreements to the other students. It was agreed to meet again on 14 February. Deputy Minister Thant Shin and Zaw Myint Pe from the Amyotha Hluttaw expressed their concerns about the possibility of students marching on Yangon, and warned that it would create a crisis. On 12 February, an ACDE delegation met with Aung San Suu Kyi to ask her to support the amendments. She did not commit to do so and merely explained legislative procedures to them.[59]

After reaching agreement on the 11 February, the protest columns from Dawei, Pathein and Monywa decided to break off their march and return home, but the Mandalay column refused to do so. On 13 February the ACDE issued a statement that they would march towards Yangon even though they had reached agreement with the government and that the Hluttaw had agreed to amend the Education Law. The president ordered the government information committee to issue another statement urging the students not to march towards Yangon and warning that the government would use all legal means to preserve public order and security in Yangon. This reflected a decision reached at the National Defence and Security Council.[60] The president and his cabinet now concluded that the ACDE and its leaders had been using education reform to create a political crisis like that of 1988. Thein Lwin gave a different reason. He explained that students from the Mandalay column were overjoyed with their success and did not listen to NNER suggestions to stop the march. They felt that stopping the march without reaching their destination would be a defeat, and vowed to stage a victory march towards Yangon. Even Min Thwe Thit, one of the ACDE leaders, admitted that if they decided to stop the march their followers would turn against them. Thein Lwin believed that whilst some students may have had a political agenda most were genuinely working for educational reform, but they could not see the consequences of their march towards Yangon.[61]

From that day the dispute between the government and the ACDE became not about educational reform but about whether the students— halted at Letpadan, Bago Division—should march to Yangon or not. On 14 and 15 February, working groups from the government, Hluttaw, NNER and ACDE drafted the amendment bill and submitted it to the Amyotha Hluttaw on 16 February. The Hluttaw bill committee invited the NNER and ACDE for hearings on 5 and 7 March, but both refused to appear. In the meantime the government had reinforced the police blockade at Letpadan, where about a hundred students, who had arrived there on 17 February, were preparing to march towards Yangon. There were negotiations between the state authorities and the students, with the NNER as an intermediary, but no agreement was reached.

On 8 March the ACDE issued an ultimatum demanding the police remove their barricades and allow them to march towards Yangon at 10 a.m. on 10 March. That was the day nationwide matriculation examinations were set to begin, and it was not possible for the government to permit student protestors into Yangon. For President Thein Sein this was the last straw. He had no further choice. On 10 March the authorities met with the students to try to find a last-minute solution, but they failed. At 10 a.m., students tried to break the police line. Someone from the student side threw a water bottle at the police and events then went out of control. Some police used excessive force on protestors, and video footage and photos of these ugly scenes spread over the Internet. Dozens of protesters were injured and arrested. Politicians, community leaders, the international community, media and even EAOs rushed to condemn the police action at Letpadan. The USDP, under Shwe Mann's leadership, did the same, distancing itself from the government and the president.

President Thein Sein's image was badly marred by this tragic incident. For nearly two months he had used every means to compromise with the students in order to avoid this. Most of his actions had been reactive in response to the situation instead of proactive with a clear-cut policy and strategy on the National Education Law and the student protests. The cabinet did not have a focal person or ministry to deal with the protests. The Ministry of Education approached the problem as a legislative issue, the Ministry of Home Affairs approached it as a security matter, and minister Aung Min approached it as a political issue. There was no concrete coordination among the ministries, and each minister directly reported to the president and sought his decision. The only cabinet meeting to have a lengthy discussion on the student protests took place on 13 February, when the president explained the situation. There was no debate on the strategy or policy to deal with the protests during that meeting. If the government had had a concrete strategy to deal with the protests against the National Education Law after November 2014, the outcome might have been different.

The tragic end to the student protests and the public outcry against the government's handling of the events of 10 March, combined with the coming election in November, resulted in Thein Sein's education reform programme losing momentum. Although the Hluttaw amended the National Education Law, the government was unable to implement it.

The NNER and students also lost. They were neglected by Aung San Suu Kyi, and although the NNER still held seminars across the country and issued education policy statements that emphasized indigenous rights, social justice, academic freedom and human rights, it has failed to gain the attention of the NLD government. The NLD government has never invited the NNER to follow up with education laws such as a basic education law or a vocational education law. Thein Lwin thought that although there were disagreements between Thein Sein's government, the NNER and students, 2013–15 were exciting years for educational reform. All stakeholders held seminars, workshops and forums on educational reform and there was active public debate on each and every issue. Everyone lost on 10 March, and the education reform programme has yet to recover.[62]

2012 Rakhine Conflict

Myanmar has suffered from ethnic and communal tensions since the colonial period. These tensions have often flared into periods of violence, which the authorities have had to suppress, often taking their attention and resources away from more constructive work, such as economic and social development. The Thein Sein presidency was not immune to this problem. In addition to conflict in Rakhine State, violence had also renewed in Kachin State when the previous ceasefire agreement reached with the Kachin Independence Army broke down.

On 28 May 2012, a young Rakhine[63] girl was raped and murdered by three Muslim men. A resident of Kyauknimaw Village, Yanbye Township, the killing of Ma Thida Htwe became the cause of public disorder between Muslims and Buddhists in Rakhine State. The local police investigated the crime and subsequently arrested three men. Initially it was a routine criminal case, but a few days later, photos of the victim were posted on the Internet by online Rakhine news websites as an instance of Muslims attacking a person of Rakhine ethnicity. The pictures spread very rapidly across Rakhine State. On 3 June 2012, a passenger bus on the Thandwe to Yangon route was stopped at Taunggoke highway bus terminal and searched by a mob. They found ten Muslim passengers. The mob dragged them from the bus and murdered them. News of the killings of the Muslim passengers also spread quickly throughout Rakhine State among the Muslim population.

On 8 June 2012, in Maungdaw, a predominantly Muslim Bengali[64] town, Friday prayer meetings were held at the West Myoma quarter Jamai Mosque and at the Myoma Kanyindan Cemetery Mosque. After the prayer meetings, a large crowd of Bengalis emerged from the mosques on to the main road, shouting in Bengali dialect, "Strength to the Muslims! Death to the Rakhine!" and "Kill all Rakhine and drive them out from this land!"[65] Some of these people then burned and looted nearby Rakhine-owned houses in the Myoma quarter, attacking and killing some Rakhine. On the same day, violence spread to surrounding areas of Maungdaw and villages to the south. Many Rakhine people had to flee for their lives.[66] Rakhine people claimed that these events were the implementation of a pre-existing plan by the Bengalis to drive out indigenous Rakhine people from the Maungdaw region and make it an exclusively Bengali area, rather than revenge for the Muslims killed in Taunggoke.[67]

After that, communal violence spread to other parts of Rakhine State, such as Buthidaung, Rathedaung, Kyauktaw, Pauktaw, Sittwe, Mrauk-U, Kyaukpyu and Yanbye, involving both Rakhines and Bengalis in reciprocal attacks, burning many homes and killing and injuring many people. In Maungdaw and Buthidaung, areas where Bengalis are in the majority, Rakhine suffered the most—in other parts of the state, Bengalis suffered the most.

The Rakhine State government and local authorities eventually managed to restore order, including issuing a curfew order in many townships, but they failed to prevent subsequent outbreaks of violence. On 10 June, President Thein Sein declared a state of emergency in Rakhine State and ordered the Tatmadaw to support the restoration of order and enforce a curfew in several townships. Also on 10 June the president addressed the nation about the Rakhine crisis. He said that the current violence in Rakhine was instigated on the basis of religion and racism. He warned that rage and hatred were in danger of spreading communal violence beyond Rakhine State. He asked the people to realize that such violence would seriously damage the country's stability and the ongoing democratization process. He also pledged to take legal action against those who committed crimes and that he would cooperate with religious organizations and leaders, as well as political parties and CSOs, to resolve the crisis. After the Tatmadaw troops were deployed to provide security the situation gradually returned to normal, but a great deal of mistrust remained between the Buddhist Rakhine and Muslim Bengali communities.

On 17 August 2012, President Thein Sein established the Rakhine Commission of Inquiry through a Presidential Executive Order. This commission was asked to inquire into the following issues:[68]

1. Investigate the root cause of the disturbance to peace and security.
2. Verify the extent of the loss of life, property and other collateral damage.
3. Examine the efforts to restore peace and promote law and order.
4. Outline means to provide relief and implement resettlement programmes.
5. Develop short- and long-term strategies to reconcile differences.
6. Establish mutual understanding and promote peaceful coexistence between various religious and ethnic groups.
7. Advise on the promotion of the rule of law.
8. Advise on the promotion of social and economic development.

Although the violence had subsided and the situation had started to improve, there were three attacks on Rakhine people in Buthidaung, Maungdaw and Kayuktaw townships in August and September, resulting in two deaths and two injuries.[69] After the June incidents, extremists from both communities issued public statements, published numerous pamphlets and distributed online hate speech to instigate further unrest.

While trying to stop the cycle of violence in Rakhine, President Thein Sein sent a team of ministers led by minister for border affairs Lt. Gen. Thet Naing Win to Rakhine to oversee relief and resettlement work. As this was the monsoon season, when living conditions are particularly difficult, the government had to provide US$66.5 million in humanitarian aid for victims in addition to US$1 million a day for food.[70] On 22 September the government hosted a two-day workshop on the Rakhine crisis. Vice President Dr Sai Mauk Kham delivered a keynote address in which he attributed the lack of economic development in Rakhine as the major reason behind the recent conflicts. Consequently, he called for the improvement of socio-economic conditions in Rakhine.

Subsequent to the June incidents, growing Rakhine nationalism and concern over the Islamization of Northern Rakhine agitated the Rakhine Buddhist community. A Rakhine peoples conference was held at Rathedaung from 25 to 26 September. This conference approved eighteen demands, three pieces of advice and six protests to the government, including the demand for tighter control of the land and sea borders and the enactment of a Bengali population control law.[71] The conference also protested at the proposal to open an Organization of Islamic Cooperation (OIC) office in Rakhine.

Then, between 22 and 25 October, violence erupted in seven townships in Rakhine State, including in two—Kyaukpyu and Myebon—that had not been affected during the first phase of violence. This time not only Bengalis but also Kaman Muslims, who are officially recognized as an indigenous ethnic group, were attacked and their homes set on fire.

By the end of October, security had been re-established but communal violence had taken a significant toll on the people of Rakhine State. Economic and social relationships between the two communities had totally collapsed. The Rakhine inquiry commission concluded that this had had four impacts:[72]

1. The physical impact, including death, injury and the destruction of property.

2. A psychological and social impact.
3. The impact on the country and its ethnic groups.
4. And the economic impact.

Overall, according to official figures, in the Rakhine State sectarian conflicts of 2012, a total of 192 people were killed, more than 265 injured and 8,614 houses were destroyed. The first phase of violence, in June, resulted in 66 deaths in the Bengali community and 32 in the Rakhine community; 72 Bengali and 51 Rakhine injured; and 4,188 houses belonging to Bengalis and 1,150 belonging to Rakhine destroyed. The toll from the second phase of violence in October saw 68 Bengali and 26 Rakhine deaths, 45 Bengalis and 97 Rakhine injured, and 42 Rakhine and 3,234 Bengali homes destroyed.[73]

After the June violence the government formed two committees for Rakhine. A committee for the restoration of peace and stability was headed by the deputy minister of home affairs and a committee for rehabilitation and humanitarian assistance was headed by the Union minister for border affairs. Three phases of relief and resettlement programmes were implemented. First, camps were established for the protection of internally displaced persons. The second phase saw the provision of humanitarian assistance. The third saw the resettlement of people in their own villages and wards.[74]

As a result of the violence in June and October, in eleven of seventeen townships in Rakhine, 111,000 people were displaced from 16,980 households. The gender distribution among those affected was 53.8 per cent women and 46.2 per cent men.[75] By the end of October the situation had somewhat stabilized, but tensions were still high between the two communities.

More than a year later, on 29 September 2013, inter-communal violence once more occurred in Rakhine State, this time at Thandwe, in the southern part of the state. That violence was triggered by a dispute over a parking space in front of a Muslim-owned shop. During three days of rioting and disorder, 110 homes were destroyed, displacing more than 500 people, and at least five Muslims were killed and many more injured in mob violence that engulfed four or five villages near Thandwe. This time most of the victims were Bengali and Kaman Muslims. The events were strangely coincident with a presidential visit to Rakhine commencing on 1 October. The president arrived at Thandwe on 2 October and inspected the affected areas. He instructed local officials to increase support for both the Buddhist and Muslim communities, "regardless of religious or racial differences", and noted that the government would bring the perpetrators to justice and rebuild damaged homes.[76] The president also met with Buddhist and Muslim community leaders, urging them to cooperate with the government to restore law and order and to work for the socio-economic development of Rakhine State.

The Rakhine Inquiry Commission submitted its report on 22 April 2013. The commission pointed out that violence affected not only the livelihoods and food security of the two communities but also affected businesses throughout Rakhine State. Attacks and counter-attacks, killings and counter-killings erupted between the Rakhines and Bengalis, leading to a breakdown in communication between the two sides. The commission urged the government to implement the following:[77]

- Agencies responsible for security should heighten cooperation and collaboration with one another.
- Security forces in Rakhine should not be withdrawn or reduced by any significant number.
- Border security should be increased. A skilled force specially trained in preventing and resolving conflict was necessary to implement preventive measures. Such a force should be trained and equipped with modern and appropriate means of conflict resolution. A bomb squad should also be established to guard against actions by extremist groups.
- In the event that intervention by the Tatmadaw was needed to prevent or stop sectarian violence, those forces should be adequately equipped with weapons for conflict resolution.
- The security forces to prevent the violence must be fully prepared and able to access all areas rapidly. To this end, they should be equipped with modern telecommunications systems, all-weather vehicles, speedboats and other suitable transport.
- The role of the navy needs to be expanded and strengthened. To this end, coastal radar stations and patrol aircraft should be established. Closed-circuit television cameras and man-made barriers are needed for twenty-four-hour surveillance along the border.
- To work closely with the navy, a marine or coastal patrol force should be established and equipped with assault boats in order to ensure effective patrolling of the Rakhine Coast.

- A Special Team comprising a civil-military mix should be established and made responsible for gathering intelligence on extremist organizations and violent groups.
- As a matter of priority, the organization of immigration service personnel (La-Wa-Ka) in Rakhine State should be strengthened.
- The Border Immigration Headquarters (BIHQ or Na-Sa-Ka) personnel in Rakhine State had issued certain administrative orders pertaining to control of the territory. Such control should be continued.
- The authorities should ensure that Rakhine State develops an excellent transportation network.
- Bangladesh has scheduled general elections for December 2013. Spillover effects, such as unrest and infiltration by extremist groups, might affect the border regions in Rakhine State. Accordingly, security and other necessary arrangements should be made well in advance.
- The authorities need to establish systems for conflict resolution, for analysis and implementation of Myanmar's laws and regulations, and preventing illegal immigration.
- The communities on both sides need to be educated on the relevant laws, regulations and policies and on the nature of sanctions for those who break the law. Rakhine State's civil service should be strengthened, in particular, the Office of General Administration and the Department of Religious Affairs.
- The authorities need to ensure that those who break the law are tried and punished swiftly following due process, without discrimination between different groups. All should be equal before the law.
- All who live in Myanmar, including civil servants, are subject to the country's laws, regulations and legal procedures and should follow these rigorously. Those who break the law or act outside the procedures and regulations should be prosecuted according to the law.

The commission also agreed that Rakhine State required large-scale socio-economic development projects. It pointed out, however, that this could only happen if the two groups were able to live side by side without conflict or tension. For the promotion of peaceful coexistence between the two communities, the commission recommended the following measures:[78]

- All groups should be able to speak the Myanmar language and understand Myanmar's traditional culture. Measures to promote such learning needed to be implemented.

- Communication and interaction should be promoted between the Rakhine people and Bengali people.
- Measures need to be taken to instill a sense of loyalty and allegiance to the Union of Myanmar.
- The human rights of all groups must be protected.
- In dealing with illegal immigrants, the government should ensure adherence to the principles of human rights, taking into account international conventions and human rights laws ratified or acceded to by the Republic of the Union of Myanmar.
- The government needs to urgently initiate a process of examining the citizenship status of people in Rakhine State, implementing the provisions of the 1982 Citizenship Law.
- The authorities need to ensure that justice and the rule of law prevail in resolving problems.
- Authorities will need to convene a task force comprising moderate leaders from both sides of the divide to oversee the implementation of the recommended measures.
- The government needs to ban the use of hate language against any religion. In particular, it needs to ban extremist teachings and activities.

In his response to the commission's report, the president asked for tolerance and mutual respect among the members of different faiths and promised that the government would respect and protect the right of all citizens to worship any religion freely. He said,

> I, as the president of the country, will do everything in my power to make sure that all the security apparatus will cooperate and coordinate to effectively perform the law enforcement duty entrusted to them. I have instructed all security forces to perform the duties entrusted to them without any bias and in accordance with the law and the public servant's code of conduct. Anyone who breaks the law and carries out violence will be prosecuted in accordance with the law in a transparent and accountable manner.
>
> We are also undertaking relief activities to help people who lost their homes and other property during the violence. We will also do everything in our power to provide secure temporary shelter for the internally displaced before the rainy season, to remedy malnutrition among children, to help those traumatized by violence, to prevent epidemics, and to create job opportunities for the people of Rakhine State. We will also swiftly undertake economic development programmes in the state.[79]

The president established a Central Committee for Implementation of Stability and Development in Rakhine State (CCISD) on 23 March 2013 to implement the recommendations of the Rakhine Investigation Commission. The government also established sub-committees on the rule of law, security and law enforcement, immigration and review of citizenship, temporary resettlement and reconstruction, social and economic development, and strategic planning on 29 March 2013. The CCISD was headed by Vice-President Dr Sai Mauk Kham and the subcommittees were headed by six ministers. The CCISD announced a Strategy for Stability and Development in Rakhine State in September 2013. The CCISD strategy was based on the "Stability First" approach[80] and had detailed plans for the restoration of law and order, rehabilitation and resettlement, and socio-economic development. From 2014 to 2015 the government was able to stop the cycle of violence and introduced economic development projects such as the electrification of Rakhine State from the national grid, implementing the Kyaukpyu special economic zone and the promotion of the tourism sector. However, it failed to implement the rehabilitation and resettlement plan, especially for Bengalis who had been staying at forty-two camps, because of opposition from ethnic Rakhine people. Also, a pilot project for the verification of the citizenship of Bengalis had little success because the Bengalis demanded to be described as "Rohingya" on their national identity cards. The stalemate continued to the end of Thein Sein's presidency as there was no prospect of a solution acceptable to all sides.

The unexpected communal violence in Rakhine State had the following profound effects on President Thein Sein's reform programme:

- Relations between Buddhists and Muslims deteriorated across the country. There were many incidents of communal violence that were triggered by small events or rumours. In 2013 in towns and cities such as Mandalay, Okkan, Moe Nyo, Letapadan, Gyobingauk, Lashio, Kant Balu and Meikhtila, such violent conflicts occurred. Meikhtila was the worst incident, and the government had to declare a state of emergency. The president delivered a speech to the nation as a consequence. Communal violence and racial hatred were constant threats to the stability of the country for the next two years.
- Radicalization of the Rakhine and Bengali communities after 2012 prevented the government from reaching a long-term solution on the Rakhine crisis as a whole.

Turning Points 181

- Buddhist concerns over Islamic threats put enormous pressure on the government. The government did not know how to handle the monks who had strong views on Muslims. Many conspiracy theories developed to explain the government's inability to control the situation. One rumour suggested that a hard-line faction in the ruling Union Solidarity and Development Party had instigated the violence behind the scenes to undermine the president's reform process. A second theory was that the strife was intended to allow the Tatmadaw to return to power.[81]
- The result was that it became no longer a religious or ethnic issue. It had become politicized, raising human rights and constitutional issues for the government.
- Because of international and domestic political pressure, the president had to disband the Border and Immigration Control Command (Na Sa Ka) and revoke temporary registration cards (white cards) from Bengalis on 11 February 2015.[82] That led to the collapse of the security network that had been developed and increased the radicalization of Bengalis in Rakhine, both of which contributed to the emergence of a new terrorist group, the Arakan Rohingya Salvation Army, or ARSA.[83]
- As the 2015 election loomed, the government became more reluctant to deal with the Rakhine issue or to stop the extremist anti-Muslim agitation of some Buddhist monks. This damaged the president's image, especially internationally, and undermined the constitutional principle of secularism.

Notes

1. *Myanmar Alinn*, 9 August 2011.
2. Ibid.
3. "CPI Director Mr. Jiang Lizhe Interview", *Modern Journal*, 15 June 2014.
4. The company is owned by the family of former warlord and drug kingpin Lo Hsing Han, an ethnic Kokang.
5. Kachin Development Networking Group (KDNG), *Damming the Irrawaddy*, http://burmacampaign.org.uk/media/DammingtheIrr.pdf, p. 19 (accessed 8 February 2018).
6. Kachin Independence Organization (KIO) letter to Communist Party of China, 16 March 2011.
7. Ibid. But CPI and Asia World agreed to pay 80 million yuan to KIO and also agreed to give some sub-contracts to KIO. Interview 045.
8. According to Kachin legend, the Great Spirit of the World, "Nign Gawn Wa

Magam", poured water from gold cups held in both hands. Water from the right hand became Mali Kha, the male river, which is wide, shallow and swift flowing. Water from the left hand become N'Mai Kha, the sister river, which is mysterious, dangerous and has a strong current.

9. Biodiversity and Nature Conservation Association (BANCA), *Environmental Impact Assessment on Hydropower Development of Ayeyarwady River Basin*, October 2009, p. 102.
10. Ibid. p. 80.
11. Ibid. p. 80.
12. Irrawaddy, *Kyaw Hsan's Job at Risk Following Tearful Press Conference*, 16 August 2011.
13. *Weekly Eleven*, 11 September 2011.
14. Interview with Zaw Min, 16 May 2017.
15. Interview 010.
16. *Myanmar Alinn*, 18 September 2011.
17. Interview 027.
18. Interview 036.
19. Later, ministers Aung Min and Soe Thane encouraged this perspective when they tried to reengage with the West.
20. Interview with President Thein Sein, 20 November 2017.
21. See chapter 7 for further discussion on this with more details about the succession issue and Shwe Mann's political manoeuvring.
22. Soe Thane, *Myanmar's Transformation & U Thein Sein: "An Insider's Account"* (Yangon: Tun Foundation Literature Committee, 2017), p. 85.
23. Interview 004.
24. Education Promotion and Implementation Committee, EPIC draft report, 6 February 2014, p. 1.
25. Interview with Tin Naing Thein, 14 March 2018.
26. Interview 047.
27. Interview with Tin Naing Thein, 14 March 2018.
28. NNER letter to Pyithu Hluttaw, 18 June 2013.
29. Interview with Dr Thein Lwin (NNER), 21 March 2018.
30. Ibid.
31. Ibid.
32. Interview with Tin Naing Thein, 14 March 2018.
33. "Interview with Zayar Lwin [Student leaders]", *People Age*, 24 February 2015.
34. Interview with Tin Naing Thein, 14 March 2018.
35. Interview with Dr Thein Lwin, 21 March 2018.
36. NNER statement, 7 March 2014.
37. Interview with Dr Thein Lwin, 21 March 2018.
38. Ibid.

39. *Kyae Mon*, 4 March 2014.
40. Interview with Dr Thein Lwin, 21 March 2018.
41. Ibid.
42. NNER statement, 7 March 2014.
43. Ibid.
44. Interview with Tin Naing Thein, 19 March 2018.
45. Tin Naing Thein still retains EPIC's official letters to the Hluttaw committee about NNER's invitation.
46. Interview with Dr Thein Lwin, 21 March 2018.
47. Ibid.
48. Interview with Tin Naing Thein, 19 March 2018.
49. NNER statement, 27 March 2014.
50. "Interview with Zayar Lwin", *People Age*.
51. Government press statement (2/2015), 20 January 2015.
52. The old student union building was demolished by the ruling military revolutionary council on 7 July 1962 following student protests and after it had become a symbol of the students' struggle against the military.
53. National Day commemorates the anniversary of the first student strike against Yangon University regulations of the British government in 1920.
54. Statement by Action Committee for Democratic Education, 24 January 2017, http://www.burmapartnership.org/updates-national-education-law-student-protest/ (accessed 5 April 2018).
55. At that time the chief minister of Mandalay Region, Ye Myint, had already decided to use force to stop the protest. Aung Min pledged to the president to allow him to negotiate.
56. Interview 047.
57. Interview with Hla Maung Shwe, 18 April 2018.
58. Interview 047.
59. *Democracy Today*, 13 February 2015.
60. As the president instructed me on the evening of 13 February 2015.
61. Interview with Dr Thein Lwin, 21 March 2018.
62. Ibid.
63. Rakhine is the majority ethnic group in Rakhine state. Whilst they make up the majority in other parts of the state, they represent just 2 per cent of the population in Maungdaw district.
64. Muslims in Northern Rakhine call themselves *Rohingya*, but the Myanmar government and people officially call them *Bengali*. Another distinct group are the Kaman Muslims, who are recognized as one of the 135 ethnic groups of Myanmar.
65. Final Report of Inquiry Commission on Sectarian Violence in Rakhine State (English version), 8 July 2013, p. 9.

66. Ninety-two per cent of the population of Maungdaw township are Bengali.
67. The Rakhine Inquiry Commission found that many Bengalis from the Maungdaw area had not heard of the rape and murder of Ma Thida Htwe by Bengalis, but only of the killing of ten Muslims by the Rakhine mob at Taunggoke. Final Report of Inquiry Commission on Sectarian Violence in Rakhine State (English version), 8 July 2013, p. 15.
68. Final Report of Inquiry Commission on Sectarian Violence in Rakhine State (English version), 8 July 2013, p. i.
69. Ibid., p. 12.
70. Speech by President Thein Sein, 16 November 2012.
71. *BiWeekly Eleven*, 5 January 2012.
72. Final Report of Inquiry Commission on Sectarian Violence in Rakhine State (English version), 8 July 2013, p. 19.
73. Ibid., p. 21.
74. Minister for home affairs Lt. Gen. Ko Ko's report to the Hluttaw, 26 October 2012.
75. Speech by President Thein Sein, 16 November 2012.
76. "Myanmar President Promises 'New Ideas' to End Rakhine Violence", *Nikkei*, 4 October 2013.
77. Executive summary of Inquiry Commission on Sectarian Violence in Rakhine State, 8 July 2013, p. 2.
78. Ibid., p. 3.
79. Speech by President Thein Sein, 6 May 2013.
80. Central Committee for Implementation of Stability and Development in Rakhine State (CCISD) report 2014, p. 5.
81. *Irrawaddy*, 29 October 2012.
82. The Pyidaungsu Hluttaw amended the Election Laws on 17 June 2015, removing voting rights for those holding temporary registration cards (white cards). The issue of white cards became a political issue and President Thein Sein decided to revoke them under domestic political pressure. That decision left the majority of Bengalis in the country without any identification papers and they lost any remaining hope of becoming Myanmar citizens.
83. Ye Htut, "A Background to the Security Crisis in Northern Rakhine", *ISEAS Perspective*, no. 2017/79, 23 October 2017.

9

Media Reform

Myanmar Media Landscape (1988–2011)

Under the military regime, the Press Scrutiny and Registration Division of the Ministry of Home Affairs tightly controlled the print media. Though administratively it was under the Home Ministry, the director was a former military intelligence officer who directly reported to military intelligence headquarters, until 2004 when the military intelligence corps was purged after the sacking of Prime Minister General Khin Nyunt. Publishing licences were awarded only to trusted people, government departments and military intelligence units. They, in turn, made a profit by leasing their publishing licences to genuine publishers. All publications were submitted for pre-publication censorship, as the 1962 Printing and Publishers Registration Law prohibited the publication or distribution of any printed material—other than that of a religious nature—without obtaining the prior approval of the government.

The government also controlled all domestic radio and television broadcasting facilities through the Ministry of Information (MOI). The official media remained propaganda organs of the government and did not report opposing views other than to criticize them. There were two private commercial TV operators and six FM radio channels that provided entertainment and sports programming. They were joint ventures with the state-owned Myanmar Radio and Television (MRTV), and they practised self-censorship. Mobile phone penetration was just 2.7 per cent of the population[1] and Internet users numbered just over a hundred thousand, 0.3 per cent of the population in 2010.[2] The government banned websites critical of the regime and blocked access to free email services and social media such as Facebook. Myanmar's freedom of expression was ranked 164 out of 168 countries.[3]

After the military intelligence corps had been abolished, the Press Scrutiny and Registration Division was transferred to the MOI and the director was replaced by another military officer who had been the editor of a military science journal. After 2004, the national convention convened again to draw up the future constitution. On 10 January 2006 the convention began detailed discussions of principles for the fundamental rights and duties of citizens. It adopted fifty principles on 27 October 2006. One of the agreed principles allowed citizens to freely express and publish their convictions and opinions.[4] As a result of the adoption of this principle, Senior General Than Shwe instructed information minister Kyaw Hsan to prepare for a new media landscape under the forthcoming constitution. Contrary to popular belief, Kyaw Hsan was not opposed to media reform. He was the minister who initiated the reform process and he actively worked to gain the confidence of Than Shwe, Maung Aye and Shwe Mann for his initiatives. However, because of the political situation at that time, his initiatives were not continuous and shifted from time to time following the opinions of the three top leaders. Thus, Reporters Without Borders reported that "The information ministry blows hot and cold on both the private press and foreign journalists. New publication titles were granted on several occasions in 2006. And in October, foreign journalists, some of whom had been banned from the country for years, were invited to cover the resumption of the work of the convention drawing up a new constitution."[5]

During that time the Ministry of Foreign Affairs conducted a series of track two dialogues on Myanmar–European Union relations. These were sponsored by the Myanmar Institute for Strategic and International Studies and the Friedrich-Ebert-Stiftung (FES). One was held on 19–20 September 2006. MOI delegates also participated and Kyaw Hsan took this opportunity to seek EU support for the MOI's preparations for future media reform. At the same time, in his capacity as secretary of the National Convention Convening Committee, Kyaw Hsan sought approval to invite foreign journalists—including those blacklisted—to the National Convention press conferences. One of them was Kyaw Zan Thar from the BBC, who was also allowed to cover the Armed Forces Day parade at Naypyitaw. He reported fairly and in a balanced manner on many issues, and Kyaw Hsan was able to prove to the SPDC leaders that openness was no threat to them. Later, he invited other foreign journalists on a case-by-case basis.

The Myanmar-EU track two dialogues continued in 2007 and the EU side became interested in the media reform plan. However, because of sanctions, they could not provide government-to-government cooperation, so FES offered to provide some training for MOI officials. Dr Paul Pasch from FES played an important role in discussions between the MOI and FES. In April 2007 the MOI and FES reached agreement on the following:

1. FES would provide experts to conduct a training needs assessment (TNA) of the three state-owned newspapers and MRTV.
2. FES would arrange for an MOI delegation to undertake a study tour of Singapore and Malaysia. FES would also provide resource persons to brief the MOI team on media laws, public service broadcasting and other countries' experiences in media reform.

In line with the agreement, Hong Kong–based media expert Cyril Pereira conducted a TNA of the three government newspapers in July 2007. Deutsche Welle Akademie radio and TV consultant Bhilaibhan Pukahuta and AIBD (Asia-Pacific Institute for Broadcasting Development) programme manager Mercel Gomez conducted a TNA on MRTV at the same time. From these assessments the MOI came to understand the future training needs for the transformation of the state media.

While Kyaw Hsan began to implement preparations for the reform process there were conflicting opinions among MOI officials. Senior officials like MRTV director general Khin Maung Htay and Newspaper and Periodicals Enterprise (NPE) managing director Soe Win doubted the TNA process and thought a future government under an elected government would continue with the current media policy. When Kyaw Hsan ordered them to translate TNA reports they used all means to delay doing so until 2011. Also, Win Tin[6]—who was general manager of NPE and Kyaw Hsan's right-hand man—strongly opposed preparations for future reform and the granting of visas to blacklisted journalists at the 25 March 2007 MOI policy meeting.

But Kyaw Hsan rejected these naysayers and in April 2007 ordered the Information and Public Relations Department (IPRD) to research the media policies of Western democratic countries. He even explained to the press that Myanmar was undertaking preparations for a democratic transition, including liberalization of the media. At this stage the MOI had to maintain pre-publication censorship, but, step by step, the roles of the ministry and press scrutiny division were being changed.[7]

While cooperation between the MOI, FES and the EU gained momentum, mass protests over fuel prices erupted across the country in September 2007. When the government used the army to crush the demonstrations, the EU protested. Four EU ambassadors in Myanmar urged the cancellation of a Myanmar-EU track two workshop scheduled for October 2007, and one EU official who wanted to attend was denied permission to do so. Retired ambassador Christian Hausewedell and the other members of the workshop decided to continue with it and were subsequently criticized for their participation. During the workshop it was agreed to finds means to support the media reform programme.

Although the EU team tried their best to help the MOI, the MOI did not make things smooth for them. The EU delegation requested that the workshop receive no publicity following their visits to ceasefire areas in Northern Shan State. They wanted to avoid any unnecessary backlash on the track two process. The Ministry of Foreign Affairs and MOI agreed, and Kyaw Hsan decided not to release news to the state media. However, General Thura Shwe Mann had other ideas. He wanted to publicize the delegation to show that the EU was still engaging with the Myanmar government, despite the September crisis.[8] Kyaw Hsan did his best by omitting details in news reports, but many of the EU team became angry when the news came out. The track two workshop programme was terminated.

Nonetheless, FES decided to continue its support for media reform. In this regard, Paul Pasch, the country representative of FES, played a very important part in the Myanmar media reform programme. Without his support at a very difficult time, the MOI may not have been able to implement the necessary preliminary work for future reforms. FES arranged a media study tour for five members of the MOI to Singapore in March 2008.[9] An MOI delegation attended a series of lectures at the Asian Media

Information and Communication Centre (AMIC) on the functions of a press council, as well as on ethical issues, the nature of public service media, community radio and media laws. Resource persons were provided by FES, AMIC and the AIBD. MOI delegates discussed an action plan for media reform with these development partners.

After the study tour, Kyaw Hsan approved the following activities in order to prepare for future reform:

1. Capacity building for English and Myanmar newspapers, if possible attaching a foreign editor to the English newspaper.
2. Conducting audience surveys for state media.
3. Conducting photojournalism training for MOI staff.
4. Capacity building for MRTV production and newsroom staff.
5. Rebranding of state media.
6. Reviewing existing media laws and preparing a new media law in accord with the future constitution.
7. Gradual relaxation of press censorship.
8. Preparation to set up media training institutes.

However, many obstacles stood in the way of implementing these. Kyaw Hsan had to manoeuvre around the responses of the three top leaders, Than Shwe, Maung Aye and Shwe Mann. Press scrutiny issues were highly sensitive, and Kyaw Hsan had to be careful not only of the leaders' opinions but also of attacks from hard-line ministers such as the minister for culture Khin Aung Myint, who was always looking for opportunities to criticize MOI policies and activities. For example, during a political and security meeting on 2 September 2008, minister for culture Khin Aung Myint and minister for industry Aung Thaung criticized the MOI for relaxing censorship rules and pointed out that the local press were writing reports critical of the government more frequently. At that time, Kyaw Hsan was away from Naypyitaw and could not defend his policy.[10] Shwe Mann ordered the MOI to tighten censorship rules again. When he returned, Kyaw Hsan was angered to learn that he had been sniped at by Khin Aung Myint. Fortunately, the preparations for capacity building and reform of the media law did not suffer from this kind of interference. The MOI sent another delegation to the AIBD from 23 to 29 November 2008 and drew up a road map for capacity building for the media sector for up to 2012 (Figure 9.1).

FIGURE 9.1
Short-term Road Map for Media Capacity Building, 2009–12

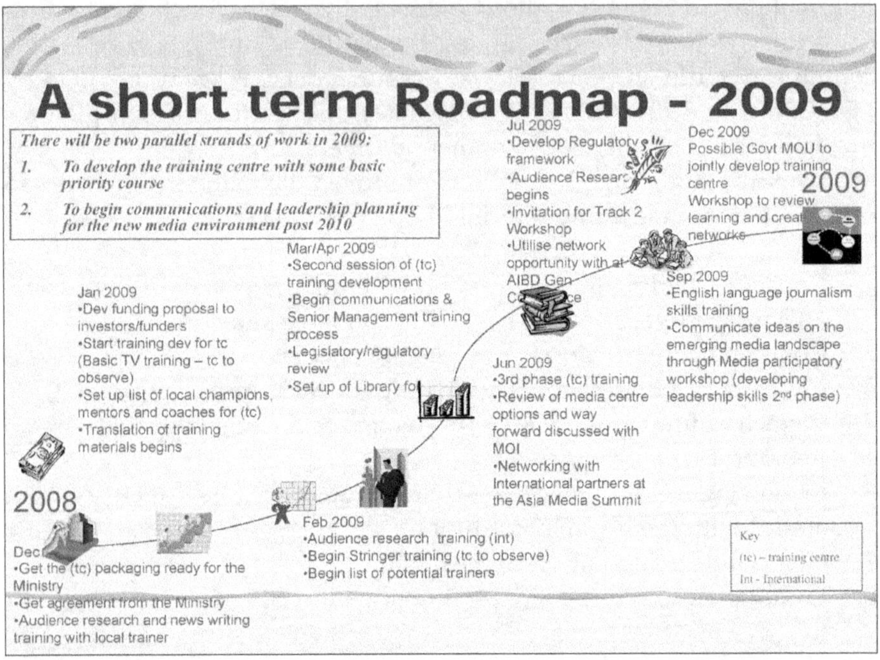

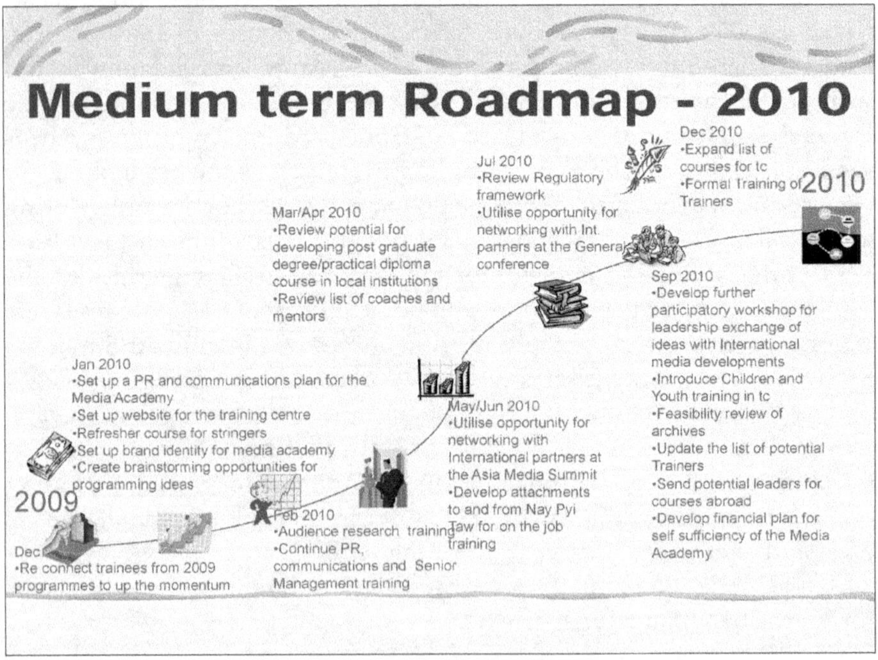

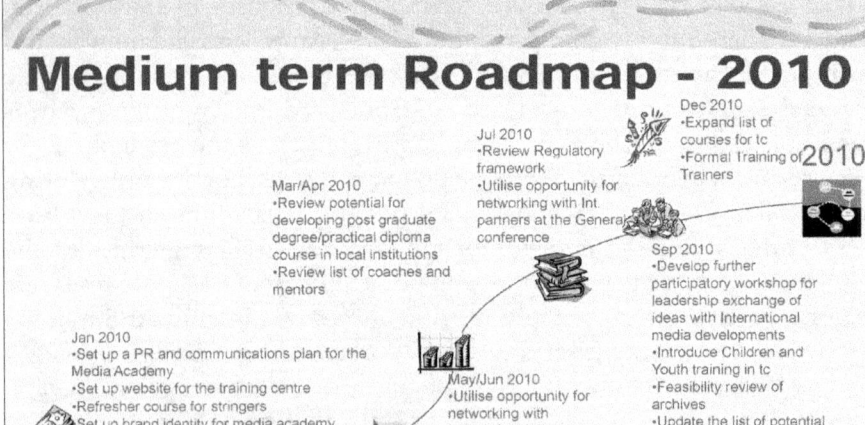

Medium term Roadmap - 2011

Dec 2011
- Review needs of new private media sector and design courses for that group

2011

Jul 2011
- Begin New media training
- Strengthen list of potential mentors and coaches

Sep 2011
- Begin training on a wider range of media related activity such as make up, set design etc

Mar/April 2011
- Plan for Distance learning
- Review publications needs
- Organise Roadshow to engage public through training and comms on new media environment

Jun 2011
- Set up an attachment programme to develop future talent
- Sponsor trainees in the media industry
- Develop partnerships with local/international educational institutions for further education programmes in media to incorporate practical training in education

Jan 2011
- Begin planning training on requirements to meet analogue to digital in 2015
- Continue motivation, team building and Senior management training
- Begin implementation of PR plan for Media Academy

2010

Dec
- Plan New Media Training in tc

Feb 2011
Plan for HD TV training

Long term Roadmap - 2012

Dec 2012
- Review communication needs for going to Digital

2012

Jul 2012
- Begin New media training
- Strengthen list of potential mentors and coaches

Sep 2012
- Introduce Distance learning
- Begin other new forms of internet training

Mar/April 2012
- Introduce courses linking schools and colleges to the media academy
- Organise Roadshow for training and communication on going digital and new media environment

Jun 2012
- Review and update attachment programme to develop talent

Jan 2012
- Review self sustainability of media academy
- Introduce more commercially focused training courses
- Review brand image and marketing techniques

2011

Dec 2011
- Implement New Media Training

Feb 2012
- HD TV training
- Develop training for going to digital

Paul Pasch understood the resistance within the government to the media reform plan. He later recalled, "The framework for media reform had from the very beginning the aim to abolish censorship but in 2007 that could not be pointed out."[11] Also, Cyril Pereira, the Hong Kong–based media consultant who conducted the training needs assessment on state newspapers recalled, "This process had to go step by step. It was baby steps."[12]

After the victory of Barack Obama in the 2008 US presidential election, there were indications that the US Myanmar policy might differ from that of the outgoing Bush administration. On 12 December 2008, a public affairs officer from the US embassy met with MOI officials and discussed press freedom and media development issues. Then, in February and June 2009, there was a second meeting, where the US embassy agreed to support the MOI training programme. Later they sent an English language trainer for MOI staff.

MOI worked with the AIBD for a broadcast law and future broadcast media development. The AIBD had advised to establish independent private broadcasters before 2010, but Kyaw Hsan thought that was too risky because it was difficult to impose censorship on live broadcasts. He proposed instead to set up a joint venture between MRTV and private companies, and submitted the idea to Senior General Than Shwe. Than Shwe agreed, and MRTV set up another pay TV channel and five FM radio stations with local business men who were acceptable to the three tops leaders.[13] These initiatives had two purposes. The first was to create human resources and infrastructure for a future private broadcast sector. The second was to keep the public away from foreign radio programmes by offering more entertainment programmes on FM stations.

The MOI also planned to upgrade the English language TV channel MRTV 3. Than Shwe wanted to transform MRTV 3 along the lines of international media such as CCTV, CNA and RT. But given a lack of funding and with limited resources, MOI had to find a local partner with which to rebrand MRTV 3 as the Myanmar International Channel (MI). Kyaw Hsan clearly understood that MI would not become an international channel, but, by fulfilling Than Shwe's wish, he received the senior general's support for his other media reform initiatives.

When the 2010 election date was announced, the government and the USDP became concerned about media reports; therefore, the MOI had to tighten censorship again, especially of political news and articles.

Because of the sensitivity of the political situation, the MOI had to stop all preparations for media reform. In reality it was hard to control the political reporting during the campaigning and post-election periods because the media had to report about the campaign, about the NLD's decision to boycott the election, election laws, voter registration and the voting process, including news on advance votes and alleged electoral fraud. When Aung San Suu Kyi was released from house arrest following the election, the situation became more difficult for press scrutiny division staff. The MOI had therefore to determine a fresh approach to press censorship in the new political environment.

During the last week of November 2010, Kyaw Hsan held important policy meetings on future media policy. All department heads, along with ministry advisors Takatho Myat Thu, Chit Naing, Ko Ko Hlaing and Win Tin,[14] participated in the discussions. The main point of discussion was how to regulate the media after a new government was formed in 2011. There were two opinions in the MOI. The first favoured gradual relaxation of censorship rules and the adoption of a new press law to replace the then current law from 1962. The second was to keep the existing censorship rules and practise the same control measures.

Takatho Myat Thu, Ko Ko Hlaing, Win Tin and Soe Win (managing director of NPE) were strong advocates of the second opinion. They argued that most of the editors of the private journals were former communists and student activists who participated in the 1988 anti-government protests and therefore it was essential to censor their articles and reports. They also demanded strong disciplinary action against journals that broke censorship rules and regulations. Other heads of departments—including the chief of censorship, Tint Swe—favoured the gradual relaxation of censorship rules.

Kyaw Hsan's main concern was the possibility of a campaign by Aung San Suu Kyi against the new government and consequent media coverage of her activities. However, he also understood that under the new constitution the MOI had to abolish pre-publication censorship.[15] There were strong debates based on the two positions, but finally Kyaw Hsan decided that the MOI should initiate the gradual relaxation of censorship with a strong monitoring system of the contents of the media. If a journal or editor failed to abide by the regulations and rules set by the press scrutiny division, the MOI would take administrative action and, in the worst case, legal action. He also considered forming a semi-governmental institution that would deal with the ethical issues of journalists.

Media Reform and Cabinet Reshuffle

On 30 March 2011, President Thein Sein, in his inaugural address, signalled that media reform would be part of his political reforms by acknowledging the media as the fourth estate of governance. He promised to abolish or amend the media laws that were not suitable for a democracy. The president's policy was different from that of Kyaw Hsan, who nonetheless was reappointed as minister for information and culture under the new government. The minister wished to implement media reform as an administrative reform under the MOI to his own timetable. He thought that if media reform was part of the political reform, the MOI would have to meet benchmarks set by Western countries for political reform. However, he had no choice but to start to implement the president's policy.

In April 2011, Kyaw Hsan held a meeting to review the existing media laws and to draw up an action plan for media reform. He decided that the media reform should meet UNESCO's media development indicators, which are:

1. A system of regulation conducive to freedom of expression, pluralism and diversity of the media.
2. Plurality and diversity of media, a level economic playing field and transparency of ownership.
3. Media as a platform for democratic discourse.
4. Professional capacity building and supporting institutions that underpin freedom of expression, pluralism and diversity.
5. Infrastructural capacity sufficient to support independent and pluralistic media.

The MOI and UNESCO agreed to hold an international media development conference in 2012[16] that would review the Myanmar media landscape and recommend an action plan for the reform process. By applying UNESCO's media development indicators as benchmarks for Myanmar media reform, Kyaw Hsan thought the MOI could avoid pressure from both within and outside of the government. According to his plan, the MOI would complete new draft press laws and abolish censorship in mid-2013.

For media laws, the priority was drafting a new press law and the relaxation of censorship. The Broadcast Law and Public Service Media

Law were secondary priorities and film laws would be dealt with last. MOI officials started to approach international media organizations for tactical support and planned for another meeting on media laws in May. Kyaw Hsan approved a Press Scrutiny Division proposal for relaxation of censorship rules and basic principles for a new Press Law on 1 May. On 2 May, an MOI team invited some editors and sought their opinions on censorship rules and regulations. Kyaw Hsan then presented his plan for abolishing the censorship regime and for media reform to the National Defence and Security Council and the council approved his ideas.[17] According to Kyaw Hsan's plan, liberalization of media would start in May 2011 and the censorship regime would be abolished in October 2012.[18] Finalized new censorship rules were explained to publishers, editors and journalists on 8 June 2011.

According to the new rules and regulations, all publications were divided into two groups. Group one consisted of arts, health, technology, sport, children's literature and other less sensitive subjects. There would only be post publication review by the scrutiny department for this group. Group two consisted of politics, economics, religion and other sensitive subjects. They would remain under pre-publication censorship but with some relaxation of the censorship rules.

While the MOI worked on media reform, other ministers and politicians also implemented their own media reform agendas. Soe Thane and Aung Min, leading figures in Thein Sein's reform programme, directly dealt with local media. The Pyithu Hluttaw (lower house or people's assembly) Sports, Culture and Public Relations Development Committee also conducted a series of hearings with editors and journalists. Journalists, who believed Kyaw Hsan to be a hardliner because of his role as information minister from 2004 to 2011 under the SPDC government, dealt directly with others instead of the MOI and the minister. There were also personal conflicts between Kyaw Hsan and Soe Thane, and also with Aye Myint, chairman of the Hluttaw committee. Kyaw Hsan and Soe Thane disagreed over the speed of media reform. Soe Thane believed in rapid reform, especially the lifting of censorship as soon as possible to improve relation with the West. Kyaw Hsan did not want to lift censorship without a proper press law to replace the existing 1962 law. He saw Soe Thane as a latecomer with no experience in media relations. For Soe Thane, Kyaw Hsan was a hardliner who was failing to implement the president's reform programme.

The disagreement between Kyaw Hsan and Aye Myint arose from their relations in the USDA.[19] Aye Myint was responsible for the Sagaing region USDA organization and Kyaw Hsan was responsible for just one district in Sagaing region. Technically he was under Aye Myint for USDA organizational activities in Sagaing region. Since Kyaw Hsan was close to Than Shwe, he largely ignored Aye Myint and directly reported to Than Shwe about USDA affairs. They also had some disputes over the selection of candidates from Sagaing region in the 2010 election. Now, as a chairman of the Hluttaw committee, Aye Myint met with journalists and displayed sympathy with their antipathy towards the MOI. He even promised to oppose the MOI's new press law even though it was still in the drafting process.[20] During November 2011 rumours began to circulate that Kyaw Hsan would be replaced with someone more acceptable to local media. Kyaw Hsan thought the rumour originated from people close to the Soe Thane–Aung Min camp, especially the leaders of Egress.

Despite the opposition Kyaw Hsan faced, he went ahead with his programme. The MOI held a meeting on 5 December 2011 to review the existing censorship regime. The Press Scrutiny Department presented their experience from July to December and recommended further relaxation. As a result of that review, economics, crime, law and educational publications were moved to group one, thus ending pre-publication censorship of these topics. Now a total of 173 journals and 124 magazines could publish without prior censorship.

The MOI held another workshop on a new press law in January 2012. At that meeting the MOI presented ten chapters of a proposed Press Law to international experts and local media practitioners, and then used the outcome of that workshop to prepare a second draft of the Press Law.[21] In February there arose a difference of opinion between the President's Office and the MOI. The President's Office wanted to form an independent press council by presidential decree in order to handle ethical issues. The MOI agreed to this idea but wanted to form the press council under the ministry as a semi-government organization. On 22 February, Kyaw Hsan met with four trusted media practitioners and selected possible candidates for the press council.[22] He kept to himself the list of nominees because he believed it was not yet the right moment to form the council.

On 19–20 March a conference on media development in Myanmar was organized by the MOI and UNESCO in cooperation with Copenhagen-based International Media Support (IMS) and Canal France International with support from the governments of Sweden, Norway and Denmark. The conference brought together Myanmar and international media practitioners, media organizations, donors and government officials to discuss media development and the action plan for media reform. Kyaw Hsan allowed members of the Myanmar exile media, including Mizzima, Democratic Voice of Burma and *Irrawaddy* magazine, as well as some blacklisted journalists, to attend the conference. He wanted to indicate the changes under way in the government's policy towards press freedom and media reform. This conference was a showcase for his reform agenda and he hoped to prove to the president that he had won support from international and local media.

The objectives of the conference were:[23]

1. To bring together representatives of the national and international media support community, the Myanmar government and civil society organizations.
2. To facilitate the sharing of best practices and lessons learned in media development, looking specifically at areas relevant to the current media context in Myanmar.
3. To strengthen cooperation and create a common understanding of the challenges and needs of media development in Myanmar between international partners, and between international and local media actors.

In his opening speech, Kyaw Hsan said, "This conference is a result of our media reforms taking place since 2008, the year in which the new constitution was adopted through a referendum." He explained that media reform would be implemented in three steps. First, relaxation of censorship and paving the way for local media to practise press freedom with responsibility and accountability. Second, drafting of a new press law that would ensure press freedom in accord with the 2008 constitution. Lastly, the ministry would abolish censorship and allow Myanmar media to practise self-responsibility under a press council. He concluded his speech with his vision for the future: "We sincerely believe that Myanmar's media sector will have more transparency and freedom in the future." At the conference, MOI participants clearly expressed the view that media reform must be evolutionary rather than revolutionary, and that the media should be free but responsible. He reminded journalists of the old axiom, "Who watches the watchmen?"

Although international media organizations hailed the conference as a major step in media reform, local media were still suspicious of the MOI's reform agenda. The President's Office also pressured the MOI to form an interim press council, but Kyaw Hsan continued to resist. He hoped to form the council after the MOI submitted the draft press law to parliament in the forthcoming July session. The censorship system would then be abolished and ethical issues and complaints would be handled by an interim press council. The MOI model for the council was based on the UK Press Complaints Commission. On 25 April 2012, the MOI and IMS jointly held a workshop on print media regulation attended, among others, by journalists and civil society members. The MOI also used the outcomes from this workshop in drafting its new Press Law.

On 15 May 2012, all novels were moved to group one and only political and religious publications remained under the censorship regime, and these with much reduced restrictions. From then on, reporting on Aung San Suu Kyi, political parties, including the NLD, parliamentary debates, and armed conflicts could take place freely. Freedom House reported that "despite rising concerns about self-censorship, media outlets continued to expand their coverage of political news, addressing topics that had in the past been considered off limits and engaging in more scrutiny of the activities of the government and legislature. Yangon-based journalists were able for the first time in 2012 to cover events in some ethnic minority areas, such as the fighting between government forces and minority guerrillas in Kachin State."[24]

When parliament's July session commenced on 4 July, instead of submitting the draft Press Law, the MOI faced another crisis with local media. During that time there was speculation on an imminent cabinet reshuffle, and the press scrutiny department instructed local journals not to report these rumours. But two journals (*The Voice* and *Envoy*) failed to abide by the instruction and published the story. Should the MOI fail to take disciplinary action against them, it would encourage similar action from others during the initial stages of reform. Kyaw Hsan decided to take administrative action instead of applying the 1962 law, which would have resulted in terms of imprisonment. Rather, on 31 July, the publication licences of the two journals were suspended.[25]

This decision faced strong criticism, not only from the press but also from ministers like Soe Thane and Aung Min. The press accused the MOI of turning back the clock on the president's reform agenda,[26] and Soe Thane blamed the MOI for tarnishing the president's image. Young journalists staged a signature campaign for press freedom, and 88 Generation activists joined them.[27] Instead of being applauded for the reform initiatives started in 2008, the MOI became a victim of circumstances.

To stop the criticism, Kyaw Hsan proposed candidates for the interim press council to the president and announced on 9 August 2012 the formation of a twenty-member council led by a former member of the supreme court. The process was rushed through and the MOI failed to seek agreement from most of the nominated council members beforehand. Some council members were surprised and said they had never met the proposed chairman.[28] Journalists, including council members, pointed out that there were only five journalists on the council, as the others were writers, scholars and former civil servants. They also opposed the duties and functions of the council, which were similar to the previous censorship regime.

Subsequently, the Myanmar Journalists Association (MJA) refused to participate in the council unless the MOI added more journalists, replaced some members with questionable ethical behaviour and amended the duties and functions of the council.[29] When he met with MJA representatives on 11 August, Kyaw Hsan said that if the press council could not function as an independent regulatory body he would have to keep the existing censorship regime. His strategy to abolish the censorship regime was to form the interim press council first, abolish censorship and replace the existing Printers and Publishers Registration Law of 1962. He said the new Press Law would be more lenient in its regulation of the media. His favourite catchphrase for this was "Light Touch".

President Thein Sein wished Kyaw Hsan to speed up the media reform process. To demonstrate that his media reform programme was not reversing, he ordered the MOI to abolish the censorship regime as soon as possible. This the MOI announced on 20 August. The abolition of censorship was welcomed by the Myanmar people and the international community, but journalists still believed that as long as Kyaw Hsan was minister the MOI would resist the president's reform programme, and this view was also shared by some ministers. The president felt he had no choice and announced a cabinet reshuffle on 27 August. Kyaw Hsan was transferred to the Ministry of Cooperatives and replaced by former labour minister Aung Kyi.

The Press Law and the Press Council

The first thing Aung Kyi had to do as minister was to restart negotiations with the MJA. Aung Kyi proposed to the president to allow the press council to draft its duties and functions itself, and the president agreed.[30] That decision removed a major obstacle between the MOI and MJA. Aung Kyi then met with MJA chairman Soe Thein (aka Maung Wun Tha) on 2 September and agreed to all of the MJA's demands concerning an interim press council. He also met with other organizations and persons to seek their support for and participation in the council on 8 and 9 September.[31] Later, the MOI and MJA agreed twenty-nine nominees for an interim press council, and even the journal *Eleven*—the most vocal opponent of the interim press council—sent a representative as a council member.[32] The council members held their first meeting on 17 September. There was a heated debate on the chairmanship as well as on the president's decree on the formation of the press council. One outspoken person was Pe Myint.[33] At that time, representatives from the MOI were afraid the deal might collapse and the council would not be formed.[34] Later, senior journalists intervened and the meeting duly elected its chairman, vice chairmen and secretary. The MOI officially announced the formation of the Myanmar Interim Press Council on 4 October.

One of the major concessions from minister Aung Kyi in his negotiations was to stop the MOI drafting process on the Press Law and to allow the MJA to work on a new law *ab initio* (zero draft).[35] Some MOI officials had reservations about this decision.

At that time, the MOI draft law had three parts: (1) Rights, Duties and Ethical Codes for Writers and Journalists; (2) Principles to be observed by publications; and (3) a Committee for the Promotion of Press Freedom and Ethical Standards, i.e., the press council. The MOI conception of the Press Law was based on a combination of the standards setting out the appropriate codes of behaviour for the media necessary to support freedom of expression and a process of how this behaviour would be monitored or held to account in the public interest.[36] They were concerned that if the MJA took over the drafting process, these concepts would be abandoned for merely a law establishing the rights of journalists, with the press council becoming just another journalist union. The new minister's decision was the result of discussions between Aung Kyi, Ye Tint and Myo Myint Maung[37] without proper discussions with department heads. Subsequently, the ministry sent some principles that they wished to be included in the *ad initio* draft to the council on 29 September 2012.

Aung Kyi intended to allow the council to draft a new law on its own in order to start the process. After the council submitted its *ab initio* draft to the ministry, the ministry would hold a workshop and invite all stakeholders to discuss the two draft laws then in existence. Following that workshop, the MOI would submit a final draft press law to the Hluttaw in January or February 2013.[38] He explained this proposed procedure to the council chairman on 29 December 2012.[39] However, the Interim Press Council believed they were the only organization that should draft the new Press Law and neglected the MOI's role in the drafting process.

The Interim Press Council began the drafting process immediately but they did not invite the MOI to their meetings, nor did they inform the ministry of their progress. The MOI sent eight letters to the council requesting information, as well as queries with regard to ethical issues created by some journals. The council did not reply to these requests until February 2013.[40] The council even failed to invite MOI representatives to their workshops on the Press Law, which were held on 25 and 27 January. The MOI only learned about the workshops from subsequent media reports. Based on the outcome of these workshops as reported, the MOI concluded that the future press council would lack the authority to enforce it decisions on publishers, editors and journalists in order to maintain high ethical standards of journalism and respect for the rights of citizens. It also excluded rules, regulations and registration procedures for publishers and printers.

Another point of disagreement between the MOI and the council was over the role of the press council itself. The Interim Press Council wished to name the future council as the News Media Council[41] in order to put broadcast media and new digital media under its jurisdiction. Not only the MOI but also international media organization ARTICLE 19 pointed out that "The [draft council press] Law fails to distinguish between different types of media, treating all print, internet and broadcast media as the same, subjecting them to the same levels and method of regulation through the Media Council. While it is important to stress that the right to freedom of expression and media freedom apply to all media types, international standards require distinction between different types of media when it comes to regulating (i.e. limiting) the conduct of those media. The regulation of broadcast media, i.e. radio and television, should be established separately. ARTICLE 19 does not believe the Media Council is well suited to this function, and that the regulation of broadcasting should be set out in a separate law."[42]

After discussing with department heads and publisher associations, Aung Kyi decided to draft a printing and publishing law as separate from the press law. The MOI took out relevant sections from the previous MOI draft law and prepared a new draft Printing and Publishing Law to submit to the Hluttaw. After cabinet approval and Hluttaw acceptance, the MOI published it on 27 February and invited the public's views on the draft. The Interim Press Council was surprised. It began a campaign against the proposed legislation and accused minister Aung Kyi of breaking his agreement with the council. Council members also met with the Hluttaw Public Relations Committee on 9 March and submitted their complaints on the draft Printing and Publishing Law.[43]

Relations between the MOI and the council reached a new low over the Printing and Publishing Law. Aung Kyi met with the members of the council on 23 March and urged them to cooperate with the ministry over the Press Law. He promised to send the council's objections to the draft Printing and Publishing Law to the Hluttaw bill committee. He also encouraged them to debate with and lobby the Hluttaw, as the draft was still in the drafting process with the Hluttaw bill committee.[44] On the draft law by the Interim Press Council (later renamed the News Media Law), he clearly said that the law should be about the rights of journalists, journalistic ethics, access to information, and complaints procedures; it should not cover the broadcasting and publishing sectors. Nor could he accept the title "Media Law", and he urged the council to title the law the "Press Law".

Ministry officials also met with international media organizations on 3 April and, based on their recommendations, removed or amended some sections that concerned the registration procedures for granting a publishing licence. The ministry also agreed a bill committee recommendation to add a new section to protect freedom of expression.[45] The ministry maintained that it did not intend to regulate publishing houses, but merely wished to establish a technical registration requirement for printers and publishers.

Later, the Pyithu Hluttaw adopted a printing and publishing law on 5 July 2013, which was neither the ministry's original version nor the Interim Press Council version. The Hluttaw added some sections and removed others based on recommendations of the bill committee. The journalists associations however all blamed the MOI for what they saw as deficiencies in the draft, and on 7 July declared they would object to the draft in the Amyotha Hluttaw (upper house or nationalities assembly). They also urged the president to kill the bill. The secretary of the Interim Press Council, Kyaw Min Swe, threatened that all members would resign if the Hluttaw and the president failed to accept their demands.[46] Finally, after much discussion between the two houses of parliament, the Printing and Publishing Enterprise Law was adopted and signed by the president on 14 March 2014. The MOI achieved its goal of a separate publishing law, but the dispute over that law deeply affected relations between the ministry and the journalist associations.

On the press law, the Interim Press Council sent their draft News Media Law to the ministry and an MOI team led by director general Tint Swe met with the council on 22, 23 and 27 April. The MOI presented its comments on the draft law and agreed to meet again to reach some compromises over differences between the ministry and the council with regard to some sections. The MOI team also informed the council that Aung Kyi was willing to submit a draft News Media Law to the Hluttaw that coming June.[47]

On 5 May an MOI team led by director general Ye Tint met again with the council and presented 26 comments on the draft law. On 31 May the council sent back their revised version. The council rejected most of the MOI comments and added new articles. The MOI then sent back 65 comments to the council and proposed another meeting. Instead of negotiating to find a compromise, the council stated that they would only accept 22 comments, rejecting the other 43. The council informed the ministry that they would not negotiate further and that they planned to submit the draft law on their own volition to the Hluttaw.[48] On 3 July the ministry responded that at least 17 major points of the original 43 had to be amended in the draft law, but the council rejected these entirely on 20 July.[49]

To resolve the deadlock between the ministry and the council, the Hluttaw public relations committee held a tripartite meeting between the Hluttaw, the MOI and the Interim Press Council on 24 July. At this meeting however the MOI and the council once again failed to reach agreement, and the MOI informed the council that unless it agreed to the final 17 objections previously submitted the ministry would not be able to submit the draft law to the Hluttaw.[50] Although committee chairman Aye Myint made no comment during the discussion, he later stated that a member of his committee would submit the draft law on behalf of the council.[51] The MOI also stated that if the council proceeded to submit the draft law without agreement over the 17 points, the ministry would argue against the draft in the bill committee of the Pyidaungsu Hluttaw (Union assembly). The council replied that they would never compromise on the 17 points.[52]

The Interim Press Council invited political parties to a meeting on 3 August and asked their cooperation in submitting their draft law to the Hluttaw. However, many parties, including major parties like the NLD and USDP, failed to attend, and some council members became frustrated, accusing politicians of neglecting the public interest.[53] Phone Myint Aung from the Amyotha Hluttaw and Thein Nyunt—a representative of the New National Democracy Party and a Pyithu Hluttaw member—offered to submit the draft on behalf of the council.[54] Later, because of time constraints in the Pyithu Hluttaw, Phone Myint Aung submitted the draft law to the upper house.[55]

Then Shwe Mann took advantage of the tension between Thein Sein's government and the press. He sent his son Toe Naing Mann and members of the Pyithu Hluttaw's Legal Affairs and Special Issues Assessment Commission to meet with the Interim Press Council on 12 July.[56] They talked very little about the News Media Law but talked generally about relations between Thein Sein and Shwe Mann, that is, the power struggle between the executive and legislative branches. After the meeting many council members felt Toe Naing Mann was more ambitious than his father.[57] Shwe Mann also personally met with council members on 13 August and explained Hluttaw legislative procedures to them.[58]

Toe Naing Mann also met with other media organizations, such as the Myanmar Journalist Network and the Myanmar Journalist Union, to discuss the dispute between the MOI and journalists. Whether these meetings were authorized by Shwe Mann cannot be confirmed, but the encounters indicated that Shwe Mann tried to use the dispute for his own political purposes by courting journalists.

The MOI tried hard to mend relations with the journalists. On 12 August, Aung Kyi met with the interim council and presented his media reform programme planned for the next thirty months. His reform was based on a model in which media freedom must be exercised with social responsibility. He invited council member's opinions and urged them to cooperate with him for the success of the programme.[59] The council members however remained cool towards Aung Kyi's proposals. They thought the socially responsible media model was another means to control press freedom and restrict the council's authority. On 13 August, the day after meeting with Aung Kyi, members of the interim council went to Naypyitaw to meet Aung San Suu Kyi to seek her support for their cause.

On 17 August, the ministry and the council met again to attempt to reach a compromise on the disputed 17 points. They agreed on 14. The Interim Press Council proceeded with the legislative process for a draft law and the MOI restrained its objections during Hluttaw debates on the News Media Law. The News Media Law was adopted on 14 March 2014, and twenty-four members of the News Media Council (press council) were officially elected on 21 October 2015.

Since the Interim Press Council was formed on 4 October 2012, the president's media reform programme had been thwarted by disputes between the ministry and the council. The ministry lost the initiative and was forced largely into a reactive posture. With regard to ethical issues in particular, Aung Kyi was reluctant to act so as to avoid any negative impression of the government. Also, the council was eager to prove it independence from the ministry and duly emphasized the promotion of journalist's rights. The council never publicly announced their decisions on complaints by the public or government or the unethical behaviour of journalists.[60] The council went so far as to declare that it was not its responsibility to settle any complaints and that it would not reprimand or take disciplinary action against journalists on ethical issues.[61]

That concept is reflected in the News Media Law (2014) and related by-laws. According to by-law section 40, the council may announce its rulings and opinions but it is not compulsory for it to do so. As a result, from 23 November 2015 to 4 May 2018, the council decided on 188 complaints[62] but there were no public announcements on council rulings or settlements. ARTICLE 19 noted this and pointed out that alternative and less severe sanctions, such as requiring the right of reply by a complainant or a correction, or the publication of the decision of the Media Council, are not provided in the law.[63] The right of reply or right of correction generally means the right to defend oneself against public criticism in the same venue where it was published. In some countries, such as Brazil, it is a legal or even constitutional right.

The lack of transparency in the council's workings led to a lack of trust in the complaint mechanism by the public and government ministries. Consequently, people sought to use other legal means to settle their complaints about ethical issues. They used section 66(d) of the 2013 Telecommunications Act, which provided for a maximum three-year prison term for anyone convicted of defaming any person using a telecommunications network. Since it was enacted, 72 cases have proceeded to court, including 65 since the National League for Democracy government took office.[64]

Because of the dispute between the MOI and the Interim Press Council, the prevailing law governing the media has many shortcomings. Among its deficiencies are a lack of protection for journalists during conflicts, provisions for access to information, a complaints mechanism, or provisions for the protection of the privacy and integrity of citizens. Instead of providing a sound environment for freedom of expression, it created more legal and ethical issues between journalists, government officials and citizens.

Public Service Media (PSM)

When the MOI began to work on media reform, the most difficult question was how to reform the state-owned radio and television stations and newspapers. After discussions with the AIBD and AMIC, minister Kyaw Hsan agreed to transform the state media into public service media, and the MOI studied various models between 2008 and 2010. After President Thein Sein took power and Myanmar's relations with the West improved, the MOI approached international partners for tactical support for the public service media (PSM) project. In July 2012, with support from IMS, Canal France International and the governments of Sweden, Norway and Denmark, an MOI delegation visited Sweden, Norway, Demark and France. A major moment in this study tour was when the Democratic Voice of Burma (DVB)—an exiled media provider and an arch-enemy of the SPDC government—coordinated the visit of the MOI delegation.[65] With the support of Deutsche Welle Akademie, the MOI delegation also visited Germany to study its public service TV and radio stations. After these trips the MOI decided to apply the Scandinavian model for the new public service media law because that model guarantees protection from political interference and commercial pressure, plus financial and editorial independence.

For the transformation of the state media, especially MRTV to a public service model, the ministry selected the German model for organizational structure because of the German experience in transforming state-owned TV and radio stations from East Germany to public service media after reunification. Germany also had two national broadcasters (Deutsche Welle and Deutschland radio) and nine state broadcast stations under state (Lande) governments. Since the MOI planned to allow state and regional public broadcast stations and community radio stations, the German organizational model was quite suitable for Myanmar.

For the governing body of public service media, the ministry selected the French model known as the Conseil Superieur Audiovisuel (CSA). The CSA is an independent public authority composed of seven members nominated by the president and the Speakers of the senate and national assembly for six-year terms.

Based on all these findings, the ministry and DVB jointly held an international conference on public service media on 24 September 2012. At this conference the ministry presented its strategy for public service media. The new minister for information Aung Kyi delivered the opening remarks, saying "We will cooperate with internal and external consultants and organizations such as ARTICLE 19 and other civil society organizations to ensure the legislative framework meets international standards of public broadcasting, which mainly include universality, diversity, independence from both the state and commercial interests, impartiality of programmes, concern for national identity and culture, and financed directly by the public."[66] During the conference, funding for the public service media was considered and four possible sources of revenue were recommended: a television tax, a tobacco and alcohol tax, the government budget, and a hybrid model (from both the government budget and advertising revenue).

On 7 November 2012, Aung Kyi and an MOI team briefed Hluttaw committees on public service media reform. Hluttaw members thought that a television tax would not be practical and that any tobacco or alcohol tax revenue should be used to fund health and education programmes. Nor did they favour providing a hundred per cent funding from the government budget. Therefore, the Hluttaw and MOI agreed on a hybrid model (government budget and advertising revenue), with an appropriate ratio between the two sources. According to the ministry's tentative plans, the two state-owned Myanmar language newspapers would commence a transition to a public service model by August 2013, and the English language newspaper the *New Light of Myanmar* would become a joint-venture with a foreign partner. MRTV would start the transition in December 2014.[67] Aung Kyi hoped all necessary laws would be approved by the end of 2013 or early 2014 and the transformation process would be completed before the 2015 national elections.

After getting initial support from Hluttaw committees, the ministry conducted eleven meetings between the MOI, UNESCO and international partners for a draft PSM law. For funding, the ministry settled on 70 per cent coming from the government budget and the remaining 30 per cent funded by commercial activities such as sponsorships and advertising revenue. That model was based on the Australia Broadcasting Corporation (ABC) and Canada Broadcasting Corporation (CBC) models, which receive between 65 and 80 per cent of operating costs from the government. This model avoided the situation of the South Africa Broadcasting Corporation (AFBC), which derived 83 per cent of revenue from advertising and commercial sponsorship and effectively became another commercial broadcaster.

At the same time, Deutsche Welle Akademie started its training needs assessment of MRTV and provided some initial training. Other media development partners such as BBC Media Action, ABC, Radio Free Asia and the Japan Broadcasting Corporation (NHK) also provided short-term training and some joint productions of radio programmes.

The MOI finalized the draft PSM law in February 2013 and sought opinions from the Attorney General's Office and respective ministries before submitting it for cabinet approval. The cabinet approved the draft on 11 April 2013 and the Public Service Media Law was submitted to the Pyithu Hluttaw on 13 May. The MOI briefed the Hluttaw bill committee on 19 May and issued a public announcement concerning the draft law on 20 May.

As with the Printing and Publishing Law, journalists strongly opposed the Public Service Media Law. The most problematic issue for them was the transformation of state-owned newspapers to public service newspapers. Newly emerged private newspapers that published for the first time since 1964 saw state-owned newspapers as business rivals and urged their privatization or even the total abolition of the state-owned newspapers. However, the ministry believed that only public service newspapers could provide information to remote regions or marginalized groups, as commercial papers were less likely to do this. Toby Mendel, a consultant from the Centre for Law and Democracy, said Myanmar had

had no private newspapers until very recently, and it would be some time before they would be strong enough to genuinely serve the public's right to know. Therefore, the country still needed public newspapers to serve this role.[68]

The Interim Press Council and other journalists' associations joined the protests against the PSM law. Their objections were not about the principles of public service media or the spirit of the law. The private sector editors and journalists just saw the public service media as another form of state media as well as competitors for advertising revenue. They failed to see that though state newspapers then held 80 per cent of the advertising market, under the new law this share would be reduced. They never thoroughly studied the law, which clearly limited the maximum space for advertising to 30 per cent of the public service newspaper columns and 7.5 per cent of public service television's daily programming. The Interim Press Council also saw the proposed public service media council as a rival to their power over journalists. They never understood that the council was to be a supervisory body for the management of public service media, and that it would not regulate or supervise print media or the press.

Most of these objections were based on personal distrust of the ministry and on their own private interests rather than an understanding of international law and the norms of public service media. However, international development partners, especially UNESCO, strongly supported the ministry's approach to public service media reform. On 8 June, the MOI and UNESCO jointly briefed the Interim Press Council and other local media organizations on the Public Service Media Law. The Interim Press Council responded with nine points of objection to the Public Service Media Council, the proposed funding model, and the transformation of the state newspapers to public service newspapers.[69] Later, the Interim Press Council also said that instead of a separate public service media law, its contents should be combined with a future broadcast media law.[70] The council launched their campaign against the PSM draft law by meeting the Hluttaw public relations committee on 9 June, and they sent their official objections to the ministry on 26 June. They then held another press conference on 7 July where they objected to the funding model of 30 per cent coming from advertising and commercial revenues, a public media council with overlapping responsibilities with the press council, and the transformation of the two state-owned Burmese language newspapers to public service newspapers.[71]

The objections from the Interim Press Council were not the only problem the MOI faced over the PSM Law. Since public service media is a very new concept for Myanmar, which has had state-owned media since 1962, some ministers and Hluttaw members could not understand the principle of the editorial independence of public service media. They believed that if the state provided an operational budget, the state must have some control over editorial policy. Aung Kyi tried hard to convince these people, and ordered the MOI to publish many articles for an awareness campaign.

Facing strong objections from the press, the Hluttaw did not take any action on the draft law until January 2014. On 14 January, the bill committee met with an MOI team and discussed the Interim Press Council's objections. More meetings were held on 13, 14 and 17 March, and minister Aung Kyi officially submitted the draft law to the Pyithu Hluttaw on 17 March. The bill committee held a hearing on the draft law on 31 May at which the ministry and the Interim Press Council presented their respective arguments. The bill committee and the ministry met again on 27 July and the Hluttaw Legal Affairs and Special Issues Assessment Commission attended both these meetings.

After these meetings the Hluttaw did not conduct a debate on the draft law. At that time the MOI faced a political dilemma. First, based on the discussions at the Hluttaw committee meetings, the MOI saw indications that some powerful Hluttaw members were eager to use a public-private partnership model for the state newspaper. President Thein Sein saw that that would lead to a media monopoly by big business groups with links to powerful Hluttaw members. However, he could not prevent that happening if the Hluttaw so decided. Secondly, the president and his closest advisors wanted to avoid a dispute with journalists in an election year after suffering prolonged fights over the Printing and Publishing Law and the News Media Law in 2013 and 2014.

After consulting with the President's Office, the MOI decided to withdraw the draft Public Service Media Law on 18 March 2015.[72] With elections scheduled for November 2015 and a subsequent change of government, the process of public service media reform was brought to a complete halt. As of the time of writing (February 2019), the NLD government has not raised this issue. Myanmar still has state media as a mouthpiece of the government, and Myanmar media reform has failed to provide public service media as a platform for democratic discourse in the democratic transition.

End of Media Reform

While struggling to mobilize support for the PSM law, the MOI faced another problem with the President's Office over ethical issues and the proposed legislation. The President's Office was willing to take legal action against journalists who broke the law or committed acts of defamation, but Aung Kyi preferred to take these cases to the Interim Press Council. He wanted to avoid a bad image for the government and media reform over press freedom. The President's Office viewed this reluctance as Aung Kyi's inability to control the private media, even in extreme cases, and therefore a failure to defend the government's reputation. The President's Office also viewed Aung Kyi as too eager to pass the law through the Hluttaw at any cost, including a compromise on state-owned newspapers ownership.[73]

President's Office ministers Soe Thane and Aung Min slowly took control of the process of handling media stakeholders and directly met with journalist associations, including the Interim Press Council. On Saturday 26 July 2014, Aung Min held a secret meeting[74] at the MPC with key members of the Interim Press Council—Secretary Kyaw Min Swe and Zaw Thet Htwe.[75] The focal minister Aung Kyi was clearly uninformed and was not invited to the meeting, although he happened to be in Yangon on that day. Likewise, other Interim Press Council members did not receive invitations to the meeting.[76] On 29 July 2014, the president asked Aung Kyi to resign and two days later I was appointed minister.[77]

With the election looming in 2015, the MOI could undertake no new initiatives for media reform and became merely reactive to circumstances in the media environment. When the MOI withdrew the PSM law on 18 March 2015, Myanmar media reform unceremoniously ended. Although the Hluttaw eventually approved a Broadcast Law, which established an independent broadcast council with regulatory power for broadcast licensing on 28 August 2015,[78] it was too late to implement the law before the November election. A Right to Information Law was also drafted, but the ministry was unable to submit this to the Hluttaw and consequently handed the draft to the new government to work on a second draft.

President Thein Sein made very important decisions for media reform by making it part of his political reform programme. That made media reform one of the top priority reform programmes and won support from international development partners. Thein Sein clearly understood that a liberalized press would be more sympathetic to Aung San Suu Kyi, but he also expected fair and balanced coverage for himself and his government. Except from a very few papers, that never materialized. Even Shwe Mann won more lenient treatment from the press because many saw him as Aung San Suu Kyi's ally. When some irresponsible press personally attacked the president and his family, they made his life miserable. But he never thought of turning back or halting media reform, and he took it as far forward as he could.

With hindsight, the failure to achieve a strong, independent press council and a public service media law badly damaged the media reform process. Myanmar is now a long way from fulfilling the UNESCO media development indicators that would provide a platform for democratic debate among its citizens.

Notes

1. https://www.mmbiztoday.com/articles/mobile-phone-users-tenfold-2010.
2. http://www.internetlivestats.com/internet-users/myanmar/.
3. Reporters Without Borders, world press freedom ranking 2006.
4. It became article 354 of the new constitution.
5. Reporters Without Borders, Burma – Annual Report 2007.
6. No relationship with U Win Tin, NLD CEC member. He is an ex-army officer who regularly wrote policy articles in state-owned newspaper. Later, he retired and served as chief editor of the *Union Daily*, the USDP newspaper under acting chairman Shwe Mann from 1 February 2013 to 30 August 2015.
7. Press conference (2/2007), October 2007.
8. Shwe Mann was chief of staff of the armed forces and the third-highest-ranking officer at that time. He chaired a daily coordinating meeting that decided on day-to-day government political and security matters, except military operations.
9. I was the leader of this delegation, which was composed of officials from the Press Scrutiny Division and state media.
10. I was present at the meeting as an MOI representative but was not allowed to participate in the discussion.
11. *Myanmar Times*, 23 July 2014.

12. Ibid.
13. One of them was Toe Naing Mann, son of Shwe Mann and who owns Cherry FM station.
14. Takatho Myat Thu is an old journalist and regular contributor for state newspapers. Chit Naing is a retired director general of the MOI. Ko Ko Hlaing is a retired lieutenant colonel from the army research department. Win Tin is an ex-army officer who regularly wrote policy articles in state-owned newspapers.
15. Article 354 grants freedom of expression.
16. The conference later became an annual conference co-sponsored by MOI, UNESCO, international media organizations and local media organizations.
17. Pyithu Hluttaw Speaker Shwe Mann was present at this meeting and agreed. But later he never mentioned this to journalists or Press Council members, and he tried to distance himself from the president's media reform programme.
18. Tint Swe, "Press Council and its Origin", Facebook post, 26 July 2018, https://www.facebook.com/tint.swe.56481379/posts/253774018683416 (accessed 2 August 2018). Tint Swe was the former head of the Press Scrutiny Division and was present at that meeting with Kyaw Hsan.
19. Before 2010 it was called the Union Solidarity and Development Association (USDA).
20. *Irrawaddy*, 9 January 2012.
21. Tint Swe, "Current Policy on Drafting Media Law", Ministry of Information 2012.
22. U Ko Ko Hlaing, U Ko Ko (RIT), Dr Tin Tun Oo and U Myat Khine.
23. International Media Support report, "Conference on Media Development in Myanmar", 2012.
24. Freedom House report, 2013.
25. They were allowed to publish again after a two-week ban.
26. *Irrawaddy*, 4 August 2012.
27. Voice of America (Myanmar programme), 4 August 2012.
28. Voice of America (Myanmar programme), 10 August 2012.
29. Myanmar Journalist Association statement, 13 August 2012.
30. Ministry of Information, letter to President's Office, 31 August 2012.
31. Myanmar Writer's Association (MWA), Myanmar Journalist's Network (MJN), Myanmar Journalist's Union (MJU), U Ko Ko (MJA) and Dr Than Htut Aung (Eleven Media Group).
32. Ko Ko Gyi, 88 Generation Students leader, later resigned due to his commitments with other CSOs.
33. Pe Myint was a strong proponent of abolishing Ministry of Information and state-owned newspapers. But after the 2015 election he became minister for information, and he not only kept the state-owned newspapers but he also expanded them.

34. Tint Swe, "Press Council and its Origin".
35. Later, how to define "ab initio, zero draft" became a major dispute between the MOI and MJA.
36. Ye Htut, "New Media Law and Regulations in Myanmar", Conference on Media Development in Myanmar, 19–20 March 2012.
37. Interview with U Tint Swe, 12 July 2018.
38. "U Aung Kyi Interview with BBC", *Myanma Alinn*, 25 October 2012.
39. Minutes by U Myo Myint Maung, general manager of Printing and Publishing Enterprise, MOI.
40. "Record of Minister Aung Kyi's Meeting with Interim Press Council", *Myanma Alinn*, 9, 11 July 2013.
41. Even though the term *News Media Council* was adopted in the new law, today the News Media Council calls itself the *Press Council* in English. The term *News Media Council* is only used in Myanmar Language. http://myanmarpresscouncil.org/index.php (accessed 7 July 2018).
42. ARTICLE 19, "Myanmar: News Media Law, Legal Analysis" (2014).
43. Interim Press Council, Annual Report, 30 September 2013.
44. "Record of Minister Aung Kyi's Meeting", *Myanma Alinn*.
45. *7 day News*, 11 April 2013.
46. Voice of America (Myanmar programme), 10 July 2013. The threat never materialized.
47. Transcription of Director General U Tint Swe's meeting with the Interim Press Council on 23 April 2013, ministry record.
48. "Record of Minister Aung Kyi's Meeting", *Myanma Alinn*.
49. Interim Press Council, "Chronicle of Interim Press Council", 17–25 September 2013.
50. According to the constitution, only a Union ministry or a member of the Hluttaw has the authority to submit a draft law for Hluttaw consideration.
51. Interim Press Council, "Chronicle".
52. *7 day News*, 31 July 2013.
53. Kyaw Min Swe, Facebook post, 4 August 2013, https://www.facebook.com/KyawMS?jazoest=265100119697912112179854912154122711071081027887555097897890507512052107105731175399112120848871696867105521195865100122112451081128773767610497656654106844569888373531201045187116516511811311772103861168374955186767581 (accessed 21 July 2018).
54. *7 Day News*, 13 August 2013.
55. Interview with U Thein Nyunt, 12 June 2018.
56. Interim Press Council, "Chronicle".
57. This information was confirmed by a member of the Interim Press Council on 26 June 2018.
58. Interim Press Council, "Chronicle".

59. Transcription of U Aung Kyi's speech from the meeting. Ministry of Information.
60. From 17 to 30 September 2013, the council received 48 complaints—37 from the public, the remainder from the government and *hluttaw*. Interim Press Council, Annual Report, 30 September 2013.
61. Interim Press Council statement (2/2013), 10 September 2013.
62. Phoe Hlaing, "Origin of News Media Council and its Future", World Press Freedom Day, 3 May 2018.
63. ARTICLE 19, "Myanmar: News Media Law, Legal Analysis" (2014).
64. Thomas Kean, "Myanmar's Telecommunications Law Threatens its Democratisation Process", *ISEAS Perspective*, no. 2017/50, 11 July 2017.
65. The MOI and DVB started their cooperation for capacity building in late 2011.
66. U Aung Kyi's speech at the Forum on Public Service Broadcasting, 24 September 2012.
67. Ministry of Information, "Media Reform Plan", presentation for Hluttaw committees, 7 November 2012.
68. Toby Mendle, Centre for Law and Democracy, letter to U Ye Htut, 27 June 2013.
69. Decisions at 30th meeting of Interim Press Council, 7 June 2013.
70. Interim Press Council, letter to Ministry of Information and decisions at 45th meeting of Interim Press Council, 24 August 2013.
71. Council member U Zaw Thet Htwe's explanation at a press conference, 7 July 2013.
72. For political reasons, the MOI only explained that it needed to redraft the law based on the latest media developments and the future broadcast law.
73. Instead of a public service model, he agreed on a public-private partnership (PPP) model.
74. I was in Washington at the time and had no knowledge of this secret meeting.
75. Su Mon Thazin Aung,"Governing the Transition: Policy Coordination Mechanisms in the Myanmar Core Executive, 2011–2016" (PhD dissertation, University of Hong Kong, 2017), p. 183.
76. Ibid., p. 183.
77. I arrived back from Washington to Naypyitaw on the same day and was surprised by his resignation.
78. The NLD government amended it on 21 June 2018, and as of 26 July 2018 an independent broadcast council cannot be formed.

Epilogue

Senior General Than Shwe

Senior General Than Shwe was the mastermind of Myanmar's transition to democracy. The 2008 constitution was his brainchild. Under the 2008 constitution, the Tatmadaw does not play a leading role in day-to-day executive or legislative matters, but it serves as a gatekeeper for the constitution. This role is ensured by the twenty-five per cent of seats in all *hluttaw* filled by non-elected military officers, ensuring that the constitution cannot be amended without their agreement.

Than Shwe laid down the seven-step road map to democracy and created the political space in which the major players in Myanmar's politics—political parties, the military and ethnic armed organizations—can work together and build trust with each other. Than Shwe always said if all the stakeholders were able to build trust, they could amend the constitution in the future. However, few believed his road map would bring a bloodless democratic transition to Myanmar.

Than Shwe created the Union Solidarity and Development Association (USDA). Later, as the Union Solidarity and Development Party (USDP), it served as a political machine to implement his road map. He also ordered the construction of many infrastructure projects throughout the country, including the future capital, Naypyitaw. Than Shwe, however, paid very little attention to institution building. The only institution he prepared to serve the new political landscape was the Tatmadaw. Even the USDP lacked the concrete foundation of a true political party, being united only by his authority.[1] When Than Shwe left the political scene, the USDP collapsed because of factionalism.

Than Shwe selected loyal and humble Thein Sein to lead the transition. He believed Thein Sein would never overstep his power but would dutifully implement the reform according to the 2008 constitutional framework. But Than Shwe made a mistake in selecting the very ambitious Shwe Mann as deputy chairman of the USDP and Speaker of the Pyithu Hluttaw. He underestimated Shwe Mann's ego and bitterness. If Shwe Mann had been president and Thein Sein Speaker of the Hluttaw, Thein Sein would never have plotted against Shwe Mann.[2] If Than Shwe had asked Shwe Mann to retire with him and Vice Senior General Maung Aye and had appointed Htay Oo (secretary of the USDP) as Speaker, the clash between the executive and the Hluttaw would never have materialized.

Than Shwe made another mistake by allowing Shwe Mann to keep the two powerful posts as USDP deputy chairman and Hluttaw Speaker.[3] When the other two deputy chairmen, Tin Aung Myint Oo and Tin Aye, became vice president and chairman of the Union Election Commission, Shwe Mann was the sole individual to run the USDP, and he misused his power. If Than Shwe had kept Shwe Mann as patron of the USDP in accordance with his original plan, the conflict between Shwe Mann and Thein Sein would have been averted.

When the power struggle between President Thein Sein and Speaker Shwe Mann intensified, other USDP leaders approached Than Shwe and pleaded with him to intervene, but Than Shwe refused to do so.[4] Than Shwe replied that if they refused to listen to his advice, he would lose face.[5] But this may not be the real reason for his refusal to intervene. Than Shwe wanted to punish Thein Sein for bringing Aung San Suu Kyi and the NLD into the Hluttaws. This damaged the USDP's chances for victory in the 2015 election. Later, Than Shwe said Thein Sein was weak, Shwe Mann was a traitor, and Soe Thane and Aung Min acted as CIA agents.[6]

Than Shwe clearly had a vision and strategy for Myanmar's transition to democracy, and for the military's role in future politics. However, he misjudged Shwe Mann and failed to build strong institutions, which led to the USDP's defeat in the 2015 election.

President Thein Sein

The man who implemented the democratic transition under the 2008 constitution was President Thein Sein. Than Shwe's selection of Thein Sein surprised everyone. However, Thein Sein's democratic reforms generated even greater surprise. From his outward appearance, Thein Sein gives the impression of being a desk-bound general staff officer. In reality, from the time he was a second lieutenant to the time he became a lieutenant colonel, he saw the battles against Communist Party of Burma insurgents with the elite Nos. 77 and 99 Light Infantry Divisions. He led the No. 109 Light Infantry that recaptured the strategic Myanmar-China border town of Panghsai (Kyu-Hkok)[7] on 6 January 1987. As commander of the Triangle Regional Command—responsible for the golden triangle area—he commanded operations against drug lord Khun Sa along the Myanmar-Thai border.

Unlike other senior military leaders, Thein Sein was very gentle and a good listener. He patiently taught subordinates and never harshly punished them when they made mistakes. He allowed them to correct themselves. He is remembered by local people for his kindness. As commander of the Triangle Region Command, Thein Sein was known as "less cruel" than other men who had held the same job. Indeed, he was the commander that the people hated the least, according to Khuensai Jaiyen, an editor of an organization that reports news about the Shan ethnic group.[8]

He never built his own clique in the army and thus had no military power base. He never tried to place his own people into important positions. No senior officer felt he belonged to Thein Sein. Even when he became president, he never used his power to try to build his own network within the Hluttaw, the business community, the civil service or civil society. His only network and powerbase was his cabinet ministers, even though some ministers felt that they owed Than Shwe and Shwe Mann more for their careers in the military.

This is in stark contrast with Shwe Mann. After he became chief of staff of the Tatmadaw, he worked hard to promote his own people as division and regional commanders. After the downfall of intelligence chief General Khin Nyunt in 2004, Shwe Mann placed his people in government ministries.[9] When Shwe Mann became Hluttaw Speaker, he recruited retired military officers, civil servants and ambassadors to the Pyithu Hluttaw's Legal Affairs and Special Issues Assessment Commission. He also used his legislative power to win over the business community, civil society and the media.

Thein Sein tried to avoid confrontation and debate. He was reluctant to force his decisions on others. After the political crisis over the impeachment of the Constitutional Tribunal, he avoided a further crisis with the Hluttaw. As an officer who abided by the laws and regulations, Thein Sein was always concerned about being accused of wrongdoing.

He not only wanted to protect his integrity but also his family. Shwe Mann understood Thein Sein's character well and threatened him with impeachment. Even though Amyotha Hluttaw Speaker Khin Aung Myint assured him that the Amyotha Hluttaw would never support an impeachment resolution,[10] Thein Sein always recalled Shwe Mann's and his supporters' threats. Thein Sein admitted that he never enjoyed the presidency, and that 2013 was the worst year of all.[11] He even decided to resign in late 2013 and wrote a letter of resignation, but his close associates persuaded him not to submit it.[12]

Thein Sein's proclivity to follow all rules and regulations became his liability in dealing with Shwe Mann. The constitution forbids the president from taking part in party activities, and Shwe Mann used this prohibition to sever all connections between Thein Sein and the USDP. However, there were means by which the president could have connected with USDP leaders. Since all USDP leaders were members of the Hluttaw and most of them were chairmen of Hluttaw committees, Thein Sein could have invited them for discussions and thus guided them on legislative issues. But Thein Sein thought to do this was contrary to the constitution, and he refused to create these opportunities. He was also concerned that Shwe Mann would accuse him of breaching the constitution and arrange his impeachment. Thus he left all legislative issues to Shwe Mann, and thereby lost his remaining influence over the USDP.[13]

Thein Sein is not an ambitious man. He merely tried to do his best whether he was a platoon leader or division commander or the President of the Republic. Even during military training, he never contested for the top spots. He did his best and happily accepted the results.[14] As president, he avoided populist policies. He never decided a policy for the sake of political popularity. There were many opportunities where he could have used the image of General Aung San, Myanmar's national hero and Aung San Suu Kyi's father, such as on currency notes,[15] or attending the Martyr's Day ceremony.[16] For Thein Sein these were not strategic interests related to his reform programme, so he did not use them for his political advantage. He did not want people to criticize former USDP leader Than Shwe by making decisions contrary to his old leader. Thein Sein was grateful to Than Shwe for allowing him to implement the democratic reform process and for not interfering in his work.[17] As his own personal decision it was correct, but as a consequence, politically, Thein Sein lost opportunities to enhance public support for himself and for the USDP.

His humble, patient and consensus-building leadership style was his strength in building national reconciliation, but it was a weakness in dealing with his cabinet ministers. His reaching out and listening to other peoples' opinions before he made decisions was interpreted by others as indecisiveness. He never forced ministers or chief ministers to implement his policy; he wanted them to cooperate with him on their own volition. Ministers familiar with Than Shwe's style of governing did not fear Thein Sein, although they regarded him as a good leader. They understood that Thein Sein would not ruthlessly punish them for their disobedience. Thein Sein was always reluctant to remove or discipline his cabinet ministers. Sometimes he waited nearly a year to take action against them.[18] When his tenure ended in March 2016, there were draft orders to remove three cabinet ministers for alleged corruption on Thein Sein's desk, but, in consideration for their previous contributions to the country, he allowed them to serve until the end of his tenure.[19]

Corruption was an issue on which Thein Sein failed to take the initiative. Thein Sein was clean and not personally corrupt. Nor were his three daughters involved in business. Thein Sein acknowledged that corruption was a major challenge for his reforms in his first address to cabinet, and he set up an anti-corruption committee led by one of the vice presidents. Later, he worked with the Hluttaw for an anti-corruption law in 2013. People who saw and suffered from widespread corruption, nepotism and cronyism under the military welcomed these initiatives and hoped to see strong action from the president, but he failed to deliver it. There were constraints on Thein Sein's anti-corruption drive. First, corruption was deeply rooted after two decades of military rule. Retired senior military officers and their families—including Than Shwe and Maung Aye, current USDP leaders and their families including Shwe Mann, Tin Aung Myint Oo and Aung Thaung—had been involved in many suspicious business deals in the past, and Thein Sein had to be very careful of a backlash from them. Second, Thein Sein did not want to publicize disciplinary action against corrupt officials. He removed some ministers and senior officials because of their corruption, but he failed to publicize these actions because he wanted to protect their families. He never believed in naming and shaming others. But these people paid the president back for this by attacking him after their forced retirement. Sometimes Shwe Mann recruited them to his camp by appointing them to Hluttaw special commissions and USDP organizational activities. He even allowed two former ministers to contest as USDP candidates in the 2015 general election.

Thein Sein believed the split in the ruling hpa hsa pa la (Anti-Fascist People's Freedom League; AFPFL) party in 1958[20] that led to the military caretaker government (1958–60) provided a valuable lesson for civilian politicians.[21] He tried hard to keep the split with Shwe Mann within the party. When the USDP Central Executive Committee (CEC) removed Shwe Mann as acting party chairman on 12 August 2015, some USDP leaders, including some chief ministers from regions and states, urged Thein Sein also to arrest Shwe Mann and remove him from the Hluttaw Speaker's post or force him to resign voluntarily. Thein Sein turned down their requests.[22] Shwe Mann had anticipated and prepared for possible arrest[23] after 12 August, knowing what he would do were he in Thein Sein's position.

Thein Sein never dreamt of becoming a politician. He had no ambition to become president or commander in chief. It was his destiny to lead the democratic transition. Thein Sein's vision for the presidency was as a means to public service, and he tried his best for the people and the country. Thein Sein was not ruthless like Than Shwe, a smooth operator like Shwe Mann, or a charismatic individual like Aung San Suu Kyi. President Thein Sein is and was too nice to be president amid Myanmar's turbulent politics. This was his strength and also his weakness during Myanmar's transition to democracy.

The Cabinet

The team that implemented the president's reform programme was the Union Government, in particular the cabinet. According to the constitution, the Union Government is composed of the president, vice presidents, Union ministers and the attorney general.

The success of the president's reform programme depended on the unity of the cabinet, but Thein Sein's cabinet was anything but a united one. Some ministers thought they owed their positions to Than Shwe, and some sat on the fence waiting for the day when Shwe Mann became president.

The majority of the cabinet members were former senior military officers who never understood the changing political and media environment. They did not behave like politicians or consider public opinion. Rather, they behaved as if they were under the State Peace and Development Council (SPDC) military government.[24] They were arrogant, not only with civil servants but also with the public. They allowed their children and relatives to be involved in business activities connected with their ministries, despite the president forbidding this. Their families led extravagant lifestyles with big mansions, luxury cars and foreign shopping trips. People knew of this from the newly opened media and Internet. Thein Sein continuously warned about these things, but most of the cabinet members did not heed his admonitions. They knew the president would never take action against them. They respected him, but they did not fear him.

There was no effective coordination between cabinet members. Each minister emphasized his or her ministry's interests and sometimes their own personal interests. They never felt that their ministries were part of the reform strategy.[25] At the end of 2012, the government and development partners adopted a "Framework for Economic and Social Reforms: Policy Priorities for 2012–15 towards the Long-Term Goals of the National Comprehensive Development Plan", or FESR. The FESR was an essential policy tool for the government to implement the country's short-term and long-term development objectives. But very few ministries based their decisions on the FESR in setting their public policy priorities and budget. They only paid lip service to the president's reform programmes. Many felt that the liberalization of government procedures would interfere with their authority, especially when instructions to do so came from President Office ministers. They used all bureaucratic means to delay or divert reforms. Sometimes they sought Shwe Mann and Hluttaw assistance to disrupt changes.

The situation was the same at the regional and state government levels. Thirteen of the fourteen chief ministers were former military officers. They ruled their respective governments like state and regional SPDC chairmen before 2011. They were involved in many controversial businesses, as well as land seizures and government contracts. As regional government policies directly affected people's daily lives, their behaviour damaged the president's image.

In the end, many Union ministries, as well as regional and state governments, failed to implement the president's reform strategy effectively. The cabinet failed to promote the government's image and deliver reform dividends to the grass-roots level. Because of a dysfunctional cabinet, administrative and private sector reforms were stalled if not derailed.

When newly elected President Thein Sein delivered his first policy speech to the cabinet on 31 March 2011, he warned them that the people would judge the performance of the government on their experiences in daily life, and his cabinet failed the test.

Union Solidarity and Development Party (USDP)

Senior General Than Shwe formed the Union Solidarity and Development Association (USDA) as a social organization in 1993. The USDA became the USDP in 2010 in order to contest the 2010 general election. The USDP was to be a political machine to implement Than Shwe's seven-step road map, but it never became a strong and effective institution.[26] When the USDA was transformed into the USDP, all of the CEC members, Central Committee members and regional leaders were selected by USDA leaders who were ministers in the SPDC government. They lacked mandates from the grass roots. When the USDP selected candidates for the 2010 election, many retired military and civil servants became candidates without having participated in any USDA organizational activities or having any knowledge of their respective constituencies. Even Shwe Mann and Tin Aung Myint Oo were involved in USDA affairs only at the regional level as patrons of the regional USDA. They were never involved in the USDA policymaking process, nor did they understand the dynamics of the organization. This created friction among latecomers (Moekya Shwe Ko) of USDP leaders and MPs and local USDP leaders who actually knew and lived with the voters.[27]

After the election, all the top leaders of the USDP became government ministers or Hluttaw members. According to the constitution, government ministers could not be involved in party activities. Hluttaw members were busy with legislative issues, capacity building for the Hluttaw and Hluttaw committee work.[28] Thus the USDP neglected party organizational activities from the Union level to the ward and village levels[29] and was not able to use the party machine to promote the president's reform programme at the grass-roots level. During the USDA days, CEC members (ministers and deputy ministers) tightly controlled their respective regions. This practice was carried over to the USDP, and elected Hluttaw members were controlled by former ministers in the Hluttaw. When Shwe Mann and powerful leaders like Aung Thaung[30] turned against President Thein Sein, the USDP-controlled Hluttaw served the interests of these persons rather than following the party manifesto and policies. If the USDP leadership had been united, the party organization would have been mobilized to support the reform programme both in the Hluttaw and at the grass-roots level.[31] But the absence of intra-party democracy combined with institutional weakness resulted in the party being unable to prevent conflict between the USDP government and the USDP-controlled Hluttaw.

In early 2014, five USDP CEC members who were concerned about the 2015 election wrote a personal letter to Shwe Mann. They said that if Shwe Mann wanted to be president (which he had openly said since 2013), first the USDP would need to win the election. They warned Shwe Mann as follows:

1. The party was becoming the victim of a power struggle between the government and the Hluttaws.
2. Shwe Mann has neglected party organizational work and is paying more attention to legislative matters in order to control the president and government. Party grass-root organizations are in disarray and have lost confidence in the party leadership.
3. Party members are concerned about relations between Shwe Mann and Aung San Suu Kyi. Shwe Mann must conduct his relations with Aung San Suu Kyi in a transparent manner. Party grass-root members cannot accept an alliance with the NLD, as it has always attacked the USDA and Tatmadaw leaders in the past.
4. MPs who are close to Shwe Mann have exhibited strong criticism of the president and of the government. This has gone beyond the need for checks and balances and is hurting the image of both the party and of the government.
5. Shwe Mann must work for unity between the government, the Hluttaws and the Tatmadaw and set aside his personal interests. This would be the only means for a USDP victory in the 2015 election.

Shwe Mann never responded to this letter.[32]

The USDP became a victim of power politics by Shwe Mann. Shwe Mann, instead of building a strong institution, used the USDP as a tool in a tug of war between the Hluttaw and the executive. Because of Shwe Mann, Thein Sein and ministers neglected the party and never tried indirectly to support the USDP, and as a result the party was weakened. This was in stark contrast to how Aung San Suu Kyi and the NLD government

Epilogue

indirectly supported and coordinated with the party at the policy level. Even the military established a distance from the USDP because of Shwe Mann and USDP representatives in the Hluttaws who were openly against Thein Sein on many occasions.

These factors contributed not only to the USDP 2015 general election debacle but also to the failure of Thein Sein's reform agenda.

President Thein Sein had great opportunities to lead the Myanmar transition to democracy between 2011 and 2016. He started reforms beyond every expectation but lost opportunities to deliver what the people anticipated. However, on the positive side, President Thein Sein was able to transform Myanmar into a more transparent and dynamic society, to bring Aung San Suu Kyi and other opposition activists into the political process, to initiate a peace process that led to political dialogue with many ethnic armed organizations, to reintegrate Myanmar into the international community after five decades of isolation, to rectify the exchange rate and encourage foreign investment, and, most importantly, for the first time since independence was regained in 1948, enact a peaceful transfer of power from one elected government to another. That is the positive legacy of President Thein Sein and his democratic reforms.

Notes

1. Interview 010.
2. Interviews 030, 044, 026 and 050.
3. Interview 026.
4. Interviews 004, 007, 026, 044 and 050.
5. Interview 030.
6. Interviews 010 and 020.
7. Chinese-backed CPB insurgents captured Panghsai (Kyu-Hkok) on 20 March 1970. Later, the CPB designated Panghsai and Mong Ko region along the Chinese border as the Northern Bureau.
8. "A Most Unlikely Liberator in Myanmar", *New York Times*, 14 March 2012.
9. In 2010, out of the five director generals in the Ministry of Information, four, including myself, had served under Shwe Mann in the army and were transferred to the MOI on his recommendation.
10. Interview with Khin Aung Myint, 13 November 2016.
11. Interview with Thein Sein, 20 November 2017.
12. Interviews 014 and 033.
13. Interviews 003, 019 and 020.

14. Interview 010.
15. Prior to 1990, all Myanmar currency notes featured General Aung San's portrait, but the military government had this removed from all new notes after Aung San Suu Kyi emerged as the main opposition leader.
16. Martyrs' Day is a national holiday observed on 19 July to commemorate the assassination of General Aung San and seven other leaders of the pre-independence interim government on that date. Successive military leaders, including Ne Win and Than Shwe, did not participate in the ceremony from some time in the 1970s, thus downgrading its visibility and importance.
17. Interview with Thein Sein, 20 November 2017.
18. Interview 010.
19. Interview with Thein Sein, 20 November 2017; Interview 003.
20. Pasapala leaders brought internal party disputes into the government and parliament, resulting in a military caretaker government. That government handed back power to one of the Pasapala factions, that of Nu, after eighteen months.
21. Interview with Thein Sein, 20 November 2017.
22. Interview 020.
23. Remarks by Shwe Mann at a discussion with the Pyinmana Book Club members, 11 May 2018.
24. Interview 017.
25. Interviews 019 and 020.
26. See chapter 3 in this volume on the Union Solidarity and Development Party.
27. Interview 070.
28. Interviews 030, 044 and 050.
29. Aung San Suu Kyi apparently learned a lesson from this and some NLD CEC members did not contest in the 2015 elections.
30. Former minister of industry and Mandalay region USDA leader before 2011.
31. Interview 030.
32. Interview 070. The author personally saw a copy of this letter.

Appendix A

President of the Republic of the Union of Myanmar U Thein Sein addresses the first Pyidaungsu Hluttaw First Regular Session on 30 March 2011

Mr. Speaker and representatives of the Pyidaungsu Hluttaw
Allow me to extend my greetings and best wishes for your physical and spiritual well-being.

I have been elected as the President of the Republic of the Union of Myanmar, accountable to the Pyidaungsu Hluttaw and to the Union Government of Myanmar. Accordingly it is my bounden duty to apprise you of the policies, principles and procedures of the newly formed Union Government.

First and foremost, I myself as well as all representatives have been duly elected by the people and are therefore the people's representatives, and as such it is our duty to honour, abide by and protect the Constitution of the Republic of the Union of Myanmar which was approved and promulgated with the consent of the majority of the people.

Since this is our given duty, I would like to urge you that it is imperative for us to be faithful to, and cherish the democratic State that is to be established in accordance with the Constitution, and that we must pledge to sacrifice our life to protect it.

Esteemed representatives,
You know that our country was once under imperialist rule for many years but that through the united strength and endeavour of all the national races

we regained our independence at great cost of life. Regrettably after we had gained independence, instead of making every effort to reconstruct our nation, armed conflicts broke out among our kinsfolk and a good deal of blood has been shed due to ideological radicalism, factionalism and racism and the people have been adrift in a sea of suffering for nearly five decades.

Whenever the country's situation became chaotic and was on the verge of losing its independence and sovereignty, the Tatmadaw, dedicated to its pledge of duty and loyalty has had to intercede many times to save the country from total collapse. In 1988 also the Tatmadaw had to resolve and remove the lawlessness and disorderliness that erupted to rebuild the nation which had deteriorated in all aspects. It then laid sound and solid foundations as a legacy for us to carry on with the task of reconstructing a peaceful, modern and developed nation.

Hence, we can now walk the path laid down by the Tatmadaw Government and cross the bridge it has built, and in accordance with the mandate granted to us by the people, carry on the task of building a peaceful, stable and developed nation. In order to achieve this task and fulfill our duties, the new government which I head will lay down suitable policies and work programmes consistent with times and conditions.

Lessons from the historical past have proved time and again that the Three Main National Tasks of protecting the Union from disintegration, preventing the breakdown of national solidarity and of perpetuating national sovereignty are categorical imperatives which not only we must act by and live by but are also truths which all future generations are to abide by for all time for as long as the world shall exist. It is also the solemn pledge of the present government to do everything in our power to fulfill these worthy tasks.

However, in order to successfully fulfill these vital tasks there are three forces that need to be strong and they are:

(1) The political forces
(2) The economic forces
(3) The national defence forces

Political force lies in national unity and solidarity. It is vital that national unity prevails in our country which is home to over 100 different ethnic races. If national unity crumbles, then inevitably our nation will collapse.

So, national unity takes priority and we must work to preserve it in the tasks that lie ahead.

Past experience has shown us that lip service and rhetoric are not enough to maintain and preserve national unity nor can it be realized at the negotiation table alone. Our ethnic kinsfolk are isolated from us by geographical factors which therefore require improved communications to overcome natural geographical barriers. Motor and railroads must be built, bridges constructed to improve connectivity to their regions. Moreover, there is an urgent need to enhance educational standards and health care and to build up economic infrastructure to raise the socio-economic life of our ethnic peoples.

The roads, bridges, schools and hospitals and clinics are the means by which the quality of their socio-economic life can be raised. The greater the number of motor and railroads and bridges, the better the communications and travel from place to place. As the saying goes "when people meet more frequently, it nurtures a sense of friendship and intimacy." So when contacts between our peoples increase, relations improve and bonds of kinship become stronger. But, our goal is not only to strengthen and improve material well-being, but also to nurture and foster the Union Spirit which is the genuine spirit of patriotism that underpins national unity.

With regard to national reconciliation, to this day, there are those both at home and abroad, groups of individuals and organizations outside the law, who are unwilling to accept the seven-stage road map and the current Constitution. These individuals and organizations are all Myanmar citizens. They therefore need to reflect and consider the fact that Myanmar is their country and that the people are their people. They also need to look upon our government as their government composed at different levels with their own nationals.

In Chapter 12 of the Constitution there is a provision which states clearly that there is a vested right to amend the Constitution in accordance with prescribed procedures. So it is incumbent on them not to dishonour and belittle their country and their fellow citizens in speech and manner.

Inevitably there will be differences in outlook but where there is possibility of agreement there should be cooperation in the interest of the country. If only people would choose to stand for elections in keeping with democratic practices to earn the right to govern lawfully, it would be blessed in Heaven and on Earth. Our government therefore has kept the door to peace open and extends a welcoming hand to all.

The second force is the economic force which needs to be boosted and strengthened. A weak economy earns no respect and is looked down upon by others. The economy is also the link to politics. When the economy is strong, the basic needs of the people such as food, clothing and shelter will be fulfilled and they are assured of a better quality of life. There will be no cause for any form of instigation from internal or external sources.

Since our country's economy is mainly based on agriculture, successive governments have given priority to developing the agricultural sector. Hence there is not only food sufficiency but also a surplus. To fulfill the food requirements for the projected rise in population new irrigation canals, dams and river water pumping facilities have been built, so there is sound agricultural infrastructure and there is no need for concern regarding food sufficiency. But agriculture alone cannot make the country wealthy. Industrialization is required for the country to become modern, developed and prosperous – a country with many employment opportunities and high per capita income.

Our country has the natural resources to set up an industrialized nation, but we need capital and energy; we need human resources in the form of intellectuals, expert technicians and skilled artisans. We already have basic human resources to some extent so if we intensify our efforts, there is no way we can fail to realize these aims. Our government thus plans to make transition to an industrialized nation while simultaneously accelerating developments in the agricultural sector.

With regard to the National Defence Forces, in order to safeguard our independence and sovereignty, reinforcement and reconstitution should be an ongoing task from generation to generation. If the nation's defence forces are feeble and weak then the country will be at the mercy of other countries. Myanmar as a nation which had existed for many centuries as a Kingdom with its own monarch and palace and royalty ended with the Konbaung dynasty when the country was easily subjugated by British imperialist forces. This was because at the home Myanmar lacked a strong and modern armed force. If we should regard the nation's defence forces as trivial we shall have to experience a modern form of enslavement under the hegemony of others. We should be aware that our country occupies a strategic position both from the geo-political and economic point of view and is therefore vulnerable to manipulation and machination of neo-colonialists.

Hence the need for a strong and well equipped world-class armed force to protect the nation. We must all contribute towards capacity-building of the present Tatmadaw, by transforming it to be a strong, highly skilled, and modernized armed force imbued with true patriotic fervor. It is the duty of every citizen to protect and defend our country. This is the responsibility of all citizens.

The Constitution of the Republic of the Union of Myanmar, which was approved by the majority of the people, has been promulgated and is now in force, and our government therefore will discharge our duties strictly in accordance with the provisions of the Constitution.

Mr. Speaker and representatives,
In the economic sector, requisite infrastructure, laws, rules and procedures were enacted in past years for the establishment of a market-oriented economy. Constitutional reforms including those for privatization have been carried out. Further efforts must be made for the emergence of a distinctly tangible market economy by raising the future socio-economic [capacity] of the State and the people as well as undertaking appropriate policy reforms for implementation in the finance, monetary and revenue sectors.

The economic policy is to pursue and implement a market economy and every effort will be made to achieve success of the economic programmes. The key to economic success is the successful realization of a genuine market economy. In the process, we will ensure that all economic forces at the State and regional level and cooperatives and private enterprises will be included to work in harmony within the framework of the market economy. Furthermore we shall extend every encouragement and assistance to the development of small and medium enterprises (SMEs) that play a key role in a developing nation such as ours.

The market economy that we aim for is for the development of the State and the people and we will therefore open doors, carry out reforms and invite investments as and when necessary. We will also make sure that the fruits and benefits thus generated will be distributed fairly right down to the grass roots level and thereby raise the socio-economic life of the entire peoples. In order to realize this aim of fair and equitable distribution of benefits to raise the quality of life for the people, we shall lay down appropriate policies and enact necessary laws.

In the international arena, there are many interpretations and views regarding the nature of the market economy and its methods and procedures. In some countries a market economy is not subject to any regulations, but in others the government exerts control on the market to a certain extent. In our case we aim for a market economy subject to a certain degree of regulation by the government. Such regulation however is not meant to control the freedom of the market but to prevent monopoly and manipulation by capitalists, the rich and wealthy and the privileged. The market will be subject to a minimum amount of control only in the national interest with no other intervention whatsoever by the government.

In implementing these measures, we shall endeavour to establish a just and equitable market economy designed to reduce the gap between the rich and poor and between urban and rural life. To fulfill the nation's need for more employment opportunities and to increase technical know-how, more efforts will be made to persuade and invite foreign direct investments, set up industrial zones while extending assistance to domestic industries of local entrepreneurs to boost productivity.

The next point is that if we really wish for a modernized and fully developed nation and if we wish our economy to flourish and succeed, we must give priority to developing the industrial sectors. For this reason the Armed Forces Government made utmost efforts to lay the ground work aimed towards an industrialized nation. At present we are equipped to take the first step towards a modern industrialized nation and therefore possess the potential for further industrial development. So in our endeavours for the realization of an industrialized nation, we must utilize the wealth generated by the agricultural sector and together with domestic and foreign investments endeavour to set up a modern industrialized nation.

We are also committed to enhance the socio-economic life of the peasants and workers. We shall take great care to ensure that laws to protect the rights of peasants are updated in accord with changing times and conditions. We shall also take action to develop the agricultural sector, to ensure reasonable prices for agricultural produce and to raise their quality. We shall also try to open up job opportunities for casual labourers who lead a hand-to-mouth existence, stabilize commodity prices, provide job opportunities as well [as] welfare and social security for workers and labourers. We shall also adjust the minimum wage scale to the contemporary cost of living. In addition to making provisions for the rights and security for workers in the country, we shall also ensure that workers employed abroad enjoy their full legitimate rights. In short, since peasants and workers are the nation's majority, our Government with unremitting effort will guarantee that they will reap benefits in proportion to their work and raise the standard of life to one of equity and social security where there need be no anxieties for the future.

Mr. Speaker and representatives,
In building a new modern, developed and democratic nation, we are in need of exceptional and superior human resources of intellectuals and technocrats. The development of the nation's entire human resources including those of new generations who will shoulder the duties of the country's future is essential. We must therefore raise the educational sector to meet international standards while simultaneously undertaking measures for human resource development as a whole.

In the education sector, 24 special development zones have been designated and in all the states and regions there are universities and colleges where students can avail themselves of higher education opportunities in their own states and regions. In basic education also there are many schools in rural areas. Efforts must be made not only to continue the present free education system at the primary school level, but it is also necessary to raise the educational standards in existing universities, colleges, high schools, middle schools and primary schools; to provide adequate teaching aids and other facilities, raise the intellectual capacity of teaching staff and promote the socio-economic life of the people and thereby encourage the rate of registration and attendance in middle and high schools. All this must be done if the education sector is to reach international standards.

To achieve all this we shall work in cooperation with international organizations, including United Nations organizations, international non-governmental organizations and civil society organizations within the country. We shall enact relevant laws to enable the private educational sector to systematically operate and provide educational services. In addition, scholarships will be made available for tertiary education abroad while providing stipends for outstanding students within the country.

With regard to the Health sector priority will be given to upgrade the quality of facilities in the larger hospitals that were set up and expanded within the last two decades while building up the capacity and proficiency of health-care workers. Promoting the standard of rural clinics and dispensaries as well as the skills of health-care employees are also on the agenda of things to be done. In implementing these measures we shall work in cooperation with relevant organizations of the United Nations, other international organizations, international non-governmental organizations and local civil society organizations. We also intend to enact necessary laws for systematic function of private health-care enterprises. The aim of the State, the people and welfare organizations is to build up and expand systematic, efficient and effective basic health care services in cooperation. In our national programmes for the prevention and treatment of the three diseases of HIV/AIDS, tuberculosis and malaria we shall work in closer cooperation with international organizations.

Mr. Speaker and representatives,
Another of our government's priorities is to ensure that our citizens in accordance with the provisions of the Constitution shall be able to enjoy their fundamental rights fully in the future democratic state. We shall provide protection for all citizens to be treated equally before the law and shall therefore build up a strong judiciary pillar. Moral turpitude debases not only the individual but also humiliates and brings dishonour on the State and the people and it is imperative that we, with the help of the people deter such malpractices effectively. Hence to ensure fulfillment of the basic rights or human rights of the people we shall if necessary amend or abrogate existing laws and enact and promulgate new laws. In order to take such measures it would be necessary to study and assess the situation as soon as possible and based on the findings submit them to the Pyidaungsu Hluttaw for the enactment of necessary legislation.

Another task that we must tackle is environmental conservation. In carrying out this task, we must focus equally on all aspects including conservation of trees and forests, reduction of air and water pollution, management and control of industrial waste and conservation of wildlife. We shall lay down a policy that strikes a balance between economic development and the need for environmental conservation. We must also mobilize the people and welfare organizations to participate in environmental conservation activities. At the same time efforts will be made to undertake research into technology for renewable energy resources that are economical and can be used extensively. Top priority will be given to review legislation on environmental conservation and laws will be revised or supplemented or new laws enacted as necessary.

I therefore pledge that we shall give priority to the implementation of domestic policies by conserving the good conditions that we have inherited and build upon them in order to achieve sustainable development; to create a Myanmar society of equity and unity and to guarantee the fundamental rights of her citizens.

To implement the domestic policies that I have just listed the Pyidaungsu Government will submit the following legislative programmes to the Hluttaws:

(1) To amend any point of law not in accord with the provisions of the Constitution
(2) To submit draft bills to fulfill the fundamental rights of citizens in accord with the provisions of the Constitution
(3) To draft a bill authorizing increase in salaries of public service personnel and pensions granted to retired government employees according to time and circumstance
(4) To study the possibility of compiling laws pertaining to the rights of farmers and to review existing laws for amendment in accordance with changing times
(5) To review legislation pertaining to creation of job opportunities and protection of rights of workers for necessary amendments in accordance with changing times
(6) To draft and submit a revised new bill on Public Health Care and Social Welfare in accordance with changing times
(7) To draft for enactment Bills towards raising the standard of education and health
(8) To amend laws of the fourth pillar concerning journalism and other media, that are no longer consistent with changing times, and enact new laws in accord with the provisions of the Constitution.
(9) To enact laws necessary for conservation of the environment and to amend industrial and mining laws to meet the needs for environmental conservation.
(10) To review and revise programmes for sustainable management of natural disasters and risk reduction and rehabilitation.

Mr. Speaker and representatives,
Having presented some important aspects of our domestic policy I shall now proceed to put forward the foreign affairs policy of our country. There have been differences in the political, economic and ideological policies pursued by previous successive governments but in their foreign relations

they have all agreed upon and never deviated from the principles of a non-aligned, active and independent foreign policy and adherence to the Five Principles of Peaceful Co-existence. So in Myanmar's foreign relations no government has ever aligned itself with any power bloc nor submitted to the influence of any Super Power; no government has ever allowed any foreign military force to set foot on Myanmar soil, nor have they ever committed acts of aggression against another nation or intervened in their internal affairs. Myanmar can take pride in the fact that in keeping with its foreign policy tradition it has never posed a threat to international or regional peace and security.

Our government will unswervingly adhere to this honourable foreign policy tradition and establish friendly relations with all countries. Moreover, Myanmar is committed to fulfilling her duties and participating fully as a member of international organizations including the United Nations, the ASEAN, BIMSTEC and other regional organizations and shall henceforth take her place as an esteemed member of the international community. So, to those countries that have been insisting that they wish to see a full-blown system of democracy in Myanmar and socio-economic development for her people, I would like to say, please acknowledge the positive changes and developments that have taken place in Myanmar and desist from their present tactics of exerting pressure, inciting and assisting anti-government groups and intimidating us from an economic vantage. Now is the time to choose the path to cooperation with our new government and I urge and invite these nations therefore to do so now.

Mr. Speaker and representatives,
From this day onwards we have started on our path to democratic reforms in Myanmar. We have taken the first step towards a multi-party democracy with the general elections but still many tasks lie ahead. Just as we need to make efforts for democracy in the State's legislative, executive and judicial sectors that are in accordance with the Constitution we must also work further to establish cooperation and mutual understanding between the Pyidaungsu Government (Union Government) and the Regional/State governments as well as between the Pyidaungsu Hluttaw and the Regional/State hluttaws. There is also the need for confidence building measures among the representatives of the legislative assemblies at different levels. Concerning those who still harbour reservations about the Seven-Stage Road Map and are reluctant to accept the Constitution, we must be

able to demonstrate our genuine good will and sincerity to remove such lingering doubts so that they will participate wholeheartedly and give their cooperation in the interest of the nation. We also need to show and convince those few nations that are still skeptical of our democratization process that we are genuinely committed to the building of a fully democratic nation.

In the process of a transition towards a democracy we need to nurture and develop understanding of democratic principles and practices not only in our representatives but in the people as well. In implementing such measures our government pledges to work in cooperation with political parties within the Hluttaw, with political forces of genuine good will outside the Hluttaw and with all civil societies and organizations. I urge all those who are dedicated to the welfare and interest of the people to work within the framework of the Constitution and not to obstruct the democratic process and rule of law and destroy peace and stability. The Pyidaungsu Government will welcome all efforts made within the bounds of the Constitution for the welfare of the country and the people, but will not hesitate to take appropriate action to prevent any moves made that contravene the provisions of the Constitution.

A democracy can succeed only together with good governance. Hence our government which must carry out assigned tasks during the period of transition to a democracy must give priority to establishing a system of good governance.

Mr. Speaker and representatives,
In Myanmar today the onus of successfully building a system of democracy that balances responsibility and freedom lie on our shoulders. The people have bestowed this task on the representatives of this Hluttaw with full trust and confidence. Likewise, the representatives of this Hluttaw have entrusted the task of the executive branch to me and the Pyidaungsu Government. To successfully carry out these onerous duties successfully we must all work together in full cooperation.

To the political parties in the Hluttaw, I would like to suggest that in carrying out our tasks we may have differing views but that we should find ways to work together in cooperation since we are all agreed that we are working in the interest of the nation. Similarly the Hluttaw members of different political parties in keeping with democratic practices should abide by the decision of the majority and respect the desire of the minority in their legislative functions. This is crucial because it is now time for us to relinquish what has become a dogma in Myanmar political tradition, that the party in power and the opposition are adversaries or antagonists; we should instead consider ourselves as colleagues working hand in hand for the national good.

For a country to have the benefit of development, stability and peace, the government machinery must function authoritatively and effectively in all parts of the country. And just as the government's authority within the country should be unconditional, so also its stature in the international community needs to be one of dignity and integrity. Hence it is essential to overhaul and restore the entire government machinery to working condition in accord with contemporary standards and make it strong and robust.

Mr. Speaker and representatives,
The Government of the Peace and Development Council beginning from 1988 to this period laid down the requisite economic, political and social foundations for the establishment of a future democratic state. We, on our part, bear the responsibility to continue these efforts for a future democracy. We wish therefore to tender our thanks to the people, members of the armed forces and government personnel who toiled to lay strong foundations for peace, rule of law and development necessary for a future democratic state. I also urge the Pyidaungsu Hluttaw to record these achievements for posterity.

In conclusion we solemnly vow to the people who overwhelmingly elected us that we shall value the trust put in us and that we shall unremittingly do our duty by the State and by the people; that we shall endeavour to the best of our ability to build a better state and a better life for the people – a democratic state that will endure, where justice, freedom and equality shall prevail. In making this pledge I wish to appeal to all to join and work with us in unity in the interest and progress of our country.

Speech — March 30, 2011
Translation — Kyi Kyi Hla

Appendix B

President U Thein Sein addresses newly appointed officials of the Executive, Judicial and Legislative Branches of the Union at ceremony to take oath of office at the Pyidaungsu Hluttaw Chambers, Nay Pyi Taw on 31 March 2011

I extend my warmest greetings to members of the Union Government and heads of Union organizations present on this occasion and wish you good health and happiness, and that you will be unremitting in your efforts to serve the nation and the people.

The Pyidaungsu Hluttaw session, which commenced on 31 January 2011, concluded yesterday. The Pyidaungsu Hluttaw has chosen and appointed the organizations and persons who will take charge of the executive, judicial and legislative branches at the Union level and likewise, the respective State and Region Hluttaws have elected and assigned similar tasks to the persons to take charge of these branches in their own regions.

So, those of us who have been elected and vested with due authority as leaders of the State and members of the government by the Hluttaw must now embark on the final step on the Seven-phase Road Map towards the realization of a modern, developed and democratic nation.

In implementing the final step of the Road Map it is essential to comprehend clearly what our perspectives should be and the policies we must follow. We as members of the executive and judiciary are responsible to undertake our assigned tasks for the establishment of a modern, developed democratic nation and as such we must be committed without reservation to accomplishing the final step of the Road Map.

This is why I would like to say that the crux of the points I wish to make and the work programmes envisaged are of vital importance for the future of the nation.

Heads of Union Government, Union ministers and deputy ministers
The most important task of the new administration is to work together to create Good Governance and Clean Government. To achieve these aims, the work of the Union Government and the state and region governments as well must be transparent, accountable and consistent with the Constitution and existing laws. The people's wishes and desires must be respected and there must be assurance of all-inclusiveness. It is also imperative that actions taken by the government be expeditious and effective.

The second task of the government is to promote and propagate democratic practices. Today, our country has a Constitution as a foundation on which to build a modern, developed and democratic nation. The legislative, executive and judicial pillars that emerged from the Constitution have come to life. The people have enjoyed the right to elect Hluttaw representatives of their choice as well as the right to stand for election. All these are sound foundations for realization of an organized/disciplined and flourishing democracy.

To put democracy into practice effectively and conscientiously on the basis of these foundations, it would require that democratic practices be nurtured and pursued in the government, in various government departments and organizations and among the people. To accomplish this, the people on their part must learn to avail themselves of their rights and freedoms in accordance with the law, culture, traditions and moral codes of Myanmar.

Administrative bodies whether in carrying out their administrative tasks or in upholding laws and procedures must take care not to infringe on the fundamental rights of citizens. It is their task to guide and help citizens to enjoy their fundamental rights appropriately without harming the interests of the Union and society.

Moreover, in carrying out their tasks they must take into consideration the perceptions and responses of the people. If the people and administrative bodies alike clearly have a sense of balance between freedom and duty and freedom and discipline and act accordingly, Myanmar society will surely become a fully flourishing democracy.

Heads of the Union Government, Union ministers and deputy ministers
Another important task is to ensure the rule of law. The rule of law is imperative for the building of a modern, developed and democratic nation. It is the duty not only of the judiciary but also of law enforcement bodies to ensure that the rule of law prevails.

Judicial bodies in carrying out their duties have the freedom to make judicial decisions in accord with the provisions of the Constitution; they have the right to handle judicial cases and pass judgment in the presence of the public except in cases under special legislative restriction. Judicial bodies must also ensure that every person is given the right to defence and appeal to which all are legally entitled. Moreover according to the Constitution, the Supreme Court of the Union has been entrusted with power to issue writs, and the first ever constitutional tribunal of the Union in the history of Myanmar has been formed. These organizations are not only to maintain and safeguard the judicial pillar, one of the nation's three main pillars from decline, but also to define constitutional provisions and scrutinize the functions of legislative and administrative bodies and thus determine whether or not they are in conformity with the Constitution.

Law enforcement bodies in performing their duties are also required to do so without fear or favour while they themselves must be exemplars in respect and abidance of the law. If the judicial pillar is upright and honorable and law enforcement bodies abide by the law and act within the law, our nation will be a nation with a disciplined democratic system where the rule of law prevails.

Another important task like the rule of law is to expedite governmental function and ensure its effectiveness. What the government needs to do is to raise the momentum for the materialization of the objects of the Five-year project that is now underway. The SPDC has laid a sound groundwork for national development and building on that we need to continue efforts for further development in the economic, education, health, transport, communications and construction sectors.

However to achieve these goals, we need to avoid negative tendencies such as flouting procedures, ignoring rules and regulations and disregarding extravagance and unnecessary waste. Furthermore since our government is accountable to the people through the offices of the Pyidaungsu Hluttaw we are obliged to consider the wishes and needs of the people. At the same time we also have to respect the role of the media, the fourth estate. We are obliged to keep the people informed about what they should know and also heed positive suggestions made by the media.

Another task to make the government's functions fast as well as more effective is improved consultation and cooperation among various ministries. Today, according to the Constitution, the nation is composed not only of the Union Government but also region and state governments which means that connectivity and cooperation among the governments is of greater importance. Nation-building tasks are so complex and demanding that their implementation is beyond the capacity of an individual or ministry alone nor can they be implemented by the Union Government, or a regional or a state government on its own. So, top-down or multi-lateral cooperation between or among various administrative bodies is a must to expedite the functions of the administrative machinery.

Heads of the Union Government, Union ministers and deputy ministers
At present, neighbouring countries and the international community are watching with great interest the kind of government that has been formed in accordance with the constitution; how it will discharge its duties, and what sort of relations and cooperation will there be between the Union government and Region/State governments?

Similarly, the people are watching the form and essence of the new government; the way it will function and what its future plans are. The people are waiting and watching with hopes for a better future. But Myanmar's democracy is new-born; it still needs to be cared for and nurtured for some length of time to reach maturity. In this process of nurturing, the role of those governmental organs in charge of administration at all levels is crucially important. Government affairs wield a great influence on the daily life of the people. The people judge whether a system is good or bad depending on how it affects their lives.

If the administrative mechanism guarantees security in daily life, if there is socio-economic security; if civil servants treat the people fairly, and if the people are able to lead a peaceful life under protection of the law, they will then have confidence in the Constitution that has shaped the administrative mechanism. And the people will put their trust in the legislative bodies and in the members of these legislative bodies.

Therefore, the first five-year term is the most crucial in building a modern, developed and democratic nation. If within this period of five years we can take the right steps, the future path of the nation will be smooth and steady. To achieve this goal, our government must be a government characterized by **Good Governance** and must of necessity be a **Clean Government**.

In addition, the government must be able in management and efficient in administration and have infinite good will towards the people. And it must safeguard and serve public interests.

The requisite of a Clean Government is the absence of moral turpitude. Bribery and corruption, tarnishes the image of the nation and the people. Therefore, we have to refrain from such misconduct not only personally but also steer away the organizations for which one is responsible from it. It is of absolute importance that we do not misuse the authority vested in us by the State to give preference to one's cronies and friends or to benefit our relatives. Only then, will our government be able to meet the criterion of a Clean Government.

In conclusion I would like to say in great earnestness that our country, as everyone is fully aware, has not yet achieved the status of prosperous nation. Compared to former times the nation made some progress during the tenure of the Tatmadaw government, but there are still many people for whom the basic needs of life have not yet been adequately met; there are still workers and labourers who lead a daily hand-to-mouth existence and the number of unemployed is high. As long as there are such numbers of impoverished people, I feel that we who are going to lead the country at different echelons of government and who are going to enjoy certain rights and privileges as befitting our responsibilities should set an example by not fully availing ourselves of these privileges.

So, the officials at the Union and Region/State levels, Self-Administered Zone or Division chairmen and executives, and the chairman and members of Nay Pyi Taw Council will not be enjoying monthly salaries in full as prescribed according to Ordinances 2, 3, 4 and 5 issued on 10 January 2011 under Article 443 of the Constitution of the Republic of the Union of Myanmar by the SPDC in consideration of the nation's present situation, its financial situation and primarily for the benefit of the people. Instead we shall continue to enjoy the same rates of salaries and benefits, as the officials who served under the SPDC government.

In conclusion, I would like to respond to the proposals put forward by some Hluttaw representatives, that there are plans to raise the rates of salaries of service personnel and pensions of retired government employees depending on the development of the nation and in proportion to governmental funds in circulation, the extent of the inflation rate, consumer price indexes and the GDP when the time is opportune.

Speech — March 31 2011
Translation — Kyi Kyi Hla

List of Interviewees

1. Aung Kyi, former minister for information under President Thein Sein.
2. Aye Maung, former chief attorney general under the SPDC.
3. Aung Min, former minister for the President's Office under President Thein Sein.
4. Aung Toe, former chief justice under the SPDC.
5. Aung Zin, former MP (2011–16), National Democratic Force.
6. Hla Maung Shwe, former member of Myanmar Peace Centre under President Thein Sein.
7. Htay Oo, former minister of agriculture and irrigation under the SPDC; former MP (2011–16); former general secretary of the USDP.
8. Htun Ye, joint secretary of the National Unity Party.
9. Khin Aung Myint, former Speaker of the Amyotha Hluttaw (2011–16); USDP CEC member.
10. Khin Nyunt, former prime minister (2003–4); secretary 1 of the SPDC (1988–2003); chief of Military Intelligence (1983–2004).
11. Thein Sein, former president (2011–16).
12. Nyan Htun, former vice president (2012–16).
13. Shwe Mann, former Speaker of the Pyithu Hluttaw (2011–16); USDP vice chairman (2010–15).
14. Soe Thane, former minister for the President's Office under President Thein Sein.
15. Soe Yin, Dr, former MP (2011–16), USDP.
16. Thein Nyunt, former MP (2011–16); chairman of the New National Democracy Party.
17. Thein Lwin, Dr, Network of National Education Reform.

18. Thein Soe, former chairperson of the Constitutional Tribunal (2011–12).
19. Thein Zaw, former minister for telecommunications under the SPDC; former MP (2011–16); USDP CEC member.
20. Tin Htut, former minister for electric power under the SPDC; former MP (2011–16); USDP CEC member.
21. Tin Naing Thein, former minister for the President's Office under President Thein Sein.
22. Tint Swe, former director of the Press Scrutiny and Registration Department; former permanent secretary of the Ministry of Information.
23. Win Than, former MP (2011–16), USDP.
24. Ye Tun, former MP (2011–16), Shan Nationalities Democratic Party.
25. Zaw Min, former minister for electric power under President Thein Sein.
26. Zaw Myint Pe, former deputy director general of SPDC office; former MP (2011–16), USDP.
27. Forty-four anonymous interviewees have been assigned code numbers.

Index

Note: Page numbers followed by "n" refer to endnotes.

A
Action Committee for Democratic Education (ACDE), 166–71
AFBC. *See* South Africa Broadcasting Corporation (AFBC)
AFPFL. *See* Anti-Fascist People's Freedom League (AFPFL)
AIBD. *See* Asia-Pacific Institute for Broadcasting Development (AIBD)
AMIC. *See* Asian Media Information and Communication Centre (AMIC)
Amyotha Hluttaw
  impeachment process, 139
  and Khin Aung Myint, 132
  ministers of ethnic affairs, 137
  vs. Pyithu Hluttaw, 88, 101, 128–30, 153n39
  Speaker and Deputy Speaker of, 102
  student protests, 170
  and Thein Nyunt, 204
Amyotha Hluttaw Law, 81, 144
ANLD. *See* Arakan National League for Democracy (ANLD)
Anti-Fascist People's Freedom League (AFPFL), 9, 221
anti-government movements, 156
anti-Myitsone movement, 156, 158
Arab Spring, 3, 72

Arakan National League for Democracy (ANLD), 21
Arakan Rohingya Salvation Army (ARSA), 181
ARSA. *See* Arakan Rohingya Salvation Army (ARSA)
ASEAN. *See* Association of Southeast Asian Nations (ASEAN)
Asian Media Information and Communication Centre (AMIC), 188–89
Asia-Pacific Institute for Broadcasting Development (AIBD), 187, 189, 192, 206
Asia World, 155, 157, 181n7
Association of Southeast Asian Nations (ASEAN)
  Myanmar's Chairmanship of (2015), 90
  Myanmar's membership of, 16
Aung Gyi, 33
Aung Kyi, 199–202, 204–5, 207, 208, 210, 211
Aung Min
  EAOs, meetings with, 169
  and Egress, 78–80
  8888 uprising, 77
  NNEP recommendations, 164
  Soe Thane and, 85, 87, 91, 162, 198, 211

student protests, 167, 168, 172
Thein Sein's reform programme, 195
2012 cabinet reshuffle, 84
Aung San, 219, 226n16
Aung San Suu Kyi
  attack on her convoy, 18
  Education Promotion and Implementation Committee, 165–66
  house arrest, 17, 20, 156
  media reporting on, 198
  Myanmar Spring and, 48–55
  Myitsone Dam project, 157, 159
  National League for Democracy, 6, 7, 10, 111
  National Network for Education Reform, 162
  national reconciliation policy, 113
  PR system, 135
  release from house arrest, 67, 196
  restriction on her movements, 1996–2001, 16
  Shwe Mann and, 112, 133, 147, 225, 226n28
  State Law and Order Restoration Council, 13
  Than Shwe and, 14
  Thein Sein and, 3, 212, 217, 225
  Tin Oo and, 21
  2012 by-election, 109
Aung Shwe, 10, 15, 17
Aung Thaung, 28, 39, 44, 141, 189, 220, 223
Aung Thein Lin, 132
Aung Thet Mann, 114, 125
Aung Toe, 19, 21, 22, 25, 30
Aung Tun Thet, 72
Aungzeya, 103
Aung Zin, 112, 131–35, 150n70
Australia Broadcasting Corporation (ABC), 208
Aye Mauk, 148n12
Aye Maung, 26, 30, 132, 137
Aye Myint, 195, 196, 203
Ayer Shwe Wah Company, 125
Ayeyawady division Peace and Development Council, 104
Ayeyawady River Confluence Region Hydropower Project (CRHP), 154

B

BANCA. *See* Biodiversity and Nature Conservation Association (BANCA)
Bengali population control law, 175
Biodiversity and Nature Conservation Association (BANCA), 155, 157
Blair, Tony, 74
Border and Immigration Control Command, 181
Broadcast Law, 194, 211
Burma Socialist Programme Party (BSPP), 8–9, 30, 41, 43, 61, 145

C

cabinet committees, 98n77
Canada Broadcasting Corporation (CBC), 208
CCISD. *See* Central Committee for Implementation of Stability and Development in Rakhine State (CCISD)
CDC. *See* Changjiang Survey, Planning, Design and Research Co.
ceasefire agreement, 155–56, 160, 173
CEC. *See* Central Executive Committee (CEC)
Central Committee for Implementation of Stability and Development in Rakhine State (CCISD), 180

Index   249

Central Executive Committee (CEC), 28, 35, 43, 66
CESR. *See* Comprehensive Education Sector Review (CESR)
Changjiang Survey, Planning, Design and Research Co. (CDC), 155
Chan Nyein, 162, 163, 165
China Power Investment Cooperation (CPI), 155–56
Chinese companies, 155, 157
Chipwi Nge Hydropower Project, 154
Chit Naing, 193, 213n14
Citizenship Law of 1982, 179
civil society organizations (CSOs), 48, 73, 164
"Clean Government", 47, 66, 68–69
Clinton, Hillary, 54
Committee on National Energy Policy, 91
Committee Representing the People's Parliament (CRPP), 16
Communist Party of Burma, 218
Comprehensive Education Sector Review (CESR), 160–62
Conseil Superieur Audiovisuel (CSA), 207
constitution, 101, 102
  article 60, 88
  legitimacy of the 2008 Constitution, 24–26
  military's involvement with, 8–9
  1947 constitution, 6, 8, 30, 31n5
  1974 constitution, 6, 30, 31n5, 61
  provisions of the 2008 Constitution, 57–58
  restrictions on executive power of the president, 26–31
  section 6(f), 99n97
  section 11(a), 26, 137
  section 12(b), 153n141
  section 15, 150n78
  section 17, 150n78
  section 18(a), 137
  section 40, 205
  section 58, 108
  section 59(f), 53, 147
  section 64, 26–29
  section 73(a), 89
  section 86(b), 112
  section 87(c), 30
  section 105, 29–30, 153n132
  section 106, 29
  section 106(c), 153n138
  section 129(b), 112
  section 161, 150n78
  section 200, 57
  section 202, 57–58
  section 203, 58
  section 224, 58
  section 228, 108, 152n131
  section 228(a), 30–31, 103
  section 232(b), 98n96
  section 232(b)(ii), 58
  section 232(i), 58
  section 232(k), 58
  section 233, 58
  section 235(c), 58
  section 262(a)(iv), 137
  section 262(f), 137
  section 320, 135
  section 321, 135
  section 322, 136
  section 324, 137
  section 327, 135
  section 334(a), 138
  section 334(a)(5), 141, 152n108
  section 445, 148n10
Constitutional Tribunal of the Union, 127, 128, 132, 134–44, 137
  functions and duties of, 136
  impeachment of, 143

Constitutional Tribunal Law, 135, 143, 147
CPI. *See* China Power Investment Cooperation (CPI)
CRPP. *See* Committee Representing the People's Parliament (CRPP)
CSA. *See* Conseil Superieur Audiovisuel (CSA)
CSOs. *See* civil society organizations (CSOs)

D

Declaration No. 1/90, SLORC, 7, 10, 12, 14
Declaration No. 5/90, SLORC, 10
Defence Services Academy, 64, 78, 103
Democratic Voice of Burma (DVB), 206, 207
democratization process, 1, 2, 24, 47
"disciplined democracy", 18, 47
DVB. *See* Democratic Voice of Burma (DVB)

E

EAOs. *See* ethnic armed organizations (EAOs)
Economic Affairs Committee, 85, 86
Education Bill, 166
Education Promotion and Implementation Committee (EPIC), 161, 164–66
Education Promotion Committee of the Pyithu Hluttaw, 162
Election Commission, 52, 131
Eleven Media Group, 156
environmental impact assessment, 155
EPIC. *See* Education Promotion and Implementation Committee (EPIC)
EPIC National Conference, 166
ethnic armed organizations (EAOs), 87, 169, 172
Executive Office of the President, 92–95, 159
Executive Presidency, 26

F

FES. *See* Friedrich-Ebert-Stiftung (FES)
FESR. *See* Framework for Economic and Social Reforms (FESR)
Framework for Economic and Social Reforms (FESR), 72
Freedom House, 198
Friedrich-Ebert-Stiftung (FES), 186–88
Friends for Democracy Group, 132, 149n38

G

Gambari, Ibrahim, 51
Gandhi Hall meeting, 7
Gomez, Mercel, 187
Government Office, 92–95

H

Hausewedell, Christian, 188
Hla Htay Win, 105
Hla Htun, 126, 170
Hla Maung Shwe, 79
Hla Tun, 84, 94, 99n115
Hluttaw bill committee, 202
Hluttaw committees, 10, 137–39, 142, 144, 196, 208
Hluttaw Education Committee, 165, 166
Hluttaw Laws, 141
Hluttaw Legal Affairs and Special Issues Assessment Committee, 210
Hluttaw Public Accounts Committee, 81

Hluttaw Public Relations Committee, 202
Hluttaw Rights Committee, 128
Htay Oo, 42–43, 66, 79, 217
Hu Jintao, 156

I
impeachment, 98n79, 127, 138–43, 219
Information and Public Relations Department (IPRD), 188
Interim Press Council, 201–6, 209–10
International Crisis Group, 1
international media organizations, 198
   ARTICLE 19, 201–2, 205, 207
international non-governmental organizations, 73
IPRD. *See* Information and Public Relations Department (IPRD)
Ismail, Razali, 17, 19

J
Japanese Kansai Electric Power Company (KEPO), 155

K
"Kabar Makyay", 107, 120n30
Kachin community, 155
Kachin Consultative Assembly, 155
Kachin Independence Organization (KIO), 155–56
Khin Aung Myint, 103, 140, 141, 219
   clash with Pyithu Hluttaw, 127–29, 139
   joint bill committee, 138
   MOI policies and activities, 189
   National Convention Convening Committee, 19, 27
   Shwe Mann and, 52, 85, 113, 118, 130, 142, 146
Khine Myae, 164

Khin Htwe Kywe, 132
Khin Maung Htay, 187
Khin Maung Phyu, 33
Khin Maung Swe, 49, 50
Khin Nyunt
   with Aung San Suu Kyi, 13–14, 19
   Operations Department, 93
   publishing licences, 185
   State Law and Order Restoration Council, 6, 18, 64
Khin San Ye, 161, 165
Khin Shwe, 114
Khin Waing Kyi, 129
Khuensai Jaiyen, 218
KIO. *See* Kachin Independence Organization (KIO)
Ko Ko, 105, 167, 168
Ko Ko Hlaing, 67, 193
Ko Ko Kyaw, 94, 99n115
"Ko Nyi". *See* Toe Naing Man
kyant-kai-yay (solidarity), 33–34
Kyaw Hsan
   and Aye Myint, disagreement between, 196
   foreign journalists, 187
   Information and Public Relation Department, 188
   interim press council, 198–99
   media reform, 186, 189, 192, 197
   MOI and MOEP, coordination meeting between, 156
   Myanmar media reform, 194
   Myitsone Dam project, 158
   National Convention Convening Committee, 19
   policy meetings on future media policy, 193
   Press Scrutiny Division, 195
   SPDC development projects, 157
   timetable for National Convention, lack of, 21

transforming state media into public service media, 206
Union Solidarity and Development Association, 66, 67
Kyaw Min Swe, 203, 211
Kyaw Soe, 33
Kyaw Win, 19, 20
Kyaw Yin Hlaing, 79
Kyaw Zan, 187
Kyi Maung, 10, 14

L
law no. 5/96, SLORC, 25
Lee Kuan Yew, 18, 114
Legal Affairs and Special Issues Assessment Commission, 114

M
Mali Kha river, 154, 156
Martyrs' Day, 226n16
Maung Aye, 51, 61, 64, 186
 press scrutiny, 189
 Than Shwe and, 20, 81, 105, 106, 109
Maung Toe, 148n12
MEC. See Myanmar Economic Cooperation (MEC)
Media Council, 205
media reform
 and cabinet reshuffle, 194–99
 end of, 211–12
 Myanmar media landscape (1988–2011), 185–93
 press law and the press council, 200–206
 public service media, 206–11
Mendel, Toby, 208
MIC. See Myanmar Investment Commission (MIC)
Min Aung Hlaing, 105
ministers in charge, 39, 40

Ministry of Education (MOE), 162, 163, 165, 166, 170, 172
Ministry of Electric Power (MOEP), 155–57
Ministry of Energy, 91, 164
Ministry of Ethnic Affairs, 59
Ministry of Foreign Affairs, 186
Ministry of Home Affairs, 136–37, 172
Ministry of Information (MOI)
 abolition of censorship, 199
 action plan for media reform, 189
 anti-Myitsone movement, 156–57
 censorship, 193, 195
 and Interim Press Council, 203, 206, 210
 media reform, 194, 197–98, 211
 and MJA, 200
 new press law, 196
 Press Law drafting process, 201
 Press Scrutiny and Registration Division, 186
 PSM Law, drafting of, 208
Min Thwe Thit, 171
MJA. See Myanmar Journalists Association (MJA)
MOE. See Ministry of Education (MOE)
MOEP. See Ministry of Electric Power (MOEP)
MOI. See Ministry of Information (MOI)
Mya Aye, 162
MyanGonMyint, 38, 39
Myanmar Economic Cooperation (MEC), 80
Myanmar Egress, 78, 79
Myanmar–European Union relations, 186
Myanmar Institute for Strategic and International Studies, 186

Myanmar Interim Press Council, 200
Myanmar Investment Commission (MIC), 86
Myanmar Journalists Association (MJA), 199, 200
Myanmar Parliamentary Union, 146
Myanmar Peace Centre, 91, 169
Myanmar Spring, 1, 46–56, 72, 75, 123
  reform agenda, 47–48
Mya Thein, 132, 135, 143
Myat Nyana Soe, 59
Myat Thu, 193
Myint Aung, 105
Myitsone hydropower project, 154–60
Myo Myint Maung, 200
Myo Nyunt, 9, 14
Myo Thein Gyi, 164–65

N
Nanda Kyaw Swar, 112, 138
National Comprehensive Development Plan, 72
National Convention, 5–8, 25, 34
  confrontation over, 16–19
  departure of NLD, 13–15
  disagreements with NLD, 11–13
  preparation for, 9–11
  reconvening of, 19–22
  working committee, 30
National Convention Convening Committee (NCCC), 9–13, 15, 19, 54, 187
National Convention Participants
  in 1993, 12
  in 2004, 21
National Convention Sessions
  in 1993–1996, 15
  in 2004–2007, 131
National Day celebrations, 166, 183n53

National Defence and Security Council, 88, 93, 108, 171, 195
National Democratic Force (NDF), 131
National Education Bill, 169
National Education Law, 160–72
National Education Policy, 160, 161, 165
National League for Democracy (NLD)
  boycott of 2010 election, 50
  disagreements with the SLORC, 11–13
  manifesto for the 1990 election, 67
  media reform, 210
  1990 election, 130
  National Convention, 13–15, 19–20
  National Network for Education Reform (NNER), 161
  Shwegondine Declaration of 29 April 2009, 48
National-level Practical Education Reform Conference, 164
National Network for Education Reform (NNER), 161–66, 171, 172
National People's Congress (NPC), 107
National Plan for Rural Development and Poverty Reduction, 73
National thirty-year electrification strategic plan, 154
National Unity Party (NUP), 43, 130
National Workshop on Rural Development and Poverty Alleviation, 73
Nationwide Ceasefire Agreement, 160
Nay Win Maung, 78–80
NCCC. *See* National Convention Convening Committee (NCCC)
NCC Working Committee, 12–13, 15

NDF. *See* National Democratic Force (NDF)
NDF Central Executive Committee, 131
Ne Win, 8, 9, 33, 226n16
New National Democracy Party, 204
News Media Council, 201
News Media Law, 204, 205
Newspaper and Periodicals Enterprise (NPE), 187
Nign Gawn Wa Magam, 181–82n8
99th Light Infantry Division, 104
NLD. *See* National League for Democracy (NLD)
NLD Central Executive Committee, 7, 161
N'mai Kha river, 154, 156
NNER. *See* National Network for Education Reform (NNER)
No. 3 Mobile Operation Command in Kachin State, 104
No. 11 Light Infantry Division, 104
No. 66 Light Infantry Division, 104
No. 109 Light Infantry Regiment, 104
NPC. *See* National People's Congress (NPC)
NPE. *See* Newspaper and Periodicals Enterprise (NPE)
Nu, 8, 127
NUP. *See* National Unity Party (NUP)
Nyan Htun, 85
Nyan Naing Win, 72
Nyan Tun, 77, 89, 91
Nyan Win, 49, 50

O
Obama, Barack, 29, 87, 192

P
Pasch, Paul, 187, 192
Pe Myint, 213n33

Pereira, Cyril, 192
Phone Myint Aung, 204
Political Parties' Registration Law, 49, 50
Practical Education Reform Conference, 161
President's Office, ministers in, 83–88
press council, 200–206
press law, 200–206
Press Scrutiny and Registration Division, 185, 186, 196
Printers and Publishers Registration Law of 1962, 182, 199
Printing and Publishing Enterprise Law, 203
Printing and Publishing Law, 202
proportional representation (PR) system, 130–35
PSM. *See* public service media (PSM)
PSO. *See* Personal staff officer (PSO)
public service media (PSM), 206–11
public service media law, 194–95, 211, 212
Public Services Performance Appraisal Task Force, 92
publishing licences, 185
Pyidaungsu Hluttaw (Union Assembly)
 amendment of the Pyidaungsu Hluttaw Law (2010), 146–47
 constitutional amendments and Pyithu Hluttaw, debates on, 112
 Constitutional Tribunal, 136
 and Khin Aung Myint, 138, 141
 Legal Affairs and Special Issues Assessment Commission, 135
 National Education Law, 167, 184n82
 and Shwe Mann, 108, 111, 124, 143
 structure and role, 101–3

Pyidaungsu Hluttaw Law, 146–47, 153n143
Pyidaungsu Hluttaw Legal Affairs and Special Issues Assessment Commission, 135, 151n92, 151n97, 152n109
Pyidaungsu Myanmar Naing-Ngan Kyant-kai-yay Athin, 33
Pyithu Hluttaw (lower house or people's assembly)
    amendment of Pyithu Hlluttaw Law (2010), 144–45
    vs. Amyotha Hluttaw, 88, 101, 128–30, 140, 146
    candidates for, 115
    committees, 85
    Constitutional Tribunal, impeachment, 112
    Declaration No. 1/90, 7
    Education Promotion Committee, 162
    electoral system for, 133
    electoral term and, 102
    Legal Affairs and Special Issues Assessment Commission, 204, 218
    National Education Law, 170
    printing and publishing law, 202
    Public Service Media Law, 208
    and Pyidaungsu Hluttaw, 29
    and Shwe Mann, 27, 68, 81, 84, 103, 114, 125
    and Than Shwe, 16, 105, 106
    and Thein Sein, 28
    Union Solidarity and Development Party (USDP), 114
Pyithu Hluttaw Education Committee, 165
Pyithu Hluttaw Law, 81, 144
Pyithu Hluttaw Representatives Group, 10

R

Rakhine Buddhist community, 175
Rakhine Commission of Inquiry, 174
Rakhine crisis, 173–81
Rakhine Inquiry Commission, 175, 177, 184n67
Rakhine Investigation Commission, 180
Rakhine Nationalities Development Party, 137
referendum commission, 25
Revolutionary Council, 41
Richardson, Bill, 13
Right to Information Law, 211
road map for capacity building, 189–91
"Rohingya", 180, 183n64
Rule of Law and Stability Committee, 138

S

Saffron Revolution, 51, 105
Sai Mauk Kham, 89–91, 99n98, 108, 175, 180
San Lwin, 33
Saw Htun, 36
Saw Mara Aung, 16
Saw Maung, 5, 7, 9, 61, 63
seven-step road map for democratization, 18, 21, 43, 66
Shan ethnic group, 218
Shan National League for Democracy (SNLD), 21
Shwegondine Declaration of 29 April 2009, 22, 48, 49
Shwe Mann, 123
    amendment of Pyidaungsu Hluttaw Law (2010), 144–47
    amendment of National Education Law, 167, 170
    Amyotha Hluttaw *vs.* Pyithu Hluttaw, 128–30

and Aung San Suu Kyi, 54
Constitutional Tribunal, 135–44
Hluttaw committees, 54
power struggle with Thein Sein, 109, 117–18, 172, 204
president's salary, 126–28
press scrutiny, 189
proportional representation system, 130–35
and Tin Aung Myint Oo, 223
2012–13 budget, 81, 123–26
USDP CEC members, letter to, 224
Sithu Aung Myint, 112, 133
SLORC. *See* State Law and Order Restoration Council (SLORC)
SNDP. *See* Shan Nationalities Democratic party (SNDP)
SNLD. *See* Shan National League for Democracy (SNLD)
SOBs. *See* Special Operation Bureaus (SOBs)
Soe Maung, 83, 84
Soe Thane, 59, 79, 80, 82–83, 85–87
 cabinet reshuffle, 80, 84
 media reform, 195, 211
 military days, 104
 Myanmar Investment Commission, 84, 86
 NNER, 162
Soe Thein, 200
Soe Win, 193
 informal meetings with activists, 156–57
 as prime minister, 35–36, 39, 64, 80, 106
 TNA process, 187
 transition from USDA to USDP
Soe Yin, 112, 113, 128
South Africa Broadcasting Corporation (AFBC), 208
Southeast Asian Games (2013), 90

SPDC. *See* State Peace and Development Council (SPDC)
Special Issues Assessment Commission, 210
Special Operation Bureaus (SOBs), 64, 84, 85
Staff Office of the President, 93
State Constitution Drafting Commission, 22
State Law and Order Restoration Council (SLORC), 5–8, 25, 34, 41, 61
 cabinet office and, 10
 Declaration No. 1/90, 7, 10, 12, 14
 Declaration No. 5/90, 10
 law no. 5/96, 25
 1999 plenary meeting, 35
 Notification No. 11/92, 9
 political and economic reforms of, 14
 reconvening of the National Convention, 19–22
 and SPDC, relations, 63, 64
State Peace and Development Council (SPDC)
 democratization process, 24
 Drafting Committee, 25
 economic policies and development projects, 81, 82
 general election for 2010, 105
 seven-step road map to democracy, 42, 66
 and SLORC, relationships, 63, 64
 State Constitution Drafting Commission, 22
Suharto, 19
super ministers, 78
Su Su Lwin, 161

T
Takatho Myat Thu, 67, 193, 213n14
Tant Lwin Maung, 162

Index

"Tarwunkhan Wungyi", 36
Tatmadaw (armed forces)
  abolition of administrative and
    political institutions, 61
  and Aung San Suu Kyi, 53–54
  and the constitution, 8
  in Rakhine State, 174, 177
  reserved seats for, 88–89, 101
  and the USDA, 34–35
Telecommunications Act of 2013, 206
Than Aung, 36
Thane Soe, 142
Than Htut Aung, 20, 156
Than Nyein, 49, 50, 131
Than Oo, 14, 161, 164
Than Sein, 33
Than Shwe
  and Aung Kyi, 51–52
  and Aung San Suu Kyi, 13–14, 17
  media reform, 189, 192
  and the NLD, 20
  political reform, 3, 18–19, 27, 34, 186
  selection of Thein Sein as president, 71, 81, 110
  and Shwe Mann, 81, 104–7, 118
  SLORC, 61, 63–65, 93
  SPDC, 70, 90
  Tatmadaw, 93, 104, 116
  transition to democracy, 9, 24, 71, 216
  2008 constitution, 5
  USDA, 34–37, 41, 43, 59, 80–81, 216
Thant Shin, 170
Thar ku (opportunists), 81
Thein Lwin, 161–65, 168, 169, 171
Thein Nyunt, 83, 111, 112, 135, 169, 204
Thein Sein, 212, 216–24
  administration, 58–60, 167
  and Aung Min, 168
  and Aung San Suu Kyi, 53–54
  education reform programme, 172
  inaugural address, 46–47, 160, 194
  involvement in USDP activities, 27
  keynote address at Practical
    Education Reform Conference, 161
  and Kyaw Hsan, 199
  legislative agenda, 30
  media reform, 210, 212
  Myitsone project, 158
  presidency, 154, 173, 180
  Rakhine Commission of Inquiry, 174
  reform programme, 31, 46–48, 71–72, 78, 103, 118, 180–81, 195, 225
  and Shwe Mann, 109–10, 113, 115–17, 123, 160
  State Law and Order Restoration Council, 17, 19
  state of emergency in Rakhine State, 174
  and Than Shwe, 113
  and Tin Aung Myint Oo, 65
  2008 constitution, 24, 57
  USDA's CEC, 43
  USDP agenda, 68
Thet Naing Win, 175
Thiha Thura Tin Aung Myint Oo, 80
Thurain Zaw, 148n12
Thura Shwe Mann, 17, 27–29, 103–14, 188
Thu Thu Mar, 162
Tin Aung Myint Oo, 89–90, 115
  as candidate for Union minister
    and chief minister, 59, 116
  drafting of new laws, 81
  "good cop bad cop", 83
  recommendations on economic and
    development issues, 81

succeeded as secretary 1, 64, 105
suspicious business deals, involvement in, 220
vs. Thein Sein, 65
Union Solidarity and Development Party (USDP), 217
USDA affairs, 223
as vice president, 77–78, 80, 97n41, 108, 124
Tin Aye, 14, 59, 92, 116, 217
Tin Hlaing, 20, 162
Tin Htut, 19, 42
Tin Maung Oo, 134
Tin Maung Than, 79
Tin Naing Thein, 68, 72, 73, 84, 86, 161–67
Tin Oo, 7, 10, 14, 17, 20, 21, 23n26, 49
Tint Swe, 193, 203
Toe Naing Mann, 113–14, 118, 204
Trade Council, 65, 80, 97n63

U

UEC. *See* Union Election Commission (UEC)
UK Press Complaints Commission, 198
UNDP. *See* United Nations Development Program (UNDP)
UNESCO's media development indicators, 194, 212
Union Election Commission (UEC), 43, 131
Union Government
cabinet reshuffles, 76–78
consolidation of presidential authority, 70–74
government and administrative reform, 66–69
Executive Office of the President, 92–95
government mechanisms prior to 2011, 61–66
Government Office, 92–95
ministers in the President's Office, 83–88
President's Office, 92–95
provisions of the constitution, 57–58
reformers and hardliners, 78–83
Thein Sein's administration, 58–60
vice presidents, 88–91
Union Government Information Committee, 153n145
Union Government Law, 81
Union Level Organizations, 117, 138, 142
Union of Myanmar Solidarity Association, 34
Union Solidarity and Development Association (USDA), 17, 28, 34–35, 96n18, 216, 223
business activities, 38–40
Central Executive Committee meeting, 66
key positions, 36–38
membership and organizational works, 40–42
organizational structure, 35–36
political party in 2010, 66
to USDP, 42–44
Union Solidarity and Development Party (USDP), 223–25
first party congress, 28, 118
Hluttaw members, 114–19
kyant-kai-yay (solidarity), 33–34
1958 political crisis, 27
Shwe Mann's attempt to control it, 123
Shwe Mann's leadership, 172
steering committee, 111
structure of, 62
Than Shwe, 216
USDA to, 42–44

United Nations Development
  Program (UNDP), 74
USDA. *See* Union Solidarity and
  Development Association
  (USDA)
USDP. *See* Union Solidarity and
  Development Party (USDP)
US Myanmar policy, 192

V
vice presidents, 88–92

W
Win Myint, 35, 36
Win Sein, 36
Win Shein, 86

Win Than, 139
Win Tin, 49, 187, 193

Y
Ye Min, 94, 99n115
Ye Tint, 72, 200, 203
Ye Tun, 112, 134–35, 141
Yin Yin, 163

Z
Zar Ta Lem, 103
Zaw Htay, 164, 167
Zaw Min Oo, 66, 158
Zaw Myint Pe, 125, 140, 170
Zaw Oo, 72
Zaw Than Thin, 94
Zaw Thet Htwe, 211

About the Author

Ye Htut was Visiting Senior Research Fellow at the ISEAS – Yusof Ishak Institute from 2016 to 2019. His research interest is on political developments in Myanmar.

He is a graduate of the Myanmar Defence Services Academy. He received his commission in 1981 and retired as Lieutenant Colonel from the Myanmar Army in 2005. He was transferred to the civil service and took up the post of Deputy Director General in the Ministry of Information. He served in the ministry as Director General (2009) and then as Deputy Minister (2012) before his appointment as the Presidential spokesperson and Union Minister.

He served as Presidential Spokesperson (2013–16) and Minister of Information (2014–16). In the latter capacity, and previously as Director General and Deputy Minister of Information, he participated in the liberalization of Myanmar's media laws and brought into that process international media assistance from the BBC, Deutsche Welle, the Asia-Pacific Institute for Broadcasting Development, Radio Free Asia and the Asia Foundation.

After Myanmar's most recent elections in 2015, he served as a member of the President's Transition Team assisting the incoming government of Daw Aung San Suu Kyi's National League for Democracy.

Ye Htut has written six books in Burmese, including *Politics and the Media*, *Bush and His Decisions*, *The Press Council and Journalists' Ethics*, *Fall of NeoCon*, and two collections of essays.

www.ingramcontent.com/pod-product-compliance
Lightning Source LLC
Chambersburg PA
CBHW070020010526
44117CB00011B/1654